Parenting 911

*

*How to Safeguard
and Rescue Your
10- to 15-Year-Old
From Substance
Abuse, Depression,
Sexual Encounters,
Violence, Failure in
School, Danger on the
Internet, and Other
Risky Situations*

Pare

nting 911

Charlene C. Giannetti
and Margaret Sagarese

BROADWAY BOOKS NEW YORK

To our husbands,
Charlene's Tom and Margaret's Michael,
for the stellar job they do as fathers.

PARENTING 911. Copyright © 1999 by Charlene C. Giannetti and Margaret Sagarese.
All rights reserved. Printed in the United States of America. No part of this book may be
reproduced or transmitted in any form or by any means, electronic or mechanical, including
photocopying, recording, or by any information storage and retrieval system, without written
permission from the publisher. For information, address Broadway Books, a division of
Random House, Inc., 1540 Broadway, New York, NY 10036.

Broadway Books titles may be purchased for business or promotional use or for special sales.
For information, please write to: Special Markets Department, Random House, Inc., 1540
Broadway, New York, NY 10036.

BROADWAY BOOKS and its logo, a letter B bisected on the diagonal, are trademarks
of Broadway Books, a division of Random House, Inc.

Visit our website at www.broadwaybooks.com

Library of Congress Cataloging-in-Publication Data

Giannetti, Charlene C.
    Parenting 911: how to safeguard and rescue your 10- to 15-year-old from
substance abuse . . . / by Charlene C. Giannetti and Margaret Sagarese.
        p.   cm.
    Includes index.
    ISBN 0-7679-0321-8 (pbk.)
    1. Parenting.   2. Child rearing.   3. Children—Drug use—
Prevention.   I. Sagarese, Margaret.   II. Title.
HQ755.8.G498   1999
498—dc21   99-18784
                                                              CIP

FIRST EDITION

DESIGNED BY RENATO STANISIC

99   00   01   02   03   10   9   8   7   6   5   4   3   2   1

Contents

*

*

Acknowledgments

*

We owe a debt of gratitude to all the parents and teachers who bought our first book, *The Roller-Coaster Years: Raising Your Child Through the Maddening Yet Magical Middle School Years.* They crowded our talks and asked tough questions. Our quest to find answers led to this book.

Once again, we want to single out the National Middle School Association and especially John Lounsbury. John has been an invaluable ally and supporter. He has devoted much of his life, intellect, and heart to young adolescents. All of us have benefitted from his guidance. Sue Swaim, Jack Berckemeyer, Holly Holland, and many others at the NMSA have helped us reach our audience. We are grateful to them all.

The NMSA has guided us toward many educators throughout the country. To many we owe much, particularly Tim Doyle (Connecticut Association of Schools) and Robert Spears (New England League of Middle Schools), who invited us into their professional networks.

Many administrators, teachers, social workers—too numerous to list here—assisted us by answering our questionnaire, hosting us in their communities, and voicing their support for our work. In addition, countless experts, including psychologists, doctors, lawyers, and researchers of many specialties, took the time to answer our questions and help us become a conduit, bringing their advice to an audience of parents.

iVillage, the Women's Network, provided us with an electronic sand-box, Parent Soup, where we could talk with parents of middlers all over the U.S. and Canada. Thanks to Susan Hahn, Susan Weaver, Karen Scott, Linda Osborne, and others who have kept us chatting on America Online and on the Web.

We'd like to take this opportunity to thank everyone at Broadway Books for making *The Roller-Coaster Years* such a success, from Dorothy Auld in sales, up through the ranks of publicity headed by Trigg Robinson, with her associate, Rebecca Watson, right on to the top with publisher Bill Shinker. For this book, we especially owe a debt of grati-tude to our new editor, Tracy Behar, who painstakingly waded through our very long first draft and guided us towards making it better (and shorter). Her faith, warmth, and encouragement made our job easier. Angela Casey, assistant editor, handled all the details with efficiency and good cheer.

Our agent, Denise Marcil, deserves an extra special note of thanks because her representation on this book took us to a new level of pro-fessional satisfaction.

Last but not least, we want to collectively thank our children, hus-bands, relatives, and friends for cooperating with our busy schedules this past year. We couldn't have done it without you.

Parenting Through Tough Times

*

*"I definitely feel that the light at the end of the tunnel
is an oncoming train."*
—Father of a fifteen-year-old girl

*"I just turned thirteen. Now my parents are thinking, 'Oh no,
she's a teen and that means trouble! We have to limit her
comings and goings.' What do I do to make them see that
I am good and don't plan on misbehaving?"*

Since publishing *The Roller-Coaster Years* in 1997, we spent a great deal of time crisscrossing the byways and the electronic highway of America and Canada talking with parents about their ten- to fifteen-year-olds. Apprehensive parents painted pictures over and over of their young tempting fate, leaning over the edge, or engaging in life-threatening antics.

Our first book chose not to scare parents with statistics and worst-case scenarios. Instead we presented information and offered strategies to sensitize parents and effect positive results. We stressed that while parents do indeed lose *control* of their middlers, they shouldn't panic. Our job is to relinquish control as we teach our middlers decision-making. We made the distinction between control and influence. Parents still retain their *influence*. In fact, at no other time in a child's growth is this more powerful and pivotal.

As middler minds expand, and budding consciences grapple with values, a parent's moral guidance is a daily duty/golden opportunity. All of the research absolutely states that young adolescents trust their parents more than anyone else (yes even more than their precious peers). Parents traded their apprehension for gratitude.

After many a proactive powwow, several parents always lingered to talk to us privately about an unreachable stepson or a defiant daughter. In our role as preteen experts for Parent Soup (www.parentsoup.com or on AOL), a steady stream of cyber-revelations added to our sea of confidences. So many parents feel trapped on a harrowing downward spiral. The health and safety of their children hang by a thread. The most common plea: *How can I get back my control?* shows that parents misunderstand their role during these years.

The stalemates, helplessness, and fears of parents, stepparents, grandparents, foster parents, older siblings, as well as single mothers moved us tremendously. A grandmother with a furrowed brow, stenciled by worry over her eleven-year-old grandson, stuck in our minds long after she pleaded, "How can I get my daughter and son-in-law to pay more attention to my grandson? He is always angry and they just don't get it. I'm afraid for him."

Just when we felt totally in sync with overwhelmed parents, middlers barricaded in their messy rooms wrenched us away to hear their side of the generation gap gripes:

One thirteen-year-old girl told us, "I'm e-mailing you because you are my *only and last hope.* Me and my mom do not know how to communicate anymore. She constantly nags me. I get uncontrollably angry and say horrible things that I don't really mean. I feel like the walls are closing in on me."

Boys were fighting mad, too, like this fifteen-year-old: "My father and I ARGUE constantly. The last time I remember us getting along was when I was eight. I don't think he cares about me at all. We argue about stupid things . . . food, my room, the computer. I admit sometimes I provoke him, but at other times he just yells. I feel like I am the child he had just so he could scream. I want things to change, but it takes two. I've tried talking but he doesn't want to listen."

Ironically, the more advanced our communications age becomes with cellular phones, beepers, fax machines, e-mail, the Internet, teleconferencing, and satellite TV, the less we are able to communicate lovingly and effectively with the ones we love.

GROWING PAINS, YOUR MIDDLER'S AND YOURS

Early adolescence is, at times, a trying interval of high emotions and low blows. Middlers do what comes naturally in terms of development: battle for independence. Separating from adults is the itinerary. Some make the transition smoothly; others fight their way free, ravaging households and hearts in the process.

All young adolescents are a little bit like Lewis and Clark trailblazing through the woods toward the horizon of adulthood. Most are unprepared for the savagery of the frontier. These children, bent on experiencing the world their way, learn life's lessons the hard way.

Watching can be excruciating for parents. We try to intervene. Too many restrictions and well-intentioned warnings only make things worse. Sheltering a child can and often does backfire. Overprotection sends the message that he can't be trusted, or she isn't competent, sabotaging a young adolescent with mistrust. Yet a permissive approach invites trouble. The wise parent stays connected by establishing reasonable boundaries and trusting a child to respect those limits. The most effective parent is vigilant, ready to step in when a middler wanders too far afield, or too dangerously off course. Sound easy? Of course, we all agree it is not.

THINK BACK TO YOUR MIDDLER AGES

Were you a breeze to raise? Fess up. You tried to put one over on your parents, whether you skipped school, snuck out, or got into a drive-in without paying. Tell us that you didn't linger in the backseat of a car until the windows fogged up. The father of a fourteen-year-old reminisces, "A buddy and I stole tomatoes from a neighbor's garden and hurled them over the house, torpedoing unsuspecting folks relaxing on their porch. We laughed until we got caught for breaking a window with a large beefsteak. My father said, 'Destruction is the work of an idiot.' I've never forgotten his words."

The truth is that each and every one of us has a rebellious, foolhardy, or guilt-ridden skeleton in our closet. A black eye, a hangover—once upon a time many of us were young rebels with lots of causes of concern for our parents. Early adolescence remains the same. It's the world that changes. The soundtrack of an eighth grade graduation dance now has the staccato of gunshots on top of the DJ's drumbeat. Racial bias crimes, steroid abuse, eating disorders, adolescent suicide, academic underachievement, all these are on the upswing, just in time for your child's coming of age.

WEAVE A SAFETY NET

It's natural for parents to lose hope that it's feasible to keep their children safe through these years in a risk-filled world. You can lose faith in a child who opts for the easy way out or marches defiantly down the wrong path. Sometimes you do feel less loving toward an obstinate or mouthy middler; that's human nature. Middlers test your love as they test the waters of independence. Children of divorce, in stepfamilies, and those who have been adopted can excel at pushing the envelope. However, the jolts that turn your family life upside down, need not derail you.

When parenting feels like a "Rescue 911" crisis, constructing a safety net is a useful response. A textured weave of attitudes, warning signs, insights, and strategies will safeguard your middler or save her during the inevitable crises that go along with young adolescent territory. We'll show you how.

Once you open this book you enter a community of others who share your problems and validate your best efforts. You glimpse into the mindset, the achy-breaky hearts, and the bared souls of ten- to fifteen-year-olds.

As we did for our first book, we devised and distributed a questionnaire with the help of the National Middle School Association tapping wisdom from middle school principals, teachers, counselors, parents, and young adolescents. Added insight came from the physicians, psychologists, and many other professionals we interviewed.

When is a young adolescent truly in danger? When should you intervene and when should you let your middler cope with the consequences? When crisis becomes the family coat of arms, we'll get you through the hard times. It's easy to love your son or daughter when life runs along without a hitch. It's when life becomes a battleground, with you and your middler on opposite sides of a silent or sarcastic trench, that you need clear-headed guidance. Your commitment is your best resource.

MISSION NOT IMPOSSIBLE

You've lived through the years when your toddler threw blocks all over the floor. You can survive the stumbling blocks of early adolescence, too. In our first book, you read about the details of the enormous physical, psychological, and emotional changes that ten- to fifteen-year-olds undergo. You learned how to help your middler navigate the middle school years. This time you stand on a precipice, in the midst of a crisis, or determined to evade one. Can you succeed? Yes.

Perspective is key. Paul Stoltz, president of PEAK Learning Inc., an Arizona business consultant and author, introduces his clients to the "adversity quotient," an aptitude to rise above hardship. Stoltz advises, "People who respond to adversity as enduring, far-reaching, internal, and out of their control *suffer,* while those who respond to it as fleeting, limited, external, and within their control *thrive.*"

In preparing for this book, we read through countless reports and studies from the best and the brightest minds. We pored over findings explaining why some middlers thrive and why other middlers succumb to drugs, alcohol, violence, and early sexual activity. Does good parenting matter? Judith Rich Harris's 1998 book *The Nurture Assumption* sent shock waves, claiming that parenting style and child-rearing practices matter little. Harris interpreted statistics to prove her thesis: Young adolescents become what they learn outside, not inside, the home from peers and on the streets.

The 1995 National Longitudinal Study of Adolescent Health, the most comprehensive and largest study to date, involving 90,000 seventh to twelfth graders, suggests the exact opposite. Dr. Robert Blum, director of the Adolescent Health Program at the University of Minnesota, found that one striking factor emerged and recurred in the life experience of all the young adolescents who passed up risky behaviors. It was having a parent who was emotionally available. Children, regardless of race, income, and number of parents, who felt connected to adults wore invisible armor. Dr. Blum commented, "We invest heavily in rule development, but that's not where the action is. The action is in connecting with kids."

With whom do you agree? Are parents a defining force or negligible? Should you throw up your hands and say, "Why bother?!" because whatever you do, it won't matter? We are not taking any chances and strongly believe you shouldn't either. Unconditional love is your (and your middler's) best asset. It is the most powerful force in any child's universe. Children between the ages of ten and fifteen may not want to be seen with you on Main Street, but don't think for a moment that they don't need you. Even if love is all you have to give, it probably is all you need to provide and all your middler needs to survive.

HOME ALONE

Remember the movie *Home Alone*? Didn't we, and a younger version of our middlers, laugh hysterically as Macaulay Culkin ingeniously outsmarts bumbling burglars with the bad luck to find him solo? The risk of being home alone is *rarely* linked to middlers. It's during that first decade of a child's life when harried working parents and single mothers obsess over baby-sitters, nannies, and day care. When a son or daughter reaches ten, they exhale.

Isn't a ten-, eleven-, twelve-, thirteen-, fourteen-year-old *old enough* to be trusted at home without adult surveillance? Not really. When and where do middlers puff and huff, lose their virginity, mutilate themselves, or take their own life? Home alone, or with a peer, but distinctly without an adult on watch.

Significant numbers of twelve- to fourteen-year-olds are home unsupervised at least two hours daily after school, says The Carnegie Council on Adolescent Development. Eighth graders from high- and low-income families are in charge of themselves for at least three hours every day according to a national survey of 25,000 young adolescents conducted by the U.S. Center for Education Statistics. In a study of 5,000 eighth graders, self-care emerged as a risk factor itself.

- Those who took care of themselves for eleven hours or more a week were twice as likely to abuse alcohol and drugs or to use cigarettes.
- Crime analysts insist that the majority of juvenile crime is committed between 3:00 and 5:00 P.M. by youngsters who victimize contemporaries.
- Self-destructive actions—suicide attempts and self-mutilation— peak in the after-school hours among ten- to fourteen-year-olds.
- The National Campaign to Prevent Teen Pregnancy reports that teen girls living with their biological parents are less likely to engage in premature sexual activity. Why? They speculate that traditional families supervise more. When parents are out working, home becomes a potential lovenest.

What's a working parent to do?

Establish strict and clear rules (and consequences) for those after-school hours. Plan the time, including your middler in the process. Chores, homework, check-in calls, social telephone time—keep your child busy.

Partner with other working parents. Trade middlers and plan outings. Have another parent include your middler on a shopping excursion or to the soccer field after school. Think of it as carpooling minus the car.

Lobby your middle school for after-school programs. While many schools offer homework clubs, sports, recreational activities, others don't. Too often most programs and clubs cater to the brightest middlers. Make sure there are programs for average children. If school falls short, find a club or program of interest outside school and sign up your middler. To give you an idea of what's available, get *The Directory of American Youth Organizations,* a resource guide describing 500 clubs, troops, teams, societies, lodges, and more.

Take your crusade to the community. A Carnegie Council report, *A Matter of Time: Risk and Opportunity in the Non-School Hours,* pointed out that 29 percent of young adolescents in need of support and guidance were not served by the existing 17,000 youth organizations. Unite with other parents for resources, leagues, and buildings to be used for youth. Start programs yourself.

Acknowledge that day-care concerns don't cease when your child grows into a young adolescent. Middlers need to be assessed from both negative and positive perspectives. They are risk-takers looking for trouble; adventurers longing for opportunity. They are also scientists, artists, inventors waiting to bloom, individuals on the cusp of many skills and talents. Their developing brain power, idealism, and activism should be captured and nurtured. Leisure blocks should be experiments in which they experience new interests, meet new people, and explore new talents.

Carve out time for your middler. "Parents are impacted by so many things—work, etc. They don't have enough time for quality in many aspects of their lives," a sympathetic teacher remarked. We know life is more hectic than ever. You put in more hours on the job, according to the 1997 Family and Work Institute's calculations, averaging 47.1 hours a week, up from 43.6 twenty years ago. Still, 60 percent of workers surveyed say they don't have enough time to get the job done. Taking your work home is the solution for more than one third. Fully 85 percent of you have families and household responsibilities. Even though your plate is full, save some room for your young adolescent.

Plan activities together. According to discretionary time studies of early adolescents, eating and TV watching are the two things families do together. As middlers grow from fourth grade to seventh, that TV partnership decreases. Listening to music preoccupies children as they grow, and parents never listen along. So unplug your middler from the portable CD player. Take in a movie or go to a basketball game. If you are harried, recruit your middler to go along on chores to the supermarket, dry cleaners, bank. Being emotionally available starts with letting your child know you value her company.

Here's what fourth graders said they'd do after school rather than go home to an empty house:

"I would like to go to the art room so I could do art projects."

"I would like to start a reading club."

"I would take a martial arts class."

"Girls could take dance and gymnastics. Boys could take karate and wrestling. We could watch movies together. There would be so much to do, I don't know how anyone could get bored."

"I would do my homework, play some sports with my friends, eat a snack, and improve my skills on the computer."

There are better alternatives to home alone. A self-destructive formula can be transformed into a constructive one. All it takes is you.

All crises are temporary. Remember that. Middler mayhem is but a phase. We live in a sitcom state of mind, where major problems wrap up in thirty minutes. Real-life problems never wrap so neatly or quickly. Some difficult situations that you encounter cannot be undone no matter how much regret, remorse, or urgency you bring to the bargaining table. That doesn't mean that progress cannot be made, even if progress means only learning something and moving forward. Sometimes living through the crisis goes a long way toward ensuring your child's survival. At times, being there is the only thing a parent can do. It is also always the best thing a parent can do.

A father of two hellions told us this moving and useful tale: "I came across an old photo recently. I was sitting in my favorite chair with my two-year-old daughter on my lap, and her four-year-old sister sitting on my shoulders as I read a story to them. From that picture, my angels enchanted me. Lately, whenever they do something that makes me angry (which they often do at thirteen and fifteen), I get out that snapshot. It helps me control my reactions." Maybe we should all get a favorite photo and keep it close at hand.

Don't lose sight of this fact: The middler years are but a chapter in the life story of you and your child. Like any love story, like any family saga, yours will feature frustrating conflicts and comic moments. With young children you write the script and control the action; with middlers you collaborate, corroborate, and coordinate. Yes, you do need a new set of tools for your parenting toolbox. Within these pages you will find them.

CHAPTER ONE

Family Life with Middlers

*

"I don't get along with my parents or my brothers.
We yell at each other all the time."
—Thirteen-year-old girl

We, our middlers, and other children are dependent on one another for love, appreciation, and a sense of well-being. Family life only runs satisfactorily and rewardingly when everyone pulls his or her weight. Families raising children between the ages of ten to fifteen get pulled down by the challenges of living with temperamental, high-flying, and unpredictable middlers.

Today's households are more than ever a melting pot of gender, race, and ethnicity, rarely resembling a Norman Rockwell portrait.

- Practically one in two households (49 percent) differ from the traditional father, mother, and child model.
- One in three families with children under eighteen is headed by a single parent, and not exclusively mom. Since the 1970s, father-only homes have increased threefold to 2.8 million.
- There are twenty million stepfamilies in America.
- Every year 50,000 children are adopted, approximately 20 percent school age or older children.
- Grandparents head households that include 3.4 million children according to the American Association of Retired Persons (AARP).
- Four million gay and lesbian couples are raising eight to ten million children, says the Gay and Lesbian Parents Coalition in Washington, D.C.

As we turn the century's corner, families—and their middlers—all have unique challenges. They share a common denominator: family stress. Young adolescents grappling with identity, independence, and separation issues disrupt every home, even though these filter through each family lens differently.

Family therapists, parents, teachers, and middlers add insights here to equip you to deal delicately with family fallout. Don't skip over any of our family forms because they often intertwine. "I am a divorced mother with one son. I recently married a man with two children. His preteens live with his ex, their mother, who adopted a Korean baby. My ex now lives with a man, a Brazilian who wants a surrogate to bear his (their) child." That quote is fictitious yet typical of the tangled family web we weave.

THE STANDARD-ISSUE MIDDLER

Control is the touchstone. "I am about to marry a man who has custody of his fifteen-year-old son. The boy has no supervision because my fiancé works. He runs wild, and doesn't follow our rules. What is the correct approach to get some control over this?"

We asked middlers, "When you and your parents disagree, what happens?" A fourteen-year-old boy from the Midwest answered, "I do what my parents think is best." We threw that one in to boggle your mind. Most of us live with a less agreeable version. In a 1998 *State of Our Nation's Youth* poll, 17 percent of fourteen- to eighteen-year-olds surveyed admitted having difficulty getting along with mom, 22 percent with dad. In our survey middlers quipped, "I wish we wouldn't all fight so much," and, "I'd make my mom nicer if I could." "I would describe my family life as basically unhappy because we don't get along," admitted a fourteen-year-old girl.

Real middlers wear us out. They are engineered to do so.

The psychological task of ten- to fifteen-year-olds is to find out who they are. Our job as parents is to set the boundaries for their field test. As our young boomerang towards adulthood, they push the limits and push our buttons. They audition our values by breaking our rules to decide whether or not those ethics are worth adopting for themselves. Young adolescents have to resist, dismiss, and even defy us, in order to create distance.

It's called a "battle for independence" because we are at cross purposes. Parents guide and mold; young adolescents experiment and rebel. In other words, parents and middlers are a volatile combination at best, wrestling for power.

MORE MIDDLERS, MORE CHALLENGES

The mother of two boys, ages eleven and fifteen, pleads, "How do I handle my younger boy's accusations that his older brother always gets more—more leeway, later curfews, fewer rules—especially because he's right. The older was easier to raise; the younger can't be trusted and needs a shorter leash."

If engineering one child through these testy times isn't challenging enough, many parents shepherd more than one middler. Others juggle children from a cross section of age brackets. Every parent knows that no two children are alike, but the more vexing reality is that children need to be raised differently. Charges ("He got to sit in the front seat last time!") escalate into more weighty and complex debates ("He was allowed to date at fourteen, why can't I go out alone?"). Parents know why, but explaining it to indignant middlers requires a smooth talk most can't sell and few young adolescents buy.

Sibling rivalry heats up substantially during the roller-coaster years. Brothers and sisters grate on one another. Ordinary sibling-to-sibling teasing feels extraordinarily vicious to fragile middler egos where worth is calculated by peer review. Favoritism appears more glaring to ten- to fifteen-year-olds who see it everywhere. Rules sting with injustice.

If your household is a civil war zone, use the acronym SPAT as a guide:

S is for Special. Ferret out and tell your child what special qualities and strengths she possesses. Treasure the positive in each developmental stage. (If you can't get in touch with the positives of the preteens, read our first book, *The Roller-Coaster Years.*) Remember most rivalries are a contest for your time and attention.

P is for Partnership. Middlers need to belong. The concept of being part of the family is appealing. Compliment your child when she is a team player. Discipline all the fighters not just the one who started it. That saves you from *the blame game* and *who do you trust.*

A is for Accountable. Inform each child that privileges and freedoms are earned by a person's responsible behavior and maturity. They are not entitlements that come with a certain age or a specific gender.

T is for Temporary. Paint the long view for your young adolescent. She is always locked in the present. Make affirmations like, "Someday you and your sister will appreciate each other more" or "In time you will be able to do all the things you are not quite old enough to do now." Point out that sibling relationships are the most enduring relationships of all, outliving and outlasting those with parents, friends, and even spouses.

The SPAT strategy can defuse mutiny, at least temporarily until the next episode of sibling strife.

"I feel I am losing control of my child occasionally," admitted 52 percent of parents in our survey. "Frequently," confessed a war-weary 6 percent. If you are stretched to your limit, don't despair. Remember that our middlers are younger than we are, and stronger.

All families struggle. Once upon a time, there was an American family with a workaholic dad and an alcoholic mother. Dad didn't make enough money and worked extra jobs (less time for the boys) while mom added antidepressant pills to her booze to cope. Their boys grew up neglected. The parents, inflexible and unaware, exiled the boys to bed at 6:30 each night and forbid them to exit until 7:00 A.M. the next day. Grandma had been notoriously over-protective, leaving the father sexually hung-up. Mom's dad had syphilis. A lot of poor role models, wouldn't you say?

The dad was none other than Dr. Benjamin Spock. Thomas Maier's book, *Dr. Spock: An American Life* notes, "Though millions turned to him for answers for family dilemmas, he could not find solutions for himself or his loved ones."

"I don't know many parents, in any kind of family, who are confident that they've got it right," says Stephanie Coontz, family historian and author of *The Way We Never Were* and *The Way We Really Are.* We intend to provide real strategies to ease your family's tension. Let's review particular crises that afflict different family forms.

TALKING TO YOUR MIDDLER

"When my parents and I disagree, what happens? I stop talking."
  —Eighth grade girl from South Dakota

Middlers go off in a huff silently or shrieking. Mothers feel cut off from their stonewalling and silent sons. Fathers feel clueless about how to communicate with the emotional excesses of daughters. There are many experts sketching out the special hurdles and communication puzzles of both young adolescent girls and boys. Take advantage of this wealth of knowledge and insight readily available to any parent who is eager to learn how to get inside the head and heart of a middler of the other gender.

Give boys time alone to lick their wounds. Boys react to hurt with a "timed silence syndrome," according to Harvard Medical School clinical psychologist and professor of psychiatry, Dr. William Pollack, who reports on his *Listening to Boys' Voices* study in his book *Real Boys.*

Fathers should focus on the feelings not reactions. Girls are highly emotional and fathers are uncomfortable with such outbursts and often retreat. Fathers can handle their young adolescent daughters' language of high emotions when they learn how girls think and respond, according to Will Glennon, author of *Fathering: Strengthening Connection with Your Children No Matter Where You Are.*

Do learn from single parents. Single parents talk *more* to their middlers than moms and dads in traditional families.

"Dysfunction in families *doesn't* come from difficulties, but from when there is a lack of communication," according to New York psychotherapist Celeste Carlin. "It's the support that people give each other that's important. In every family there's some crisis somewhere—it's how the family handles it that matters: Are they talking about it or shying away from it? Fostering self-esteem by staying connected, letting children know that you care and that you think they are great (if not applauding their behavior)—if you do that, they and you will be able to weather all life's bumps and bruises."

Here's a gem from our first book, *The Roller-Coaster Years.* When a middler says, "I don't want to talk about it!" what he or she means is "I can't talk about it now, ask me later." Bedtime or in the car works best.

DIVIDED FAMILIES, SINGLE PARENTS

"My daughter is a handful. My divorce proceedings with her father were slow and terrible. She used this to her advantage and blamed everyone but herself for her failures. My ex and I have tried to give her everything: good private schools, vacations to Europe, etc. but she always wants more, and never appreciates what we give her!"
—Single mother of a fourteen-year-old

The proportion of adults currently divorced more than tripled from 1970 to 1996, from 3 percent of the adult population to 10 percent. The number of children living with only one parent has more than doubled from 12 percent to 28 percent. Single parents forging a new life often underestimate the impact of a splintered family. A report from the Search Institute, *Youth in Single-Parent Families: Risk and Resiliency,* found that young adolescents in single-parent homes are more likely to binge drink, use illicit drugs or cigarettes, become sexually active, and be involved in theft and vandalism than peers in two-parent families.

Divorce is hard on children, *even harder* on young adolescents. Alas, there is no equivalent for losing that "happy" two-parent home, even when it wasn't all that happy. Nothing satisfies a middler who secretly hopes (as most do) to reunite estranged parents. "Contrary to what some people think, older children are no less affected by divorce than are younger children," insists Barry Frieman, a professor at Towson State University and clinical social worker with the Children of Separation and Divorce Center in Columbia, Maryland.

Children from divorced families tend to be more aggressive, demanding, disobedient, angry, and less affectionate. Boys have greater difficulty adjusting than girls. Processing this emotional maelstrom is daunting because middlers experience all emotions in an exaggerated way. Furthermore, preadolescent girls (and boys even more so) have trouble recognizing and expressing their feelings.

During the years from ten to fifteen, children crave a sense of belonging. They depend on family to steady them in an increasingly complex world. They are shattered when this family sanctuary disintegrates. An already pressing sense of powerlessness increases.

Does this mean that *all* divorce offspring are destined to become troubled miscreants? Critics of divorce-dooming research point out that studies of divorced children are biased. A 1991 *Science* journal study, which analyzed more than 17,000 families, found that children's behavioral problems were present *before* the parents separated, and therefore cannot be linked solely to divorce distress. Other studies use no control group, and are questionable.

Aren't young adolescents "old enough" to grasp the reasons why marriage fails? Although that sounds logical, it doesn't play out that way. A middler's understanding of the divorce, and why it happens, actually complicates relationships. They live in an "it's not fair" mode. That injustice frame of mind makes them take sides with the "wronged" parent. According to Judith Wallerstein, Ph.D., nine- to twelve-year-olds exact revenge on the parent they hold responsible for the break-up. Middlers are recruited easily by an angry parent to wage war against the other.

How can you tell the difference between a temporarily traumatized middler and one who requires professional help to adjust? "There are no hard and fast rules about when to get children help," explains Douglas Darnall, a psychologist who specializes in divorce and custody conflicts. "You have to trust your instincts. You know the hurt is not healing if, in a reasonable time, your children don't return to their old selves."

Generally, middlers who act out should be able to express remorse, regret, or guilt about misbehavior. After a tumultuous bout a young adolescent should offer some explanation. Even though middlers resist hugs in public, they should still want closeness and support. Seek professional advice when:

- Your middler defies you relentlessly.
- You suspect substance abuse.
- He acts aggressively, hitting siblings or getting into fights.
- Withdrawal is an ongoing pattern. (This should not be confused with the normal young adolescent love affair with hibernating in one's room.)
- She has less interest in all formerly favored activities.

Love and support from *both* parents is the best stabilizer. Your residual fury with your ex is not reasonable grounds for cutting off access. A study by Hetherington, Cox, and Cox found that the less conflict between parents after the divorce, the better adjustment level the children showed. Children who have a positive relationship with the noncustodial parent perform better academically and socially.

Middlers become torn when parents malign one another. Dr. Darnall's book *Divorce Casualties* identifies "parental alienation"—conscious and unconscious brainwashing. Read his checklist and if you are guilty, change your ways:

> I cringe when the children talk about having a good time with my ex-spouse.
> I believe my ex-spouse lets the children run wild.
> I remind my children that we don't have enough money because of the divorce.
> I ask my children about my ex-spouse's personal life.

Two Hurdles: Visitation and Custody

"Recently for unknown reasons, my ten-year-old son's father has stopped seeing him on the weekends that he's supposed to. He gave no explanation. My son misses his father. I don't know what to do. I never told my husband that he couldn't see his son. In fact, I have always had an open door policy."

An unreliable noncustodial parent is heartbreaking, especially painful for a young adolescent trying to figure out: Who am I? A middler attempts to answer a cosmic "Am I lovable?" question. This psychic calculation can only be made with access to both parents, and acceptance by each. A noncustodial father or mother who ignores a child levies a weighty blow. A neglectful parent leaves a middler feeling unworthy. An unreliable one triggers, "Will I grow up to be a bad parent, too?"

Talk to your ex. If talking fails, steer your middler to aunts, uncles, and grandparents for nurturing.

What about the opposite—the noncustodial parent who waits in vain for a middler? They become suspicious of the motives of the custodial parent. Try these strategies:

Require your middler to explain. Hearing a fourteen-year-old giggle about the sleepover party she doesn't want to miss is less likely to make the noncustodial parent paranoid.

Encourage your middler to negotiate changes with your ex. How can they adapt their schedules? Meeting for dinner on a weeknight to catch up instead of sleeping over on Saturday night?

Empathize with your ex-spouse. Say, "Our son is pulling away from me, too." Talk about how this is normal behavior for all young adolescents.

Agree on what's important: being there. It is not the household, or the time that counts, but emotional availability.

Musical Households

Many middlers suddenly want to move in with the other parent. A father wrote, "My thirteen-year-old son lived with his mother until two years ago. Then he wanted to come and live with me. Now that I have given him a good home, he wants to move back. His mother doesn't care whether he goes to school, to bed at a decent time, or eats a healthful meal. He says I'm too hard on him. I expect help around the house, respect, bed at a certain hour, and homework done in a timely and correct way. How can I persuade him to stay?"

Mothers get rejected, too. "Help! My daughter ran away at thirteen to her dad's greener pastures. She's turned her back on me. We used to be very close (I raised her basically alone for her entire life). It's like she's hiding from me. I don't know what I should or shouldn't do."

Look at these maneuvers from your child's point of view, not from your own. A middler needs to know both parents to understand who she is. She moves toward the parent she knows the least, whether the parent *deserves* this attention or not. Don't automatically assume that a middler is looking for a better life, later curfew, or rejecting you.

The Search Institute report, *The Troubled Journey: A Portrait of Sixth–Twelfth Grade Youth,* identified liabilities children in single-parent homes have: too much time alone, overexposure to television, and economic stress. Despite these, the study found that some thrive anyway. What distinguishes successful single-parent families?

Children are supported emotionally. No matter how busy you are, set up times when you touch base with phone calls, evening meals, or late-night snack times.

Standards prevail. Preach your values often. Ten- to fifteen-year-olds are formulating ideals and need your "ten commandments." Show your child how to build positive values with gestures of kindness and a commitment to hard work.

Children are monitored. Know your middler's whereabouts at all times.

Discipline is enforced. Compliment your middler when she takes on responsibility and proves herself. When your child gets out of line, attach consequences.

The Search Institute concludes, "Family structure does not, in and of itself, explain adolescent well-being. What matters most is what happens within the family." Family structure is not destiny.

STEPFAMILIES—STRANGERS AMONG US

"I have two families. I never wanted it to be this way. One is made up of me and my two children, now fourteen and sixteen. The other is my husband and myself. We've all been together six years. I'm never at peace. I'm always feeling guilty, either about my kids not accepting their stepdad, or my husband having to put up with their endless bull_____."

If you walked down Main Street this afternoon, rounded up a few stray youngsters and one adult to live together from this day forward, what would happen? That's a stepfamily. The blended family is a hotbed of conflicts. The rate of divorce among the remarried with children is 60 percent. The first two years are the make-it-or-break timeframe for stepfamilies. Family is supposed to provide sanctuary. For stepchildren there is no such sanctuary. Instead, there is umbrage ("You're not my father so don't act like it!") and hard feelings over territory ("What do you mean I have to share my room with his son!").

Remarried newlyweds encounter treacherous pitfalls, but new research promises hope and, yes, even success. Dr. James Bray, clinical psychologist and associate professor at Baylor College of Medicine, conducted a nine-year study of stepfamilies sponsored by the National Institutes of Health. The bad news is that 20 percent of children have behavior problems compared to 10 percent in nuclear families. Bray has good news, too: "A strong, stable stepfamily is as capable of nurturing healthy development as a nuclear family. It can imbue values, affirm limits and boundaries, and provide a structure in which rules for living a moral and productive life are made, transmitted, tested, rebelled against, and ultimately affirmed."

Turning a brooding bevy of reluctant middlers and disillusioned adults into a cohesive, supportive unit takes time, effort, and commitment. The linchpin strategy is to let go of unrealistic expectations, and to factor in the development cycle of middlers. The following do's and don'ts will help you.

Do let go of the instant love fantasy. Bonding takes years. Stepmothers and stepfathers don't automatically love a spouse's children. Most think they will; the truth generates guilt. Biological parents need to understand that no instant love exists. Build your new family dynamic with patience. Hold off on the love, a concept for the future.

Don't assume all adults are rightful authority figures. Middlers chafe at rules and regulations. Two parents are hard enough to bear. Having an additional one, a stepfather or stepmother, means another adult giving orders. Middlers with two homes have a double dose of authority. A Horatio Alger Association national study on young adolescent attitudes affirmed that the stepfamily relationship is significantly more difficult for middlers, more so for girls than boys.

Draw the lines of authority clearly. Biological parents should discipline, not the stepparent. When a stepmother is the primary caretaker, it's critical that she and her stepchildren understand where her jurisdiction begins and ends.

Do expect family cacophony during the middler ages. Even in stepfamilies who have coalesced, children in the roller-coaster years take the family on a rough ride. Watching progress come undone is disheartening for adults and confusing for young adolescents. "Don't talk to your mother that way," reprimands a stepfather. "You're not my father so butt out," barks the stepdaughter. Stepparents can have a harder time dealing with middler mouthpieces.

"I noticed that biological parents have this *forgiveness gene* that stepparents like me don't have. I can't just forget about the nasty jabs or the cold shoulder. I carry a grudge that I can't let go of," said the stepfather of two girls, ages twelve and fourteen. *All middlers are horrid some of the time to any parent in all households.* Repeat that in times of distress.

Do attend to sexuality issues. All young adolescents (even those in intact traditional families) are extremely uncomfortable with the idea of their parents as sexual beings. Seeing a parent kiss, embrace, or flirt seductively with a stepparent is upsetting. Discomfort is magnified by feelings of jealousy and loyalty conflicts. Those love vibrations fly in the face of every divorced child's fantasy that someday their biological parents will get back together.

Newlywed stepparents display affection toward one another because their romance is new. If coldness and fighting characterized the former marriage, they think this is valuable for stepchildren to see. Sounds right? Wrong! Curtail passionate kisses in your middler's presence.

"Help, I've just discovered my stepson and my daughter are having sex with each other," wrote the mother of a fourteen-year-old girl about her daughter's romance. Blended family preteens are roommates without blood ties. Family incest taboos are not in place. Young adolescent boys and girls are live wires hormonally. Have separate sleeping arrangements for different genders. Discourage young adolescents from lounging around scantily clothed.

Don't take a young adolescent's anger or rejection personally. Middlers feel powerless. Stepchildren feel *more* powerless because their lives have been shattered by divorce and reconfigured by remarriage without their consent. All are supersensitive and resentful about change. They are forced to make new relationships with stepparents and stepsiblings. Managing these relationships is the biggest obstacle middlers face according to 50 percent of teachers we asked. The simplest request can seem like a major injustice. "Say thank you to your stepfather" can take on major overtones.

Being rejected angrily or being treated invisibly is standard treatment for stepparents. "I have a fourteen-year-old stepson who came to live with us five years ago. His mom had a drug problem. You can imagine that lifestyle! Living with him has been pure hell since he turned thirteen. Everything I do is wrong. He claims I don't treat him like I treat my biological children. He walks around either ten feet ahead of us or ten feet behind wherever we go. When I tell him I love him all I get is a blank stare. He ran away recently and told the police officer he wasn't loved. This was a slap in the face!"

Some middlers in blended families are so preoccupied with maintaining their ties to biological parents and working through loyalty conflicts, they are oblivious to stepparents. Others use stepparents as whipping posts. Anger needs to be vented. A stranger is preferable to a parent. If you are the parent, realize that you cannot force a child to behave lovingly toward a stepparent.

Don't expect gratitude. Parents and stepparents sacrifice financially; they work hard, donate countless hours of time, emotional energy, and devotion to middlers. Many truly feel they are providing a better life.

"I am raising an eleven-year-old boy and a fifteen-year-old girl, my husband's children from his first marriage. Essentially, life at their mother's was chaotic. We provide structure, rules, and discipline (believe me, we are not strict). No matter what we say, the fifteen-year-old ignores our rules and responds in an incredibly disrespectful manner. She says she can do what she wants at her house. Why are we trying to change her! She says she can't deal with having to be so different when she's with us."

If you are determined to rescue your stepmiddler, beware. Your good works always imply, and even amplify, what a failure the other parent is. A middler will defend even an indefensible parent. Consequently your best efforts backfire. It's not fair, but it is a normal rhythm for children of divorce.

Do learn what's normal. Dr. Bray's book *Stepfamilies* outlines their unique cycles, forms, and hurdles. Share your blended family struggles and steer your middler to do so as well. Join a support group. Go online and tap in to a stepfamily community. Hold your tongue, hold out for a better future. The best for stepfamilies is ahead.

THE ADOPTED MIDDLER

"Even though I've always been open about my daughter's adoption, now at eleven she wants details. I'm not looking forward to that."

For this age group, *not talking* about the circumstances of being adopted is standard behavior. Wondering or feeling uneasy about the circumstances of a child's birth and adoption is definitely on middlers' minds, and their parents', too.

When the family feuding of the middler years gets underway, nearly all adoptive parents fret. In the air hangs a 1990 finding by researchers Grotevant and McRoy revealing that adopted children undergo psychological treatment two to five times more frequently than nonadopted peers. Are adopted middlers bound for turbulent sojourns?

Not necessarily, according to the largest study of 715 families and their adopted young adolescents. *Growing Up Adopted* by Peter Benson, et al. followed adopted children (including 33 percent of mixed ethnic heritage) between the ages of twelve and eighteen for four years. These children mostly appeared well-adjusted. They demonstrated optimism, competency in school and social life, and possessed self-esteem. Seventy-three percent met the criteria for well-being, compared to 62 percent of the nonadopted sample.

What explains the dueling destinies predicted? Adoption covers many situations. It includes children adopted at birth, others who suffered poverty and warfare in foreign countries before being adopted, and still more who ricocheted in and out of foster homes. The problem-child statistics arise from "clinical" populations, drawn from files of psychiatrists and mental health centers. The optimistic research comes from parents who smoothly adopted infants. All this contradictory data means that there are many factors that influence what kind of adolescence your adopted son or daughter will have. No crystal ball exists.

Parents should consider how adoption dovetails with young adolescent issues. Being a middler and adopted creates riddles and conflicts. During the years from ten to fifteen, every adopted middler sizes up the phantoms of the past. Adopted young adolescents typically contemplate these questions:

"What will I look like?"

The growth spurt kidnaps middlers, sending every one into a self-conscious tizzy. The average child grows twelve inches in height. This sprouting is always too soon, too late, not enough, or too much. A weight gain of twenty to thirty pounds occurs, happening too fast, or slow, and not in the right places. Bodies feel out of control. "What will I see in the mirror next month, next year?"

Children with biological parents, brothers and sisters, cousins, aunts and uncles, have a blueprint. Adopted children have only mystery and suspense. In *Growing Up Adopted,* 65 percent of the adopted young adolescents wanted to meet their birthparents. Why? To find out what they looked like, said 94 percent. Motivations were curiosity, not turmoil, as 80 percent wanted to tell their birthparents "I'm happy."

"Am I lovable?"

As brains grow, grasping a more complex and abstract world, adopted children sometimes feel another loss, their original parents. Being placed with another family entails being "rejected" by birth parents. Of those in Benson's survey who wanted to meet their biological parents, 72 percent wanted to know: *"Why didn't you want me?"*

"Am I sexual?"

Emerging sexuality includes blossoming sensual body parts as well as the sensations of lust. This is emotionally explosive to adopted ten- to fifteen-year-olds who carry a unique weight alongside the issue. Elinor Rosenberg, a clinical assistant professor in psychiatry at the University of Michigan and author of *The Adoption Life Cycle,* explains, "What the pubescent adoptees do know about their birth parents is that they were sexually active and usually irresponsible about birth control. Observing their own characteristics can be a distressing and complicating factor, evoking both the wish and the fear of being like their birth parents."

Because of these two salacious, risk-taking ghosts, some young adolescents are afraid of their sexual feelings. Others are compelled to become sexually active, even pregnant, to understand *by experience* what their birth parents went through and how it felt to lose one's baby. Although there are no conclusive studies linking adopted adolescents to earlier intercourse, most child welfare workers say that adopted adolescents act out sexually more often compared to those who are not adopted, increasing pregnancy risks.

Since these fears are unconscious, parents need to mine this secret territory with sensitivity. Do focus on sexual decision-making skills. Be careful how you cast sexually impulsive young adolescents, because you are talking about your child's birth parents.

"Am I different?"

Middlers dress to duplicate whatever uniform their friends wear, from the barrettes in the girls' hair to the brand of sneakers on the boys' feet. Conformity is clearly the marching order. When wanting to be exactly like your peers is the goal, to stand out in any way is undesirable. To be adopted is to be different.

In science class, students work on a lab about genetics. At a sleepover, girls giggle over astrology and each needs to know the exact hour they were born. A class project assigns a genealogy chart. Travel plans lead to passport applications requiring birth certificates. Any one of these require an adopted middler to confront the past, and provide information that may have been lost.

What Parents of Adopted Adolescents Can Do

Adopted middlers wear their own scarlet A. They recognize it during these years even when no one else does. Some wear it effortlessly. Others feel branded. In Benson's study 27 percent reported that adoption was a big part of how "I think about myself." Most middlers have fantasies and theories about the nature of their birth parents, and about that choice made not to nurture. As their curiosity about the character and characteristics of birth parents increases, the adopted child simultaneously struggles with feelings of disloyalty to the only parents he has ever known.

When parents try to address their middler's qualms, they find daughters and sons who refuse to talk. When a child acts out and their history is brought into the discussion, the middler often verbally lashes out. These are difficult years to have meaningful calm conversations about the child's history. To prevent your middler's internal search from becoming a search and destroy mission for family equilibrium, use these strategies:

Expect adoption to resonate through all the usual psychological, social, sexual, and emotional rough spots. An adopted child may withdraw. He may sequester himself in a prison of fears and a prism of loyalty conflicts. Use your judgement if your child demands more information than you feel he can handle.

Rely on your parenting skills. Mothers and fathers who adopt had to qualify—pass a test—to become parents. You are *more* skilled than other pools of parents. When compared to parents who didn't adopt, adoptive parents score better on measures of stability, communication finesse with their young adolescents, staying involved in the education process, and being supportive. Your edge shows. In the *Growing Up Adopted* survey 74 percent of the twelve- to eighteen-year-olds said, "I get along well with my parents."

Stay connected. Prepare yourself because your child may contemplate searching for her biological parents and fantasize about reunion. Don't take these reunion fantasies personally or seriously, because young adolescents rarely take action. They are merely feeling out your attitude as they feel their way through their history. With a past marred by disconnection, middlers need security. Say, "I'll always be here no matter what, through good times and bad."

Remember that all middlers, adopted or not, are in the process of separating from parents, biological or otherwise. It's easy for adoptive parents to assume all rejection, mouthiness, or misbehavior is because of adoption, when sometimes it's simply adolescence.

When in doubt, consult a professional who understands adoption. If your middler veers out of control, an expert can help you and your child figure out how adoption issues swirl through the turbulence. A small number of adopted youngsters run away. An adopted middler who flees is not trying to get *away* from his family as much as he is trying to run *toward* understanding. He is re-living his birth parents' actions, as they "ran away" from him as an infant.

Adopted middlers do think about a lost home, but they will return with family ties soddered by love, and not by blood alone.

GAY, LESBIAN, AND BISEXUAL PARENTING

"My husband and I found out that his daughter (my stepdaughter) has been sexually active since twelve. She asked me to take her for birth control pills. She has problems with her mom who is gay, and has her girlfriend living in their home. I wonder if the reason my stepdaughter started having sex so young is because she fears she might be gay like her mother!"

Gay people are more open than ever before. It began with a roster of high profile homosexuals and lesbians such as Sandra Bernhard, k.d. lang, and Elton John. Next came the love stories, most famous Ellen De Generes and Ann Heche. The issue of gay, lesbian, and bisexual parenting is a natural progression. Celebrities like Melissa Etheridge opt for artificial insemination to have a child in a lesbian coupling. Many divorce and remarriage scenarios over the last decade have included a coming out subplot.

Children with at least one gay, lesbian, or bisexual parent range between six and fourteen million according to estimates. Adoption agencies say that requests from gay couples have increased. Sperm banks, too, report that homosexual applicants are on the rise.

The question plaguing gay, lesbian, and bisexual parents and couples is: Are they fit to be parents? Will their sexual preference sway their middlers toward homosexuality? Such questions launch much debate, and pit the religious right (who believe that homosexuality is a choice and not an involuntary orientation) squarely against the gay rights activists (who insist sexual preference is genetic and unalterable).

From studies published in respected publications, including *Child Development* and *The Journal of Child Psychology and Psychiatry*, the scientific consensus finds that children reared by gay or lesbian parents are no more likely to be gay or lesbian than those brought up by heterosexuals. Other research proves that these children are *not* afflicted with more psychological problems compared to offspring from non-gay parents. When the team of Harris and Turner looked at twenty-three gay and lesbian parents and sixteen heterosexual parents, few differences in parenting styles surfaced. Only minimal problems cropped up.

This is not to say that having one gay, lesbian, or bisexual parent, or having two lesbian moms or gay dads is without drawbacks. When Epstein (1979) and Bosett (1980) focused on children who had gay fathers, three areas of difficulty emerged. Children in gay families experienced ridicule. They felt alienated from their classmates. They expressed discomfort with their father's sexual orientation.

For middlers, such conflicts are incendiary. Peers become more important to self-image and self-esteem. Socializing is rife with barbs. As puberty begins, the concept of sexuality and sexual orientation takes center stage. Middlers are often confused about sex, making homophobia a fearful fixation for this age group, and a universal putdown.

When a middler has a gay, lesbian, or bisexual parent, or lives in such a home, he or she may have more anxiety: *Am I gay because of my parent?* If word gets out about gay parents, add worry over harassment.

What Gay Parents Can Do

If you are a gay parent, or if your ex-spouse is gay, the experts endorse the following measures.

Prepare yourself for a young adolescent's emotional reactions. Expect anger, confusion, regret, and even remorse during the middler ages. Be sensitive and patient and let your middler know that you empathize with his dilemma.

Face the sexual orientation legacy head on. Tell your middler that homosexuality is not hereditary. Who you are sexually attracted to is not determined by your parents. Explain exactly what homosexuality is—a consistent sexual attraction and desire to choose the same sex. Make certain you discuss same sex crushes (a normal part of growing up for some). Helping your child understand sexual identity is part of a parent's most profound job.

Separate the issue of divorce from the issue of homosexuality. Don't make sexual orientation the issue in custody or visitation wranglings. All parents love their children, regardless of race, color, creed, or sexual orientation. Explain your reasons for divorce as larger than simply the sexuality issue.

Prepare your middler for prejudice. "The only disadvantage to having a gay dad are those people who can't accept it. It hurts me when people are homophobic, because I think how much I love my dad and his boyfriend and all those people I know who are gay." That confession is from *"What About the Children?"* Frankly discuss gay bashing, discrimination, and hatred. Reassure your child that tolerance is growing. Since the late 1980s, the percentage of Americans who disapprove of gays and lesbians according to a National Gay and Lesbian Task Force survey has declined from 75 percent to 56 percent.

Teach your middler that disclosure is a matter of privacy, not shame. Do heterosexual parents talk about their intimate selves? No. Teach your middler that the sexual orientation of an ex-spouse or a parent is no one's business. Disclosure is not about humiliation, but about whose right it is to know.

Link your middler to support groups. The Gay and Lesbian Parents Coalition International can direct you and your young adolescent to support groups, books, and an online community. Doing so obliterates feeling isolated. Meeting rainbow families "normalizes" the experience, introducing your child to how others live, react to criticism, and cope.

All gay parents who are true to themselves are happier. What middlers need from parents on any spectrum of the rainbow is love, support, and good values.

FAMILY BREAKDOWNS IN ANOTHER LANGUAGE

American shores receive more than one million legal and undocumented candidates every year. In the Pacific region, one-fifth of the population was born elsewhere. In Los Angeles, four out of ten people are foreign born; in New York City, three out of ten. The 1990 Census included ninety-five racial and ethnic categories and subcategories. For instance, there are eleven types of Asians, and fifteen Hispanic varieties. Parents and young adolescents don't always speak the same language. In some families this is true literally.

In 1997, we asked teachers to reflect upon the cultural diversity they experienced in their classrooms. Our survey turned up a truly international scope, including Thai, Vietnamese, Puerto Rican, Jamaican, Indian, Native American, Muslim, Polish, Hindu, and Iranian, along with Asian, Hispanic, and African American groups.

Foreign-born parents neither embrace our language nor American culture with the same zeal that their middlers do. Monica McGoldrick, LCSW, Ph.D. et al., experts in family therapy and culture, have coedited the manual *Ethnicity and Family Therapy* and explain, "Adolescents reject their parents' ethnic values and strive to become Americanized. Intergenerational conflicts reflect the value struggles of families adapting to the U.S."

In these Old World to New World families, early adolescence has a new cross-cultural twist and wrinkle. Ten- to fifteen-year-olds don't want to appear different. Cultural ties exaggerate those differences at a time when middlers downplay whatever sets them apart. A young adolescent's task is to act like other American youth. A child conforms in order to be liked by a new group of friends. Parents who emigrate with young adolescents in tow have a double burden, adjusting to migration stress while managing middlers who battle with them over values.

The definition of family itself differs across culture. African Americans define family as extended networks of kin, Chinese as a heavenly body of ancestors. In America, we favor individuality and independence and we launch our children out into the world. Other cultures prefer interdependence, and teach their young to bow to the family and learn their place within its fold.

When two generations envision the middler issues of identity, separation, and family so divergently, the fireworks can be painful. The Asian parent wants to honor the past and preserve it. She doesn't like her son's non-Asian girlfriend. Americanized middlers want to "speak their mind" in the good old USA free-speech tradition to parents who value "holding one's tongue." Chinese parents are distressed by sons and daughters who not only show no respect, but curse their ancestors! To foreign-born patriarchs and matriarchs this behavior betrays sacred concepts like honor and brings on shame.

Parents of assorted ethnic and mixed culture middlers know they are in crisis, but how they react to these family problems varies. Family therapists suggest negotiation, but combining cultural nuances and the generation gap makes the process complex. Family counseling practitioners use these guidelines:

Recognize your middler's determination to become American. Parents steeped in ethnic and religious traditions face increasingly rebellious middlers who become Americanized. They want to fit into a new peer group. It's normal. All second generation immigrants assimilate.

Preserve your traditions but be patient. Allow your young adolescent space to rebel against, even reject, your values. Each middler undergoes this process in order to decide which values are worth adopting. Look ahead, because your grandchildren will rekindle the old ways. Third and fourth generations are more adept at balancing the new culture while holding on to their heritage.

Use support systems within your family and community to bridge your rapport. Find role models that emulate the best of both worlds, the old and the new. Encourage your middler to interact with these chosen few.

Give your son and daughter a language to express their conflict. "I had no language to talk about how all this affected me," laments Japanese-American poet David Mura and contributor to *Half & Half*. Expose your child to voices that articulate culture struggles.

Your middler is a culture broker; so are you. You are both evolving as you embrace your new land and make a new home and future. "Ethnicity is marked by an ever ongoing cultural evolution," say the experts of *Ethnicity and Family Therapy*. "We are all always in a process of changing ethnic identity, from incorporating ancestral influences to forging new and emerging group identities." Your young adolescent is doing this, too. In time your differences will not be as glaring.

Helping Middlers Handle Illness . . .

Cancer, AIDS, lupus, cerebral palsy—25 percent of children under age seventeen manage chronic illness. Kelly Heugel, diagnosed at twelve years of age with Crohn's disease, authored *Young People and Chronic Illness*. Her tips for parents will also help their middlers.

Support don't smother. Encourage independence. Help a young child identify goals he or she can accomplish despite this illness.

Empower your middler to actively manage her illness. Educate her about her disease. Discuss options. Make decisions together.

Don't ostracize or isolate a sick child. Encourage siblings to talk with the sick middler about how the illness affects all members of the family.

LETTING GO . . . A PAINFUL PASSAGE FOR ALL

Living with middlers as they separate, battle with us, and discover who they are is a stretch of wills and a test of love. A wonderful piece of advice came from a thirteen-year-old New England girl. Next time you are locked in a fight with your child, recall this gem. "I go into my room and come out the next day and forget about it."

Sometimes out of the mouths of middler babes comes the best strategy.

STRATEGIES: CONTRACT FOR THE ROLLER-COASTER YEARS

This contract takes into account the fundamental needs of ten- to fifteen-year-olds. A safe house is craved to escape from the pressures of growing up and trying to fit in. Their need for privacy emerges around age twelve, and so parents need to understand it, respect it, and not automatically be suspicious when a middler sequesters herself in her room.

Our contract tackles issues, strives to develop skills, encourages good communication, and attempts to negotiate typical middler conflicts. Conscience is forming during these years, and so debating values is good practice. Allow your middler to argue, because it fine tunes decision-making skills and fosters independence. Since "it's not fair" is every middler's middle name, including two sides to this contract satisfies a middler's sense of

. . . AND COPE WITH DEATH

The death of a parent is the most life-altering trauma a ten- to fifteen-year-old can experience according to The Adolescent Life-Change Event Scale. A parent's death propels a young adolescent into an unwelcome spotlight. This embarrasses a middler, forcing the child to process humiliation (and the guilt it unleashes), along with feelings of helplessness, anger, and abandonment.

Oftentimes a middler has the added burden of regret. During these years the parent-child relationship is often marked by harsh words and cold distances. Death allows for no second chances to make things right. Here's a primer on typical middler reactions and how to help:

"If I start crying I won't be able to stop." Middlers feel out of control because of their unpredictable body growth and emotions. They feel if they start grieving, this, too, will snowball. Explain grief as a natural process with stages.

"I don't want to talk about it." A parent monopolized by grief hits this stoic wall and assumes this child is "a rock." No child is. He is feeling intense loss, whether capable of expressing it or not. Encourage him to express his grief.

"Now I'll never really know my parent." "I had just begun to see my parents as people, not superheroes," said a fourteen-year-old. "When my father died [of a heart attack], it cut off a whole beginning of getting to know him as a person." Share memories. Continue talking about the parent who died. Answer any questions your middler has.

Dawne Kimbrell, Ph.D., a clinical psychologist and Vanderbilt University assistant adjunct professor of psychology, advises, "Give her time and room to absorb the loss. Reassure her. Try 'It takes time, but you will get through this'." Middlers live in the now. When the present is so sad, steering them toward a peaceful tomorrow begins the healing process.

justice and sensitivity to injustice. It is a blueprint to guide your family business. (As with all contracts the sooner you get a commitment from your young adolescents, the better your chances of having this contract work.) If privileges are earned, your middler is less likely to voluntarily engage in behaviors that undo what he has worked so hard to achieve.

We, the undersigned, pledge to fight for our rights and live up to our responsibilities as follows. When we fail, we will take the consequences set forth.

RIGHTS OF MIDDLERS AND OF PARENTS

- To be treated with respect and dignity.
- To be spoken to in a civil manner (even when pissed off).
- To be loved and appreciated for who I am.
- To be given an opportunity to argue my case.
- To be allowed a cooling-off period during all disagreements in the privacy of my room.

RESPONSIBILITIES

OF MIDDLERS	OF PARENTS
To get an education and perform to the best of my ability.	To supervise the education of my child and help when required.
To discover and nurture the special talent I possess.	To identify and nurture my middler's talent.
To remain drug, alcohol, and smoke free.	To monitor the safety of my middler and ensure s/he remains drug, alcohol, and smoke free.
To contribute suggestions for rules and consequences when they are broken.	To include my middler in the rule-making process and in defining consequences of misbehavior.
To follow the rules in the household regarding curfews and chores.	To set reasonable boundaries and behavior codes.
To perform the consequences when necessary.	To be consistent and fair in disciplining.

We, the undersigned, agree to this contract.

_____   _____

CHAPTER TWO

Friends, Friendship, and Falling in Love

*

"My eleven-year-old daughter doesn't have friends. Not at school, not in the neighborhood. She is involved in outside activities, but hasn't had much luck. I'm concerned about what this is doing to her. Is there anything I can do to ease things for her?"
—Mother

The sting of being ostracized pelts nearly all young adolescents at one time or another during middle school. When the sun rises and sets on peers, *"I have no friends"* or *"I hate my friends"* are serious laments. Chances are your middler will be the butt of cruel teasing. Tending to your middler's social insecurities is only one side of the coin. *"I hate my daughter's friends"* intensifies once the romantic component kicks in. *"What does my son see in that girl?"* We repeatedly hear *"I hate my son's girlfriend"* from exasperated mothers and fathers.

This chapter is about relationships, the platonic and the romantic kind. Who is responsible for teaching friendship and social skill–building? You are. Since few of us are prepared, we'll give you the curriculum. When it comes to romantic entanglements, a parent's role is more precarious, yet even more important. When the dating games begin, both you and your middler need assistance.

FRIENDSHIP LESSONS

Listen to this eighth grade girl: "Who's coming to your party so far? Hopefully, Dana's mom won't let her go. I hate her so much! I think Dana needs new friends. And Paul is really getting on my nerves. He's always looking at me and talking to me in such nice ways—he makes me want to puke!"

The hardest course for middle school students to understand is the social scene. Most young adolescents are clueless about why their friendships are so unstable. They ask themselves, "Why do my friends act the way they do?" Not helping your middler grasp the social turbulence maroons your child on an island of confusion and pain.

Friendship class, for boys and girls, should begin about fourth grade when children are on the cusp of struggling (or galloping) toward independence, and grasping onto peers for support. This curriculum jumps off old words of wisdom. Since these adages are easy to remember, and well known, if you attach a little lesson, you can effectively teach a middler what she or he needs to know about friendship.

I cannot tell a lie. A good friend is trustworthy. She can keep a secret. She will not spread a rumor. When we surveyed students, parents, and teachers for our first book, we found that lies and rumors, scribbled on notes and traded all day long, are the currency in middle school. Teach your child not to get sucked into the rumor mill. Trust is the cornerstone of friendship.

Birds of a feather flock together. What qualities do good friends have? Companionship. Caring. Fun. A friend shares your child's interests and makes him feel good about his achievements. When your child and his friend are together, there should be good times. He should feel liked and accepted for who he is. The warmth between the two of them should make him feel good about himself and about his life.

Never a borrower nor a lender be. Avoid situations that stir up social crises. Students confessed that homework and test-taking were triggers that set off many feuds among classmates. Smarter students are pressured to let an unprepared student cheat off their work. Experts tell us cheating is epidemic. Many students pester to borrow the homework to copy all the math equations. You're damned if you do, and damned if you don't conspire. The middler who sidesteps such landmines keeps friendships and integrity intact.

No man (or woman) is an island. Teach your child that if he is being ridiculed, he should not keep it a secret. Let your child, especially if it's your son, know it's not wimpy to talk about upsetting peer situations. It's not snitching to reveal the cruelty of tormentors to an adult.

In our survey, many young adolescents (36 percent) admitted to being shunned by a group. How did they respond? Only 15 percent confided in their parents, and a mere 2 percent in teachers. Keeping their humiliation a secret was the strategy of 8 percent. "I decided to get tougher," reported nearly 20 percent. Toughing it out, with only humiliation for company, is not acceptable. Middlers need your help to process hurt and learn from social disasters.

If you can't say something nice about a person, don't say anything at all. According to experts, cruel remarks are most potent and damaging in middle school. (Harassment and bullying will be fully discussed later in Chapter Ten.) Young adolescents, in the midst of an awkward growth spurt, all have physical flaws, and they all know it. Teach yours not to push that hot button with derogatory digs.

Do unto others as you would have them do unto you. The golden rule is the ultimate mantra to teach your young adolescent. If you want your child to exhibit kindness, empathy, compassion, sharing, and helpfulness, talk about these values. Ask your child to emulate them. A New York soccer coach wisely recommended to his preteen, "I tell my daughter, if you want to have a friend, be a friend."

Having conversations about friendship, exploring your middler's experiences with finding it as well as losing it, is worth the effort. According to researchers, young adolescents who have friendships of high quality—which means they include intimacy, prosocial behavior, trust, loyalty, affection, and emotional support—develop high self-esteem.

Don't worry too much at this age about a middler's dependence upon peers. As one mother lamented, "I don't want my daughter to surrender what is unique about her. That seems to be what she is doing. The way she dresses, it's like she has to wear a uniform. Where she goes, with whom, it is all so dictated by the group." Psychologist John Gottman, Ph.D. points out in his book, *The Heart of Parenting,* that conformity is healthy. Being able to pick up on social cues and mores, and adapting to fit in is a social skill which is a valuable asset in early adolescence and throughout life.

CLIQUES GET MANY MIDDLERS' GOATS

"My twelve-year-old daughter has been complaining about the social climate at her school. She hates the snobbishness of her fellow students and their routine of deliberately hurting those who they feel are different and inferior. Lately some of her friends have been ignoring her. She thinks it's because a former friend suddenly hates her and has made statements to that effect. Now she wants to change schools, maybe even enter a foreign exchange program. She even asked me if I could homeschool her. How can I counsel her?"

—Mother

When your daughter wants to escape to her version of the old French Foreign Legion, you know you are in clique-land.

While boys, too, are targeted by their peers, they don't experience cliques the same way girls do. Boys are ostracized to be sure, but not as regularly or as adeptly. Physical intimidation and violence more often characterize boys' social humiliations (see Chapter Ten for more on violence).

Being singled out for ridicule, ignored, or talked about behind your back by a group is officially coined "scapegoating." This cruel clique syndrome emerges in middle school as young adolescents begin to define themselves by belonging to groups. As if to psychically steady themselves from moving away from their parents, middlers reach out to their peers. When being included counts so much, being excluded is part of the game.

Because the search for identity and the longing to fit in is so central, being shunned can be immobilizing. The typical social humiliation scene replays over and over again, usually taking center stage in a young adolescent girl's life. Her role becomes one in a Machiavellian masterpiece theater, played out before an audience of former friends and classmates. The child is left out, twisting in the wind. School becomes a daily torture chamber.

Typically, the ostracized girl looks at herself, figuring she is to blame for all this. "What did I do? Did I say something wrong?" She scours her behavior and replays the conversations she's had in the last few days or hours, searching for the explanation that will make some sense out of this painful experience. "Is it the way I dress? The way I look?" she worries, scanning every part of her person and personality for clues to this mystery.

"Young adolescent girls have no sense of loyalty or commitment," observes Felice DiDonna, CSW, a middle school social worker and family therapist. "Many are best friends one day. Overnight they have a new best friend, and they are viciously picking on yesterday's best friend. It may be sad, but it's a true fact of life at this age."

Girls don't understand what's going on. The victim is the joke. Rarely is she let in on it. "I was shunned. The girls had been my friends! They wouldn't tell me why they were shunning me, teasing me, or putting me in this awkward situation," said one thirteen-year-old Connecticut casualty.

According to Lynn E. Ponton, clinical psychiatrist and adolescent specialist, "The language of girls this age can be confusing; it includes the following questions, asked silently or even aloud on a daily basis: *'Do you like me? Are you still my friend?'* The language clouds the underlying issues."

Ah, here's the rub. Those underlying issues aren't really about camaraderie or companionship at all. They are purely concerned with power and control.

When your child becomes ostracized, what do you do? Social ties, bonds, and binds are the real, unrecognized agenda of middle school. And yet, there is no custom-made instruction given to our young adolescents. We, as parents, have to teach our middlers about cruelty and coercion. To assist you in emotionally medicating and healing the power bouts of early adolescence, here's a list of things you can do when scapegoating happens.

A Clique First-Aid Kit

Define cliques and their mean maneuvers to your child as agendas of power and control, not friendship. Since everyone this age feels insecure, they struggle with being accepted. Some try to forge their own sense of self by controlling others. Some attempt to make themselves feel better by ridiculing the shortcomings of others. Witnesses of the persecution don't speak up or rush to defend a victim, even a good friend, for fear of being rejected, or worse, targeted next. Ask your child to observe the central features: Who is included? Who is not? Who decides? Who agrees? Does anyone ever disagree? Have a discussion about what happens if someone reaches out to rescue a shunned victim.

Immediately reassure your child that being shunned is not her fault. Tell her that nothing she did, or *is* deep down inside or on the outside serves to explain what is happening. Girls who are socially ridiculed develop negative body images, concluded Dr. L. Kris Gowen after studying 157 girls between the ages of ten and thirteen. Victimized girls mistakenly think, if they were just prettier or thinner, then they wouldn't be teased. Tell your child that this kind of mean-spirited torment is unfortunately part of early adolescence. Unless young adolescent girls are let off the blame hook, they can come away permanently scarred and carry on lifelong searches to understand their humiliation episodes.

The sea of confessions from mothers who, to this day, recall vividly their own similar war stories has truly amazed us. Even celebrities, famous for beauty, charm, and achievement, such as Kim Basinger and Hillary Rodham Clinton, have gone on record with tales of preadolescent trauma. Share your own memories of scapegoating.

Turn your child from victim to victor. Admit that you can't always make the painful drama disappear. You can talk to your child's middle school teacher, who can work to eliminate the behavior in school. Brainstorm with your child to get her to identify options. This is hard, to be sure. It's not as easy as picking up her lunch tray and sitting at another table in the cafeteria. Middle school is no picnic.

However, there are choices. She can ignore the tormentors rather than trying to befriend them again. She can start looking for new friends, among the boys in school, or in groups outside of school. You want to explode the image of powerlessness your daughter may have of herself, along with a belief that she is at the mercy of others. This twelve-year-old girl's rationalization is healthy: "I figure I have other friends, so if I have one or two less, it won't kill me." All young adolescents need hope and a view that includes possibility. At no other time does this count more.

Don't join the fray. Some mothers telephone the offending girl's mother. What begins as a mature and logical step can turn the clique crisis into an adult catfight. That's what happened with two ten-year-old classmates in a Detroit suburb. The young pair had a history of name-calling and harassing phone calls, which soon got their mothers involved. Did this intervention help? Hardly. The moms made headlines with "Sugar and Spite and a Legal Mess Not Nice." Each, taking her child's side, took the social umbrage to the next level of police reports, orders of protection, all the way to the courtroom.

Promise your hurt, clique-weary child that this, too, will pass. It will. We promise.

WALKING THE GANGPLANK

"How do I go about discouraging my twelve-year-old from hanging out with friends that I'm afraid are not good?"
—Mother

Suppose you and your middler don't agree on the choice of friends. Parents from a variety of locations across the country registered these complaints. Although expressed in many different and passionate soliloquies, it boils down to "I don't like my child's friends." It's interesting to note that when we asked the teachers in our survey to list the problem situations their students encountered, "in with a bad crowd" topped the bad news list. Two-thirds checked that problem, making it more prevalent than drugs, major depression, or acts of violence. Why do so many middlers make such appalling entrees into undesirable rat packs? Is dabbling in a legion of losers or slinking around with a loose list of brash flirts some kind of universal detour for many? Is this bad crowd obsession a figment of teachers' overactive alarm bells or parents' overprotective imaginations?

A young adolescent's choice of friends is a new frontier. At this age, middlers pick their own friends, choices over which parents no longer have any control. It's common for middlers to shed old friendships like obsolete snakeskins. Why? Youngsters grow in different directions, at uneven paces, and simply apart. Oftentimes, mothers and fathers are unfamiliar with this new band of companions because middle school brings together new faces from all over town.

The upside to this new potential pool is its diversity and social opportunity. The downside for parents is being bushwhacked by an unknown fourteen-year-old hip-hop derelict or an eleven-year-old bare-naveled Lolita rudely raiding your refrigerator. Your formerly delightful child looks on, amused by your reaction. Your dismay is part fear of the unknown, and part good old nostalgia for the days of sandbox socializing when you were in control of who came for the cookies and milk.

Expert Eda LeShan explains that strange or even unsuitable friends can be part of a young adolescent's "wish fulfillment." The argument goes like this: Such companion choices meet a child's inner need somehow. Picking someone daring, or totally different, is part of exploring and experimenting with identities. Think of it as your child's researching how the other half lives. A shy girl befriends an outrageous daredevil with blue fingernails and azure-streaked hair. A bright and studious boy suddenly begins hanging out with the star underachiever (who overachieves with the girls). Middlers search for other selves and other perspectives. These partnerships are not usually permanent.

The best course of action for parents to take initially is caution. Hold your tongue. *Middlers are extremely sensitive to criticism of their friends!* Reserve your judgment until you know more about this new friend, and more about what your child finds so compelling. The friendship may end quickly, as mystifyingly as it began.

In the meantime, *be on the lookout for harm that may result.* Don't stand by idly or silently if you observe the danger signs of substance abuse or violence. Be sure you have concrete evidence, not just suspicion, before you act.

"I didn't think I'd ever have to think about my son joining a gang," a father reported emotionally. "We live in the suburbs for heaven's sake, not some inner city. But right here in our town I've found out that gangs are a growing problem. I've talked to the local police who confirmed this is true. Can you tell me how to gang-proof my son?"

Could "the wrong crowd" be a gang? Is the popularity of *Grease,* the movie and the musical revival, a case of art imitating real-life trends? Unfortunately, what this father stumbled upon, the spread of gangs, is happening in communities all across America. It no longer matters which side of the tracks you live on, or whether you reside in a small town or a downtown metropolis.

Organized gangs are on the upswing. Nearly twice as many twelve- to nineteen-year-olds in 1995 told researchers there are street gangs in their schools compared to those surveyed in 1989. In central cities, students reporting gangs went from 25 percent of those polled up to 40 percent. The suburban gang observers nearly doubled, from 14 percent to 26 percent. In what were defined as nonmetropolitan areas, which covered small towns and rural enclaves, those who witnessed gangs nearly tripled, going from 7 percent of students reporting gang activities to 20 percent.

Why Gangs?

What could make hanging out in gangs, notoriously linked with misbehavior, so increasingly appealing to our young adolescents? The answers are intriguing. They raise more questions which we, the parents and adults in our communities, will have to answer.

Inner cities no longer have the monopoly on economic hopelessness and chaotic family life. Even though we are now enjoying a booming economy, not everyone is reaping the benefits. Many families have had members lose jobs over the last decade due to corporate downsizing. The disparity between the haves and the have-nots has widened considerably. Gangs flourish in this climate.

Dysfunctional families come in many forms. They can be bruised by divorce with invisible and vicious subplots of domestic abuse. Still more have members who are addicted to alcohol or other substances. Even in the best of families, with two working parents or one single parent, many experts believe that today's youth are left alone too much of the time.

The Carnegie Council on Adolescent Development report *Fateful Choices—Healthy Youth for the 21st Century* points out, "The sad reality is that young adolescents at every economic level are very often neglected by adults—even within their own families—or get lost in the mass, victims of large institutions that undermine their healthy development. They return from school to empty homes and suffer the consequences of anonymity—a scourge of modern society and a condition that makes people behave at their worst."

Roaming through their adolescent years without adults to guide and amuse them, young adolescents turn to one another. Middlers are at a time when they desperately need to belong. If the family fails to provide them with a viable support system, they are vulnerable to the overtures of organized gangs.

Diversity and cultural trends play a role. Answering the "Who am I?" and "Where do I fit in?" questions is one of the major tasks of young adolescents. For many in minority cultures, the ethnic identity puzzle is harder to assemble. African American, Hispanic, and Asian adolescents struggle more and require more time to understand themselves and their places in society. According to a consensus at a recent Black Psychology Conference, standard psychology fails minority teens because it doesn't take into account their deep history and the impact of racism.

Furthermore, cultures collide. Mixed marriages have created middlers who don't fit neatly into either group. Among newer immigrant groups, the young reject their Old World–steeped parents. A self-imposed generation gap widens. Gangs provide a homogeneous identity to middlers struggling with ethnic conflicts and confusion.

Gang glamour is cool. The youth culture's music and fashion endorses gangs. This media melange has blurred racial and cultural lines, enticing many middlers to dress, talk, walk, and act like ghetto guys and dolls. The total influence of ethnic and youth culture, family, and community has made many of today's young impressionable and vulnerable to gang cultures. Gangs promise a cultural definition, guarantee a feeling of fitting in, and yet exact a dangerous price for belonging.

HOW TO PROTECT YOUR MIDDLER FROM BAD BOYS AND GIRLS

If you find one of your middler's friends dangerously intimidating, take a closer look to see if a gang connection could be lurking nearby. Safeguard your child from being vulnerable to a bad crowd, or worse a juvenile gang, by asking yourself these questions:

Do I spend enough time with my middler? Does our family schedule offer enough opportunities to deliver that coveted feeling of membership? What kinds of recreational activities do we regularly pursue? Do we take on any projects as a family or as a one-on-one team? Building a shed, planting a garden—many things make good family projects.

Has my middler joined any groups? Is she or he a member of The Boys Club, the YMCA, the YWCA, or Girls, Inc.? Does he attend a church youth group of any kind? Does he play a sport at school or on a community team? Of all the middle school clubs available (do you know what clubs your middle school offers?) is your son or daughter active in any? Seven out of ten young people do not belong to any club or organization according to a 1997 national poll called *Kids These Days*. If you want your child to befriend a different mix of young adolescents, steering him towards a new club provides him with a clean slate of possibilities.

Have I given any thought to the questions (or mixed feelings) about eth-nic, racial, or cultural membership my young adolescent may be grappling with? Does my child attend any rituals, either family or community, that positively help her feel good about being part of this heritage? Am I too at-tached to the old ways of my ethnic group, and not open enough to the American customs that my middler wants to embrace?

Is my child getting a satisfactory sense of belonging from a group of friends? When sixth graders were studied as they grew into eighth graders, approximately 75 percent spent their time in groups. These cliques were organized around popularity, revolved around sports or aca-demics, or were simply configurations of just average middlers. Nearly half the girls felt cliques were very important, but another third of all the middlers gave mixed reviews. What about the remaining middle school students? They reported spending most of their time alone or with one close friend. If that is your young adolescent, make sure that sense of be-longing is provided in other nonschool settings.

ROMANTIC RELATIONSHIPS

"He sat next to me on the bus ride home. His hands were freezing. I held them and rubbed them. I loved every minute of it. He is so gorgeous. I don't believe that you can be in love at the age of thirteen, but in this case I'm as close as humanly possible."
—Seventh grade girl

Parents dismiss the romantic feelings of the young. If a young mid-dler professes she's in love, adults call it "puppy love" and scoff. Worse, the pubescent infatuation becomes the family joke. Make no mistake, young adolescents think about these matters differently. Sixty-two percent of children ages ten to thirteen told a Roper Starch poll that the opposite sex was important to them. Only half of the parents polled be-lieved their youngsters were so romantically inclined so early.

Young love takes many forms. Sometimes it comes and goes quicker than even Cupid can shake an arrow at it. Two weeks is a common length of middler couplings. Those who aren't falling in and out of love are act-ing as the "love brokers." A messenger often carries the "I want to go out with you" intention as well as the "I want to break it off" swansong. What follows are the different faces and phases of middler romantic passion along with strategies to deal delicately with each one.

Fantasy Land

One father told us, "My thirteen-year-old daughter asked me if she could pin a poster on her bedroom wall. I said fine and even gave her a hammer out of my toolbox. The next thing I knew her walls were a collage of newsclips and teen magazine centerfolds. I got the picture. She was fixated with Nick Carter, one of the Backstreet Boys. With all these photoshoots, when did this kid have time to sing? All I could think of was dingy apartments of serial killers I'd seen in movies or books, where obsessive unbalanced people create shrines like this to the object of their affection. Was my daughter on the road to becoming a nut case?"

This father was gripped with concern. Mothers react with less alarm because they have more experience with dreamboat-itis. When Paul McCartney's wife, Linda, died of breast cancer in 1998, many of us recalled when Paul, John, George, or Ringo was the center of our universe. Charismatic faces change. Frank Sinatra. Elvis. Leonardo. What doesn't change is a young adolescent girl's descent into an imaginary world. Her crush defines her life, her binder, her locker, her wardrobe, and her bedroom walls.

Boys go through this, too, as record-breaking poster sales of Cindy Crawford prove. Why do you think the *Sports Illustrated* swimsuit issue flies off the shelves? *Playboy* has given way to the Internet, where today's young boys surf for centerfolds. Young adolescent boys may be propelled more by curiosity than crushes, but they are preoccupied with fantasy, too.

Aligning fantasy and reality into a seamless scenario allows our middlers a dress rehearsal for true love. In the privacy of their room, they can get up close and personal with a range of new and overwhelming sensations, including lust, love, and jealousy. Falling for rock stars, models, or athletes is safer than actually displaying such intense passions for the boy or girl sitting at the next desk in middle school, not that that doesn't happen, too, or even simultaneously.

Such dreamy crushes give mothers and fathers wonderful opportunities to have those first discussions about relationships. One mother told us, "On a summer's day at the beach, my twelve-year-old daughter and I spent an hour comparing her favorite boys. Who was the cutest? The rock star, the basketball player, or the Russian hockey defender? I asked, which one did she have the most in common with? Well the rock star loved scuba diving and she loved to snorkel. She loved basketball, too, and was a talented athlete. What qualities would she like to find in the idol of her dreams if she got to know him face to face? She didn't want to find out he was an egomaniac. I'd never seen my tight-lipped child so willing to talk with me."

Spending time in fantasyland with a middler sets up a communication precedent. The content of the talks covers critical ground. When you establish this relationship-talk ritual now, your young adolescent will feel comfortable discussing romantic choices with you later.

The "Real" Romance

The relationship conversation is easier to launch with girls. Getting your son to open up on this topic may be more taxing, but press on.

"On Valentine's Day," the mother of a thirteen-year-old boy told us, "my son brought his girlfriend along with us to a restaurant. She was wearing a beautiful heart-shaped gold locket that I admired. She blushed and said it was a gift from my son, which was news to me. I could tell it was expensive and a very personal choice of gift. Two weeks later, the material girl ditched my son. He was left with a broken heart and an empty wallet."

Feelings and connections aren't the stuff that little boys are made of. Processing the intense emotions that swirl around the issue of girls isn't easy for them. As this mother learned too late, her son could have used some guidance. Only mothers can unlock the mysterious nuances of how females define love for their sons, not to mention how girls behave and what it all means. Only fathers can explain the great divide that exists between how the two genders react to romantic overtures and commitments. Whether it's golden gift giving or extending one's heart on a silver platter, boys need as much, perhaps more, loving counseling.

Adventure Land

One boy remarked, "My sister wants to go out on dates with her boyfriend. She's only thirteen but all she thinks about is guys. And I think she thinks about sex! Isn't she too young to date?"

The desire to date is emerging sooner, reflecting an earlier onset of puberty (as you will read about in Chapter Four). Many middlers jump onto the dating gameboard faster (and with less emotional maturity) than they did in the past.

The average age that American middle class children go on their first unchaperoned date is fourteen or fifteen for girls, and fifteen or sixteen for boys, as pinpointed by a Temple University researcher. Dating tends to occur earlier within disadvantaged communities. It's wise to follow these norms because 80 percent of young adolescents who started dating at age twelve, engaged in premarital sex before the end of high school.

Our own survey asked middlers to tell us what happens on a typical date. Many hadn't dated at all yet, but some had. An eighth grade New England boy gave us the silent gender's version of the fifth amendment, stonewalling with, "I will not say," implying that if he talked it would be self-incriminating. Obviously he's not the kiss-and-tell type. "We go to the movies and just have fun," chronicled a South Dakota thirteen-year-old boy. A precocious Arizona desert rose, age twelve, said, "We go home, eat, and go to bed." We hope she misread the question and is telling us what happens *after* the typical date.

Romantic Choices and Pairings

A father said, "My daughter's got me very upset. She's fifteen and so far has apparently no interest in picking a boy from a similar background. She's zeroed in on this sixteen-year-old boy from the other side of town, with a significantly different socioeconomic profile. Last week she spent her allowance and what she earned baby-sitting on clothes for this boy since his parents can't afford much. When they go to a movie, she pays. Quite honestly I am at a loss. I realize taking a stand would probably cement their relationship more. I don't want to drive a wedge between us. I'm trying to give her space, but I can't help but worry that this boy is going to get her into some kind of trouble."

If you relate, you are in good company. This father's comments depict vividly the two basic conflicts that parents have concerning the romantic lives of their young adolescents. First, they fret over the choices sons and daughters make. Does this boy come from a good home? Is this girl smart enough for my college-bound son? Secondly, they express concern over whether their young impressionable child will be led astray. Will this flirt seduce my son into sexual behavior too soon? If I let my daughter go out with this rebellion poster boy, will substance abuse dog the match?

Let's be clear about one thing right off the bat. The romantic choice is not yours. You already know that. You realize that if you express outright disapproval for a heartthrob, it's bound to intensify the attraction. It's a Romeo and Juliet catch-22. Do you say nothing about a match that your antenna says spells trouble? Or do you argue your case? Not exactly either. Here's what you can do.

Investigate your first impression further. Perhaps, this underprivileged boy that your princess has picked is a success story in the making. Find out more about him. What does she see that you don't? Perhaps he is smart and an achiever in school. Or maybe he has talent in art or music. It could be he has a personality bound for leadership. Invite him over for a casual dinner (stress the casual so he doesn't feel like he's in a lineup), or include him when you are giving a family party. Remember to give yourself and your partner the lecture you've given a million times about appearances. Don't judge by his outside packaging. Go deeper.

Offer observations not criticism. If you have scoured his personality and you are more convinced this is a disastrous pairing, don't tell your daughter why in no uncertain terms. Instead give her observations. For example, "Johnny always puts down school. Does that mean he doesn't plan to continue his education? Have you ever tried to explain to him why you *do* want to go to college?" Or, "Jennifer seems so affectionate and romantic. Does she play sports? What does she want to be when she grows up? Do you think she will want to get married right out of high school?"

The answers may not come out of your middler's mouth right then. Young adolescents live in a touchy here-and-now zone. They lack instant wisdom, and perhaps that on-the-spot willingness to acknowledge what you are saying. Don't despair. What you are posing is a framework for them to think through. It's a "what if" web that you are spinning. Your child will get caught up in it if not today, then tomorrow, or down the road.

Young adolescents are just beginning to learn to take their emotional temperatures during romance. In our survey, 36 percent had boyfriends or girlfriends. One-fourth said they were happy with their romantic choices, while 4 percent admitted they were stuck. Why didn't more answer? Making sense out of love is still too new. It takes time for brains to catch up to hormones. Some relationships, like this next one, are not delivering happiness or satisfaction.

A mom worried, "I have a son who has been dating his girlfriend for a year. She's sweet enough but they spend more time arguing than anything else. They don't seem to respect each other. Worse, they call each other names, like 'moron' and worse. I've tried to explain to him that it's not good when two people are constantly fighting. It's not like he learned this arguing stuff at home. His father and I rarely argue, and when we do, we try not to do it in front of our boys. Doesn't this sound like an unhealthy relationship?"

Mom's correct in pegging this an unhealthy pattern. Can Mom break it off? No. Can she comment on the badmouthing? Absolutely. "Where do you think your girlfriend learned that name-calling?" Can she express concern over the frequency of fighting? She could say, "It seems you two spend a lot more time being miserable and angry than having fun with one another." It's not a healthy romance, but the middler needs to draw that conclusion.

Allow young adolescents to explore good and bad matches. Choosing a companion is a decision-making skill. It isn't something we can squirt into a child's Gatorade. Making appropriate choices takes grasping a number of questions and possibilities. It involves calculating the future, and forecasting where these two lovebirds will be heading, together and individually. Above all, picking well takes practice. Falling in love and out of love entails some hard lessons, like realizing he is not what you wanted or she is not the person you thought she was.

When you levy a final verdict on your middler's boyfriend or girlfriend you deprive your child of the process of evaluating the choice. Good decision-making requires making mistakes. Don't we all learn more from our failures than our successes? (You've been told that one a zillion times too.) This is part of the romantic training arena.

Cultivate your middler's personal voice. "My eleven-year-old daughter has fallen for what I see is a typical womanizer. He asked out her best friend, then lied about it. She forgave him. Now I admit this is only fifth-grade soap stuff here, but I'm worried that my daughter is showing the early signs of a willingness to be a doormat for guys."

Do you admit to being romantically challenged? Have you made mistakes in your love life? Gotten divorced? Are you a lightning rod for losers? Did you play Sir Galahad to a maiden who wasn't worth the rescue effort? Few of us feel like experts. When we don't exactly exude "romantic confidence," how can we impart that ability?

Not only do we feel ill-equipped to teach relationship lessons, but our students, too, are handicapped. Young adolescents are insecure. Girls are worse off than boys. Studies show that feminine self-esteem declines around age eleven, and bottoms out between twelve and thirteen.

According to Carol Gilligan, an expert on girls and self-image, this chronological disadvantage has romantic side effects. She found girls at age eight who were dumped by boys, recognized their anger, and spoke up. Fast forward to age twelve. These same girls now weren't clear about how they felt. They traded in their righteous ire for confusion. As girls get older they begin to question their gut intuition when they should be honing it.

Have lots of talks with your daughter and son about locating that personal voice. Use every opportunity to ask her what her romantic gut is suggesting. Teach her to connect with her instinct and to act on its internal wisdom.

Use training manuals to help you. There are many books written to explore the nature of romances, the mistakes lovers make, and ways to analyze your good and not-so-good love connections. An example is *Love Is a Story,* by Robert Sternberg, Ph.D. Apparently, our relationships are stories, tales within us. Some of us think love is a recipe; if we mix patience and affection, it will work. For others, love is a drama where characters wrestle for control. There are gardening tales, collector scenarios (the old notch on the bedpost set), and scripts which feature trust or sacrifice.

By reading and talking with your middler about a book like this, or any other, you are saying that romance requires an education. It does. Join a mother/daughter reading club and choose a book with a romantic theme. Take your child to a father/son luncheon where the speaker will be addressing socializing issues. If no such opportunities exist, organize them!

Wouldn't it be nice if our sons and daughters could learn the lessons about broken hearts and faded dreams we've learned over a lifetime? You can give your child a head start. If you make relationship talk a priority, middlers can learn these "heart smarts."

Never trivialize your middler's romantic feelings. Whether you agree or disagree with your child's pining, avoid "You'll get over him." Instead, when your middler is nursing a broken heart, say "I know how betrayed (angry, sad, surprised) you must feel." Don't poopoo with "You're too young to feel that way." A better comment on unrequited love is "It's wonderful to see you are capable of feeling love so completely. You will have another chance, if you let yourself."

Validate all the emotions your middler experiences. Attach a name to each. Then your middler learns to recognize feelings and take responsibility for them. Giving your child the encouragement to articulate all of the emotions that occur during romantic ups and downs is one of the best gifts you can ever give. Strengthening your middler's romantic voice is the best insurance that she (and he) will continue to improve those invisible emotional, ethical, and moral choices.

There are times when you will need to intervene in a young adolescent's romance, and in the next chapter we will explore those circumstances.

The ages between ten and fifteen may not be the most opportune time for young adolescents to begin their love lives, but they do. Friendship feuds and backstabbings can be as hurtful as broken hearts. When toddlers begin walking, they wobble. When young adolescents begin fantasizing, socializing in groups, entering exclusive couplings, they wobble socially and romantically. Parents ever-so-gently have to stabilize them. The friendship standards, the choices, voices, and conclusions that middlers exercise will put into motion patterns that will last well into adulthood. Watching a middler fall in love, fall out of love, fall off the popularity poll, or never get on it in the first place, is tough. The best part is being there to catch your child after the fall. Let them know you will.

Strategies: Encourage Good Social Decision-Making
Remember to:

Ask your middler why he has selected a new friend or become infatuated with someone. Discuss first impressions. "What makes you like that boy?" Then agree to talk in a few weeks to see if that initial opinion was right or wrong. Stop short of forbidding or endorsing a child's choices. Nudge with observations instead.

Supervise your child's party plans. Discuss the guest list of a birthday party beforehand to ward off scapegoating. Teach your child to be sensitive.

Monitor whether your child is the dumper or the dumpee. Help your middler attach names to the feelings he encounters in the social whirl that is adolescence. Remind him that he must understand his anger, or that she must know why that person triggers disgust. The bad feelings of rejection, betrayal, and hurt need to be acknowledged as well as the good feelings of camaraderie, fun, and love.

Discourage early dating by encouraging group dates. If your young adolescent wants to date by twelve or thirteen, suggest she go out in a pack. She can be with her "beloved" and part of a group, too.

Provide alternate social opportunities. If your middler has little experience in the friendship department, boost her confidence with a pen-pal. This arena delivers social acceptance and helps her build conversational skills. A pen-pal can be an excellent distraction during painful clique periods. Try these Internet sites for penpal possibilities:

Cybersisters (www.worldkids.net/clubs/CSIS/csis.htm) has an active pen-pal program.

G.I.R.L. (www.worldkids.net/girl) links girls from eight to fourteen all over the world.

Conduct a postscript after a social event. After a dance or date, ask, "Did you have fun?" Let your young adolescent know she is strong enough and smart enough to calculate who is enjoyable company. Let your middler understand that ultimately, she is going to be solely responsible for deciding what is right and wrong, who is good for her and who isn't.

CHAPTER THREE

Sexual Encounters and Fatal Attractions

*

> *"Our twelve-year-old girl just unintentionally introduced us to a new game called Lemons. After a recent get-together, we found these pieces of paper. On one set were the names of the boys and girls she had over, the players. On the next set were the places: 'shower, library, closet, and bedroom.' Yet another group listed body parts: 'penis, vagina, butt, and tits.' The last scrap read: 'bite, lick, suck, and squeeze.' We are very concerned. Her thirteenth birthday party is coming up and we don't know what to do. Are you familiar with Lemons?"*
> —Father

Remember Colonel Mustard in the drawing room with the noose? The Lemons game sounds like some erotic version of Clue. Luckily this game is not well known, but Lemons makes a parent long for that old Spin the Bottle, doesn't it? Our last chapter explored friendship and love, and now we are going to add sex to the mix.

All parents want their middlers to grow up, fall madly in love, get married, enjoy a fulfilling sex life, and have children, *in that order.* Unfortunately many young adolescents are not following our preferred progression of intimacy.

Many of us have to deal with the reality that our young adolescents are sexually active. A report from the National Campaign to Prevent Pregnancy reveals these findings:

- Twenty-seven percent of fifteen-year-old boys have had sexual intercourse.
- Among seventeen-year-olds, 90 percent of Black, 18 percent of White, and 35 percent of Hispanic teenage boys are no longer virgins.
- By the time boys reach nineteen, 85 percent will be experienced. Girls are neck and neck.
- Twenty-five percent of fifteen-year-old girls reported they have had sexual intercourse. By nineteen, 77 percent will join these ranks.

Did you know that 80 percent of all Americans first had sexual intercourse as teenagers? Chances are you know that statistic better than you are willing to admit. Actually, the number of teenage boys and girls having sexual intercourse has declined. For the first time in twenty years the numbers are down by some five percentage points, according to the *1995 National Survey of Family Growth*.

What is thrilling for young adolescents is chilling for parents. Sex with the wrong person, even one time, can be a point of no return at best, or a fatal attraction at worst. With higher stakes and less capable, younger sexual decision-makers, parents shudder as the proof of sexuality emerges, and stutter as they try to counsel coherently.

This chapter is going to prepare you for sexually explicit and explosive news from your child. We canvassed sex education researchers for guidelines to help you handle sexually charged situations. How do you have a conversation with a middler who says, "My sex life is none of your business!"? We will show you how to become fluent in the language of sexuality advice. Are you thinking that you can skip this chapter because your son is only ten or your daughter not yet twelve? Think again.

"We all went to a drive-in movie recently. My daughter, twelve, and this eleven-year-old boy were leaning all over each other. Both we and the boy's parents disapproved. This weekend they went off to sleep-away camp. When we went up to visit, she and this boy were inseparable. I was disturbed! My daughter and I have a good relationship. She has never been a problem child, nor has this young man. Am I supposed to HOPE nothing will happen or has happened? Am I jumping to conclusions?"

Today's young are doing what comes, and has always come, naturally. When so many of us have told our sons and daughters "Don't do

IT!" we can't help but collectively wonder: What part of this message don't they understand?

Many middlers are unclear about the definition of the "IT" part. What does "IT" stand for? Intercourse, oral sex, kissing? Young adolescents reject the "Don't" part. If all of our instructions begin with "don't," we leave middlers with no leeway, no room to experiment, and no choice but to ignore our stand. Hormones are turning them on, and so they must turn us off when we stand rigid.

We are afraid to do otherwise. By affirming the value of a good, fulfilling sex life, we run the risk of endorsing sexual activity. According to John H. Gagnon, a sexuality expert at the State University of New York at Stony Brook, "It is hard to get people to say we ought to teach people to have good sex. It is hard to be pro-sexual in America." Where middlers and sexual messages are concerned, this is even harder. When we see our young bombarded with sexually gung-ho messages in the media, we assume our job is to counteract these.

Even though intellectually we know that it's normal for young adolescents to have sexual feelings, and even to experiment sexually, when we discover the evidence, our response, in very emotional terms is "Don't do it *again.*" That won't do. Instead start with these:

Create a climate of trust. When the news broke in May 1998 that young pregnancies were down, experts wondered why. The National Campaign to Prevent Teen Pregnancy argued the credit goes to parents, not to condoms or abstinence messages. They said a major variable shows that the stronger the connection between adult and young adolescent, the less likely the child will behave irresponsibly.

Get a good sex-education yourself. Learn all you can about young adolescent sexual behavior.

WHAT INFLUENCES MIDDLERS TO HAVE SEX?

To do IT or not to do IT—why do some answer "yes" and others "no"?

A sampling of 720 girls, aged twelve to nineteen, polled by Mark Clements Research sheds light. Four out of five blamed boyfriends, explaining that girls felt pressured by their boyfriends or were afraid of losing them if they said no. Girls pressure one another to get into the sex act, according to 70 percent. Boys influence one another, too, said 86 percent. A little over half believe that movies and TV fan the flames. Perhaps the biggest aphrodisiac, though, is alcohol, cited by 85 percent as a major factor.

In our survey, 19 percent of middlers felt pressured to become sexually active. One Connecticut middler girl admitted, "I was at a party with a new group of friends and felt pressured to play Truth or Dare." "I have done everything of my own free will," said a thirteen-year-old who was part of the 66 percent who didn't feel coerced.

In a 1998 National Campaign to Prevent Teen Pregnancy statistical portrait of sexually active fifteen- to nineteen-year-old girls, several influential factors came to light. The first was family stability. By age sixteen, 22 percent of girls from intact, two-parent families had become sexually active compared to 44 percent of girls from other kinds of families. No one is sure why. It could be that two-parent families live in a higher stratum, and provide more activities and distractions. Or perhaps they work less and have more time than single parents to supervise.

A "like mother/like daughter" pattern emerged in the study, too. A daughter was less likely to have sex if her mother had completed high school and not had her first child during her teen years. If you didn't finish high school, or were a teenage mom yourself, realize your daughter may be at risk.

George Rekers of the University of South Carolina found that girls in father-absent homes were more likely to engage in promiscuous activity. If you are a single mother, make a note of this, but don't lose sight of the fact that a fifth of young adolescents from the "ideal" two-parent family said "yes," too.

What kept virgins that way? The National Campaign to Prevent Teen Pregnancy discovered that values stopped virgin girls from saying "yes." Religious or moral reasons were reported by 44 percent. Fear motivated others. Twenty percent attributed their holding out to being afraid of getting pregnant. Worry over contracting STDs stopped 13 percent. Romance played a part in decision-making for 20 percent, who said they just hadn't met the right person.

Boys are programmed biologically and culturally "to score" with bravado and no thought to the consequences. Sexual intercourse is the closest thing we have to a rite of passage for males. That is hardly news. What is coming to light is that information about boys' sexual behavior (other than condom use) has been *less* scrutinized than girls. For instance, The Alan Guttmacher

ORAL SEX—A NEW GENERATION'S LIP SERVICE

"My seventh-grade daughter came home from school in a panic because she lost her notebook. Her upset seemed out of proportion. When it was recovered she showed me some highly sensitive, X-rated verse:

> *Donny has a great dick*
> *I went to take a lick*
> *It was quite a kick*
> *I never got sick . . . from that great dick.*

I was floored."
—Mother

No wonder this middler was afraid of reviews! Seventh-grade middlers, and younger, are talking about oral sex. By ten, they know what oral sex is. In a national 1994 Roper Starch poll, 26 percent of high school students admitted having oral sex. A study of California high school virgins done by Dr. Mark Schuster, a Los Angeles pediatrician, found that 10 percent had engaged in oral sex. Boys and girls were equally likely to be on the receiving end.

"Do you spit it (the semen) out or swallow?" is a typical seventh-grade question, says Dr. Cydelle Berlin, health educator at New York's Mt. Sinai Medical Center. Its increasing popularity boils down to the fact that this generation is the first to be raised in a world where intercourse is labeled dangerous, even lethal. It's a one-word lesson—AIDS, followed by a laundry list of sexually transmitted diseases (STDs) covered in health class: syphilis and gonorrhea, chlamydia, genital warts, herpes, and the HIV virus.

Institute's 1995 study *How Old Are US Fathers?* notes that no data is available on the father's age in four out of ten births to adolescent women.

Researchers are starting to assess boys' motives. Depression, wanting to hurt themselves, feeling alone or "no good" about themselves was confessed by 88 percent of a 1992–1994 study of 1,780 males who visited family planning clinics (14 percent of whom were fourteen years old or younger, 50 percent were fifteen to seventeen, and 36 percent were eighteen to nineteen). Having problems in school, with communicating with family and friends, with alcohol, or grieving over the death of a family member also played into the profile of these sexually active young and older adolescents.

The "sex is dangerous and deadly" lessons begin in preschool. Strangers are potential perverts. As they grow, so does a sexually frightening vocabulary including date rape and incest, reiterated on countless TV movies and talk shows.

Despite the warning label, the urge to get physical persists. So this generation adapted. Oral sex equals sexual intimacy and enjoyment without the risk of STDs, the HIV virus, or certain death. So goes their reasoning. Young adolescents could sneak in a little oral sex because, after all, they were technically abstaining. Abstinence refers to intercourse, right? Girls who wanted to remain virgins could engage in fellatio and cunnilingus and still remain "pure." For girls afraid of getting pregnant, or for boys afraid of getting a girl pregnant, oral sex fit that bill, too. Middlers could keep their steadies satisfied and happy and keep their reputations intact. All these calculations occurred even before President Clinton's erotic indiscretions made fellatio a national conversation.

Do parents accept oral sex as a lesser of two evils? NO. Even growing up during the sexual revolution of the 1960s and 1970s hasn't prepared them. They are comfortable with oral sex between two adults in the context of intimacy, but not comfortable with this generation's casual definition. Equally alarming is the fallacy that oral sex is safe.

Instruct your middler that oral sex is not safe sex. The HIV virus and other sexually transmitted diseases can be contracted this way by those who may have open sores in the mouth or by those who have had recent dental work. Think of all the adolescents walking around with braces.

Underline that condoms are imperative for oral sex to be made safer.

Discuss the personal consequences of having oral sex. Ask your middler: Does its practice incite gossip, or a reputation? Do boys feel entitled to it?

Knowing how these facts and figures relate to your middler's world is essential. Think about them. If you discover your middler is having sex, understanding the context will help both of you.

WHAT TO DO IF YOUR MIDDLER IS SEXUALLY ACTIVE

"How do I tell my mother that I am sexually active and maybe pregnant?" a fourteen-year-old asked us. Here's a parent with such a child: "It was quite a shocking eye-opener to pick up my video camera and discover the tape of my fifteen-year-old daughter having sex with her boyfriend. To say

I was stunned doesn't even scratch the surface of the range of emotions that coursed through me. My first thoughts were horrible. Who held the camera? Were tapes like this, my baby doing Deep Throat, how she and Loverboy entertained friends? Suddenly I flashed back to myself at sixteen, trying to talk my teenage girlfriend into posing for my camera. Yesterday's camera is today's video. With that thought the urge to kill faded, but I still knew I had to say something."

Once you suspect your son or daughter is sexually active, what's next? In our survey we asked both parents and teachers what should follow the discovery. Overwhelmingly, parents (76 percent) and teachers (83 percent) recommend using the incident as an opportunity to discuss relationships.

It's extremely hard for mothers and fathers (sometimes more so when it comes to their little girls) to react rationally, and productively, to the probability or fact that their child is having sex. Yet, facing this issue, not ignoring it, is absolutely critical. Your child's future depends upon courage, your finesse, and your skill. This question-and-answer format will help you proceed through these hot waters skillfully.

Are you jumping to conclusions? Are your suspicions real or imagined?

Once you have proof (or a reasonably strong intuition), approach your middler carefully. Don't rush in with inflamed accusations because that is guaranteed to end your conversation before it begins.

Start the talk with, "I'm concerned about you. I've heard this or I've noticed that and I want to make sure you are not in trouble, here." Use sensitivity. Keep an open mind. If your middler denies the truth or refuses to talk, affirm that you are ready to talk whenever she or he is.

What is the nature of your middler's sexual adventure?

There are many ways to be sexually active. The Centers for Disease Control (CDC) now acknowledges that there are degrees of sexual activity among fourteen- to seventeen-year-olds. They have left behind the salt and pepper approach that divided young adolescents into sexually active and sexually inactive. In its place is a new labeling system, closer to the patterns of our youth. It characterizes as "delayers" those with no intention of having sexual intercourse, "anticipators" those who intend to in the next year, "one-timers," "steadies" those with a history of one partner, and "multiples" those with a history of intercourse with multiple partners.

Was this a first-time encounter or is your child in an ongoing romance where sex is frequent? Are you privy to gossip that your child and his friends are all experimenting with oral sex? Do you suspect your child has had several partners?
Your middler is the only one with the answers. You may get the truth, you may not. One young adolescent said, "I am not a virgin. I wish I could tell my parents, but I feel that I just can't, even though they have told me in the past that I could. It's not enough to tell your kid that you'll understand. You have to mean it! I won't tell my parents because I know they will be upset. *We don't want to disappoint you.* So if you want us to talk to you, then talk to us as someone who has been there before and maybe you'll hear more truth."

As parents ourselves, we know all this is easier said than done.

How can you help your middler come to terms with sexual behavior?
A thirteen-year-old boy wrote this to his girlfriend, "I really like going out with you, although we haven't done much yet. You think you're not ready. I respect that, but I would still love to stand by you until you are ready." Even the nicest boys come with raging hormones and that ever-present "but."

Once a young adolescent decides to have sex, help your middler understand what's really going on beneath those sheets.

Here are questions to get started. If your child clams up, slip the list under her pillow.

- Was the decision to engage in this sexual act your idea?
- What were your motives? Curiosity? Love? Fear of ridicule? Peer pressure?
- Were your friends influential in your decision?
- Were you forced in any way?
- Had either of you been drinking?
- Did you ask your partner if s/he had ever done this before? Were you asked?
- Did you answer honestly?
- Whether you had oral sex or intercourse, did you use a condom?
- Were you upset or worried in any way afterward?

Add a note that says, "You may not want to give me the answers to these questions but you should know the answers yourself. I'm here to help. I want you to be in control of sexual decisions, and to act responsibly."

When your middler takes you up on this invitation, slip in these facts.

- The younger a person is the first time she has sex, the more often the sex isn't voluntary.
- Lots of young adolescents lie about partners.
- In surveys, four out of ten don't tell if they have the HIV virus. Those with one partner tell more often than those who have had several.

This exercise leads a middler to realize that she—not hormones—controls what happens. Mastering sexual intimacy takes forethought, not just foreplay.

Do you discipline a sexually active child?

"Sexuality and its behaviors should not be punished," says Monica Rodriguez, Director of Education for SEICUS (Sexuality Information and Education Council of the United States). "Sexuality is a natural and healthy part of life." Your middler may be partaking too early, but sexual experiences should not be defined as inherently bad. Oral sex and even sexual intercourse are not crimes. Punishment isn't the answer.

If grounding or curtailing privileges isn't the right tack, what is? Clearly and firmly explain that you do not sanction the activity. Pay closer attention to the situations you allow your young adolescent to get into. Experts say most sex between adolescents happens in the afternoon and in the home. Don't make it easy for your child to have sex.

Is it too late to turn back the sexual tides? Once young adolescents have tasted the carnal pleasures, is it possible for them to abstain?

Yes. It's not all ecstasy on the sexual roller-coaster. Listen to a girl who found anxiety, not bliss: "My mother found out I was sexually active. I couldn't look her in the eyes or talk to her for days. I felt like I was falling off the edge of the earth. Why did I feel so bad? I knew I was wrong and that she understood that I was sorry for doing what I did, but still!"

If you subscribe to the theory that once a person has sexual intercourse, or oral sex, there's no turning back, think again. Consider that 84 percent of 1,000 sexually active girls in a Georgia survey wanted to learn how to say "no" without hurting the boy's feelings. Young adolescents of both genders, even the sexually experienced, want and need advice on how to take a step back.

One sexual experience doesn't mean sex becomes automatic. Even if you are the most approachable parent, your young adolescent may resist discussing such intimate details. Sexually active middlers need this message to be reinforced: if they had oral sex or intercourse once, it doesn't follow that they must repeat that performance on the next date. Or in the next relationship.

Teach them face-saving refusals. For instance, "Yes, I like you but I'm not ready for that deep an involvement." Or "I know you don't want to force me into doing something that I'm just not ready for." Explain "no" is more effective than "I don't think so." Tell them to add strong eye contact. Avoid staring down.

Boys need these lessons as well. Furthermore, boys need face-saving lines to level at friends who question the manliness of a boy who says "no." Brainstorm with your son. Try this one. "Leading a girl down that path opens up risks I'm not eager to take, yet." Or, "I'm not sure who she has been with and I'm not looking for AIDS."

It's never too late to let middlers know it's okay to hold the line or even go back to *not* having sex. Look into the many programs that teach young adolescents to reclaim their virginity.

Suppose your child is enthusiastically engaged in a sexual relationship. You better have good intelligent arguments handy.

When do you believe sexual intercourse is allowed?

"Okay, so you think I'm too young," your young adolescent says. *"How old is old enough to express my love sexually?"* What do you say? Remember most of us are stuck in the no, not, never mode. Clarify your beliefs by answering these:

- How old is old enough for sexual intercourse? Oral sex? Engaging in the fondling of breasts and private parts?
- What situations would make sexual experimentation acceptable? Being thirteen and curious?

- Does being in love make it right?
- Is marriage the only circumstance in which any sexual activity is allowed?

You have to know where you stand, morally and chronologically, before you can deliver your sex ethics code. Once you know where you stand, then you can say, *"Your behavior is not what I think you should be doing."* The *why* comes next. Speak honestly and frankly. Sexual intercourse is an adult activity. Becoming sexually active, even if that's only oral sex, still entails the risk of contracting sexually transmitted diseases. Bringing sexuality into a relationship intensifies all the emotions that a person feels. When the relationship ends, which is frequent during early adolescence (and make that point), high-velocity feelings make breaking up even more painful.

Tell your middler that sex has a way of monopolizing all your energy. A person gets side-tracked, preoccupied with sex and the aftermath, from rumors to rejection. Your middler will know just what you are referring to. They've all heard "sluts" reviews. Being the star of an X-rated love story prevents a middler from concentrating on school, and developing skills that will be important to defining who he is and what he will become.

Mary Ann Lewis, Tennessee Department of Education expert says, "Encourage your child to establish personal goals." Does your daughter plan to go out for track or to go away to college? Does your son want to work part-time or become an astronaut? Help your child create short- and long-range goals that mirror interests and talents. Project those dreams into the future. Then talk about how sexual decisions and activities might affect these dreams.

Is there any help out there?

Enlist older teens to back you up. When we asked young adolescents in our survey, "What would help you sort through your doubts and questions about sexual activity?" thirty-nine percent said, "Having a program where older teens talk about their experiences."

Many health agencies, communities, and school districts around the country have peer programs (see the resource section). Teen-to-teen sex education works because peers are extremely influential. One curriculum, "Postponing Sexual Involvement" (PSI), created by Marion

Howard, a professor at Emory University, uses trained teen leaders to counsel seventh and eighth graders about delaying their sexual activity. PSI grads were four times *less* likely to become sexually active in eighth grade than those who weren't. One third were *less* likely to become sexually active a year later.

Are you dismissing the contraceptive issue?

Always take a sexually active young person in to see a pediatrician or gynecologist who specializes in treating adolescents. This is a respectful way of giving your middler the opportunity to consult alone with a knowledgeable, nonjudgmental adult. No matter how liberal or sensitive you may be, some middlers are not comfortable talking about their sexual experiences with parents. So provide an alternative.

Make sure your daughter and son know about safe sex. A sexually active child who doesn't use contraception has a 90 percent chance of pregnancy (or getting a girl pregnant) within one year. Aside from the risk of conceiving, there are a host of medical drawbacks to think about:

- About one quarter of the 40,000 new HIV infections each year occur among thirteen- to twenty-one-year-olds.
- Every year, one in four sexually experienced teens acquires an STD, often hard to detect because the symptoms are silent, masking disastrous effects in both males and females, including the ability to have children in the future.
- Chlamydia, the leading cause of infertility, has shown up in 10 to 29 percent of teenage girls tested in some settings, and in 10 percent of teenage boys.
- Genital warts caused by human papillomavirus (HPV) can lead to cancer of the cervix. In some surveys 15 percent of teenage girls were infected.
- In a single act of unprotected sex, your child has a 50 percent chance of contracting gonorrhea.

Technically the only safe sex is no sex. Say that. Then move on to talk about contraceptives. According to the Institute on Child and Adolescent Sexuality expert, L. Brown, African American girls reported difficulty initiating discussions with their boyfriends about condoms, believing it wasn't their role to do so. Tell your daughter to speak up. By the way, scare tactics don't work on boys ages fifteen to seventeen. These are the invincible years. So inform, don't threaten.

Are abstinence-only programs better than sex-education courses that include information on birth control and contraceptives? For the record, abstinence-only programs funded lavishly by the government ($850 million in one year) were compared with sex-education programs that promote abstinence, but cover contraception. What works best? The answer is neither and both. When compared in terms of results, they yielded the same impact. In California, 10,600 seventh and eighth graders were split, with each half getting one of the different instructional approaches from 1992 to 1994. After a year and a half, there was no difference between the two groups' pregnancy and STD rates.

What is fact (not speculation) about the behavior of students who have condoms at their fingertips in schools? Studies done in New York, Chicago, and Philadelphia, among others, show that making condoms available in high school *does not* increase the rates of sexual activity. So if your middler is not sexually active, risky behavior is not being given any green light. It does, however, increase the frequency of using condoms during sex. Translated, this means supplying condoms makes already sexually active adolescents practice safer sex, and decreases their risk of contracting AIDS and STDs.

A final note: less than half of teenage boys who had intercourse during the last year said that they used condoms 100 percent of the time. The contraceptive talk with girls and boys is a must.

Getting back to "don't do IT." Intercourse is for adults and not for young adolescents. What's okay, yes even wonderful, for adults is not appropriate for middlers. Expand on what the *it* means. What's allowed? A mother shared this at one of our talks: "I told my sexually active almost sixteen-year-old son that masturbation was okay. He shot back with an annoyed 'Mom, masturbation's boring!' My comeback, 'If it's boring then you're not doing it right.' "

Take a deep breath or a gulp, and face up to a sexually active middler. It takes courage of conviction, sensitivity and, yes, even a sense of humor.

OLDER BUT NOT WISER MATCHES

"My thirteen-year-old is pretty, an A student, and a good girl. The problem is that she looks older than she is. A junior in high school took her to his prom. He just turned seventeen. Now she is moving into an older crowd. I know if I forbid her to date him, our nice even keel around here will be history."
—Mother

Mom's right to be leery. When fourteen- to seventeen-year-olds from New York, Alabama, and Puerto Rico were studied, girls linked romantically to boys three years older had intercourse earlier than those dating same-age peers.

Developmentally, a thirteen-year-old is light years behind a seventeen-year-old. Older adolescents are further along on the continuum of sexual experience and expectations. A younger besotted girl (or boy) is less likely to say no to sexual advances and more likely to be timid about discussing safe sex. A pair of young adolescents will ask a parent to chauffeur; an older boyfriend will take your daughter in his own car. What's more troubling: how fast he drives or how fast he is when parked? There's a riddle with no reassuring answer.

Younger adolescents with older romantic partners are at higher risk for pregnancy. Seventy percent of teenage mothers-to-be had partners who were twenty years old or older. Because older adolescents have had more experience and sexual partners, they pose a greater risk of AIDS and STDs.

How do you intervene?

Talk honestly to your middler about this troubling research. Start with, "Here is why I am concerned . . ." Have this discussion whether your middler is the older or younger in the coupling.

Explain the power balance issue. Ask your middler: Should the older one have more authority? Get your middler to think this through and state her opinion. The point of view of the younger may be the voice of innocence and inexperience, but be certain that your young adolescent knows this voice deserves equal weight in any relationship.

Keep the dialogue going. Should you forbid your middler from seeing this older boy or girl? If you can, then do. However, your middler may resort to sneaking out and defying you. Remember, it's prestigious to be dating an older guy or girl. It's an ego boost. Focus your middler on who this person is, not just on the age factor. Limit where you allow her to go. Watch closely.

Fatal Attractions

Our website had its own cyber soap opera featuring dating violence. Here's a snippet:

The parent: "How can I help my precious daughter see the light? She's involved with a boy of fifteen who has skipped school, admitted to drug and alcohol use, and is under house arrest. I think he may have pushed her as well."

The girl: "THERE IS NO VIOLENCE IN OUR RELATIONSHIP, SO LAY OFF. I don't care what you think about me being your precious little girl. I'm fifteen now! Drop the thing about the push. You guys are tearing my heart apart."

The boy: "I have made mistakes in my life as everyone does. I had depression. Yes, I did shove her, but it was to come back to the house 'cause she wanted to walk out in the street and it was late."

A kiss is still a kiss, but is a shove just a shove? According to Rhode Island College psychology professor David Sugarman, Ph.D., one in four teenagers becomes victimized by dating violence. While the most common scenarios are boys mistreating girls, experts say that girls can be abusive. Gay, lesbian, and bisexual middlers are in jeopardy, too.

Abuse starts out with verbal threats and can escalate into physical assault, even murder. In a 1995 poll conducted by *Family Circle* and *YM,* 8 percent of their sampling admitted to being hit, 14 percent to being shoved, and 31 percent to being verbally abused. More than half the mothers didn't believe this could happen to their daughters.

Getting wrapped up in a romance with an abusive young adolescent can happen to the nicest middlers. "Generally inexperienced, adolescents have difficulty managing the complexity of feelings, decisions, and conflicts that arise," says Barrie Levy, author of *Dating Violence.* "Romanticizing about love and relationships, they often interpret jealousy, possessiveness, and abuse as signs of love."

How can you tell if your middler is flirting with a potentially violent attraction?

- Your middler has given up all the friends and activities once enjoyed.
- Grades are down for more than one month.
- Your middler acts secretive, hostile, or depressed.
- Your middler has complained that her boyfriend is jealous or possessive.
- Your middler confided that this person discourages her from doing things, seeing friends.

How should you handle this situation?

Express your concern calmly. If your middler will not talk to you, steer her to a trusted counselor at school. Provide her with a hotline she can contact in confidence.

Explain the issue. Dating violence is not a one-time occurrence. It is a pattern of violence established in a child's family and passed from one generation to the next. If domestic violence is part of your family history, get counseling.

Work on your middler's self-esteem. Many girls remain in abusive relationships because they need the attention of a boy to make them feel good.

Alert the abuser's family. They may already know and be in denial. If so, inform them that you are determined to protect your child. If they don't know, they might be on your side and work to correct their child's actions.

Notify the police if your middler is in any danger. If the abusive suitor refuses to leave your child alone, obtain a criminal restraining order. If these are not granted to juveniles in your state, get a civil restraining order. Violation of a criminal court order leads to the abuser's arrest. If he violates a civil order, you can take him to court. In either case, you are warning him off. Notify the school of your action.

This may be one of those battles you have to fight on behalf of your young adolescent. Not to do so courts the danger that bad romantic judgment could turn into a fatal attraction.

TEEN PREGNANCY

"Just into high school, with a bright future ahead, my gorgeous, intelligent, bound to be successful daughter became pregnant. I just knew she had ruined her life. Her growing tummy reminded me every day of the grief, embarrassment, and confusion that I knew she was feeling. There were tears and turmoil. Being a nurse, I had seen so many babies having babies. I always hoped, as I held those tiny infants, that it would not happen in my family, but it did."

Although our teen pregnancy rates are higher here in the U.S. than in other countries, the teen pregnancy rate has been falling since 1974, down 12 percent between 1991 and 1996. It's down 21 percent for African Americans, a striking decline. Only two in ten of unintended pregnancies happen to teenagers. Even with this good news, young and older adolescents still give birth to 13 percent of all the babies born.

How do you proceed when you have a pregnant daughter, or a son who has learned that a girlfriend is carrying his child?

Expect to be awash in waves of emotions. Anger. Guilt. Pity. Sadness. Learning that a middler, who just yesterday was blasting CDs in her room with not a care in the world, is destined to become a mom in a few short months is bound to throw you into an emotional tailspin. Realizing your baggy-trousered basketball fanatic is a father-to-be will make your heart nearly stop, after you feel it crack, that is. "I would be hurt, angry, and disappointed at first, but then I would help her," confesses a Connecticut mom who echoes many others.

Help your child explore the options. Having the baby, carrying the infant to term and then making an adoption plan, or abortion—these are the choices. This pregnancy was a consequence of your young adolescent's actions, thus the responsibility rests with the child. This is a decision that you should not make for your child. For the rest of her life, she will have to live it.

Should the boy get an equal say in pregnancy decisions? It's easy to forget that this crisis is happening to the boy and his family, too. Listen to one: "The toughest decision I've ever had to make was to become a father at fifteen. I'm not talking about simply becoming a father in the physical sense—anyone can do that—but being a real dad. It was funny because I was really scared, but at the same time I thought that having a child would somehow make me a man. People talk about teenage pregnancy all the time, but they usually only talk about the girls. Most people assume that the teen father won't stick around for long. I'm happy that I decided to live up to my responsibilities. But sometimes I wish I had been more careful, taken school more seriously and focused on growing up first."

Fourteen percent of sexually active fifteen- to nineteen-year-old teenage boys reported that they had gotten a girl pregnant. Six percent of those fathered the child. If your child is Black or Hispanic, the pregnancy odds are higher for him.

Here are the options to go over one by one with the parents-to-be.

Having the Child

The stigma of having a child out of wedlock has diminished. Think of Jodie Foster or Madonna. Your real mother-to-be is not a celebrity with nannies and investment counselors. So she's going to depend on your support. "Our family supported our daughter's decision to have her baby. She planned on the boy being in on the raising part, but he never agreed. We encouraged her to stay in school and make a life for herself and this child. I was never prouder of my daughter than the day I watched her graduate from high school, with my adorable granddaughter bouncing on my lap. We have all survived."

You can't put a Pollyanna luster on this option. This choice entails sacrifice, hardship, and strife. Yet, if this is what your pregnant child wants to do, then you need to help her. Take her for prenatal care. Find parenting classes, for her and the father-to-be. Help her create a child care plan that doesn't interfere with school. Seven in ten teen moms finish high school but are less likely to go to college. Encourage her to include the father in decision-making, financial planning, and care. A young adolescent mother-to-be is going to need a parent's shoulder, understanding, and love every step of the way.

Adoption

There is no shortage of childless couples. Yet, today's young often don't choose adoption. From 1989 to 1995, less than 1 percent of never-married pregnant women ages fifteen to forty-four made adoption plans for their children.

The reasons why vary. Adoption gets bad press. You've seen the stories. Good parents adopt a child who grows into a demon because of being abused as an infant, or having fetal alcohol syndrome.

According to the 1997 Benchmark Adoption Survey, most people believe that adoptive parents are generous and lucky (although not as lucky as birth parents), and make fine fathers and mothers. A majority think adopted children grow up to be well-adjusted and secure. Yet, the institution triggers doubts and mixed feelings. Some hold the view that adopted children are insecure, more likely to suffer behavior problems, and perform poorly in school compared to other children. A notable portion of those surveyed disapprove of adoption, characterizing the decision as hardhearted or irresponsible. The more educated people are, the more merit they see in adoption.

The Benchmark survey went on to say that Americans are divided about whether or not it is better for pregnant teenagers to choose adoption for their babies or keep them; they are divided as well over what would be better for the child. This widespread uncertainty, imagined distress for the adopted child, and even downright disapproval, combine to prevent young mothers-to-be from evaluating adoption sensibly.

Did you know that six in ten Americans have had personal experience with adoption? These folks, the ones who know firsthand about adoption, are *more likely* to endorse this option. Have your daughter and/or son talk to adoption agencies in your area. Look at the open adoption and closed adoption circumstances. Listen to parents who are providing loving and happy homes for the children they were given the opportunity to parent. To ignore this option severely limits choices.

Abortion

A father told us, "I found out that my now sixteen-year-old daughter had an abortion last summer. Accidentally I intercepted her e-mail. She says her sex life is her own business, not mine, end of discussion. I'm trying my best to be low key with her but I'm going ballistic on the inside."

Getting an abortion is a much more difficult path to pursue even though most Americans approve (about 60 percent according to a 1998 *New York Times*–CBS poll). There has been a 24 percent drop in the abortion rate among teenagers. Is this good or bad? Of course that depends upon your religious convictions, with which no one can argue.

The decline bears examining. Abortion clinics have become targets, magnets for protesters, arsonists, and even bombers. Women who choose abortion are defined as murderers. Physicians who perform the procedure have been effectively villainized as killers—some have even been executed by misguided zealots for their "crimes" in some eye-for-an-eye biblical retaliation. An increasing number of hospitals and doctors no longer perform abortions because of the possible consequences. Eighty-three percent of counties in America have no abortion provider.

Abortions are not covered under Medicaid. Now they have legal strings attached. For a minor seeking an abortion, twenty-eight states have mandatory parental involvement laws in effect, so many young adolescents who want to pursue this option can't without telling their parents beforehand, a big obstacle for some.

Actually, 61 percent of minors who have abortions do so with their parents' knowledge, the great majority with their approval. Nearly half of all daughters tell their mothers or fathers. Yet, the strictures, stigmas, and risks serve to make abortion a non-choice in the eyes of many already terrified and immature mothers-to-be.

If abortion is your middler's choice, ask if it really is her idea or if she feels pressured by the boy. Make sure your child understands what the abortion procedure entails physically. Planned Parenthood Federation of America offers counseling that covers all these issues. Accompany her the day of the procedure.

Pregnancy Denial

Could there be anything worse than dealing with a pregnant daughter? Yes. "Pregnancy denial" is a new vocabulary term. A rundown of some recent cases includes two New Jersey sweethearts who killed their newborn. A New York teen secretly gave birth five months prematurely and hid the infant in her closet for two weeks before it was discovered. A party girl at her prom gave birth in the ladies room, trashed the infant, fixed her make-up, and returned to the dance floor. An Arizona teen hid the surprise infant in a coffee can.

Experts explain that denial is a defense mechanism that takes hold when circumstances are so overwhelming that an adolescent cannot face them. Because she can't bear telling her parents, or often anyone, the pregnant child blocks out the physical symptoms of pregnancy, hides the fact with baggy fashions, and effects a Scarlett O'Hara *I'll think about it tomorrow* strategy. She seeks no medical care, no tests, and no advice.

Apparently, this syndrome can touch any girl. Cases have included disadvantaged adolescents, and daughters blessed with two parents and a comfortable life, even the overachieving cheerleader prototype.

A common denominator in several baby-killings or neonaticides, according to Dr. Phillip J. Resnick, a professor of psychiatry at Case Western Medical School, is the girl's inability to reveal her pregnancy. His groundbreaking study underlined that teens feared telling both parents, but especially mothers. Another Columbia University College of Physicians study by Dr. Margaret Spinelli, director of a maternal mental health program, found that an intrusive and hyper-vigilant father played into the denial profile.

In our survey we asked ten- to fifteen-year-olds whether, if they got pregnant or got a girl pregnant, they would tell their parents. Seventy-seven percent said they would. Typical reasoning ranged from "My parents would find out sooner or later" to "My telling would help the baby." If you think your middler wouldn't confide in you, make sure there are other adults in her life who are approachable.

SEXUAL ORIENTATION

"My thirteen-year-old son has me in a panic. I have caught him twice wearing my pantyhose. The first time he was eleven. Now again. When I asked him about the pantyhose, he admitted he had the urge to try them on. Is this an Oedipus thing, a gay thing, a RuPaul thing, or normal? He says he wants a girlfriend like the other kids. Boy, I'm confused."
    —Mother

Parents who worry about a child's sexual identity have a steeper hurdle than parents discovering heterosexual sexcapades.

A 1997 *New York Times* article, "Elite Schools Face the Gay Issue," reported that girls were sexually experimenting with one another and discussing bisexuality with a cavalier tone. Shocked and queasy parents wanted to know: What did this sexual experimentation mean?

In recent years, gay, lesbian, and bisexual activists have launched a noble campaign for respect and acceptance, and have made inroads. Yet discomfort, even disgust, is still rampant. Alan Wolfe, a professor at

Boston University and author of *One Nation After All,* found that four times as many Americans condemned homosexuality as were willing to accept it positively. Words like "sick," "perverted," "immoral," "untrustworthy," "abnormal," "sinful," spilled out of homophobic mouths.

How does a parent distinguish between same-sex crushes, brushes with homosexual or bisexual behavior, and the *certainty* that a ten- to fifteen-year-old child is gay, lesbian, or bisexual?

Early adolescence is a cloudy time for some boys and girls. When the National Commission on Adolescent Sexual Health reported on seventh to eleventh graders, 11 percent described themselves as "unsure" about their gender issue, and 1 percent said "bisexual," compared to the 88 percent who knew they were heterosexual. Among twelve-year-olds, 26 percent weren't certain about their sexual identity. Only growing older clarifies the sexual identity issue.

Parents should proceed slowly and follow these guidelines:

Fend off panic. Richard Friedman, a Cornell University expert on homosexuality, counsels that same-sex experimentation, more common among girls, isn't a final verdict on homosexuality. For some, such experimentation confirms their heterosexual nature; for others it is the beginning of understanding that they are gay.

Work through your disappointment. If your young adolescent appears to be growing up gay, lesbian, or bisexual, experts recommend that you admit your disappointment to yourself. Don't condemn yourself for these feelings. All parents want their children to grow up the way they are, sexual preference included. Realizing your son is not going to grow up straight, marry the girl of his dreams, and father your grandchild, or that your daughter is never going to marry Mr. Right is a blow.

Don't blame yourself. "A child does not become a homosexual simply because of something a parent did or did not do," according to Wayne Pawlowski, a sex education expert.

Reassure your child. Convey your unconditional love. "Your child is the same person he or she was yesterday," reminds the Parents, Families, and Friends of Lesbians and Gays, a support group. Tell him that he is still your child—gay, straight, blue, green, or purple. Deliver the acceptance he so desperately seeks.

Concentrate on your child's struggle. Being homosexual or "bi" in a straight world is a staggering dilemma for a preteen. A gay middler has no group of similar peers with whom he can share "different" sexual feelings and fantasies. If he shows his sexual colors, what he can expect absolutely is humiliation and scorn.

So gay- or lesbian-inclined middlers carry their difference in secret, in silence, and as a shameful burden. In a 1998 study, Harvard Medical School's Dr. Rob Garofalo analyzed data from 4,159 high school students, and found that gay and bisexual children carry weighty risks. Twice as often as their heterosexual peers, they have sex before age thirteen and engage in unsafe sex, or try cocaine, marijuana, or begin drinking alcohol before that age. Some turn to the Internet to escape a profound sense of isolation. They are desperately in search of companionship and validation that they dare not look for in the real world.

Find role models. Who prepares a gay or lesbian child for life and for relationships, for finding love and fending off discrimination? Examine your family tree. Almost every family has a gay or lesbian member. Share these stories with your child. If possible, encourage your son or daughter to spend some time with this person.

Get support. If you have friends who are homosexual, this shows your child that you value people of different orientations. If you don't, take advantage of support groups available. We are no longer in the dark ages when it comes to issues of gay, lesbian, and bisexual life. Our resource list offers many opportunities to help you evolve, and absolve yourself and your young adolescent of the bias toward being sexually different.

Barry Giles, a Connecticut teen, liked wearing skirts to school. When he was suspended for his alternative fashion sense—one purple and yellow peasant dress—eight other boys came to school in dresses, and twelve girls donned suits and ties to offer support. This was no laughing matter for the principal, the school board, the Connecticut Civil Liberties Union, or the parents in the community. It's hard to find the light side of sexual identity issues, even harder to find compassion and tolerance, but hardest of all to find goodwill and respect.

If your child tells you that he is gay, the truth is that you have already done something *right,* not wrong. Your child trusted you with a very profound secret. Cherish that trust.

The answers to love are as profound and elusive as the answers to life. If parents can accept the sexuality of their young, advise, and deal with the consequences, they will be able to counsel their child toward responsibly handling (and yes, postponing) one of life's greatest pleasures.

Strategies: Be Prepared

When a thirteen-year-old boy has his body pressing against a willing sweetheart, when both are trying to kiss, breathe, and make decisions simultaneously in a passionate instant, we as parents want them to be prepared. Ideally they have given thought ahead of time to their passions and the consequences. We need to do the same.

Let your emotions pulse through you. If your middler is sexually active, pregnant, or gay—cry, scream, rage. Then detach from the shame and the pain.

Talk to your partner. Discuss all the options and actions you could, should, should not, and would take. Keep your child's best interests in the forefront, not yours, nor what the neighbors will think.

Rehearse what you will say to your child. And what you will not say. Accepting your child's sexuality or sexual orientation is a stretch for all parents.

Involve your middler in these discussions because this is her life, her future. The immediate crisis atmosphere will pass. Your relationship has years ahead.

Be there for your child. He will need your level head and a forgiving heart. Reprimand, perhaps, counsel, yes, but love unconditionally.

CHAPTER FOUR

Risking Life for the Perfect Body

*

"I believe my thirteen-year-old is starting to have an eating disorder. She tells me almost nightly that she wishes she could die because she is tired of having to watch what she eats. She complains that all the girls in her class weigh less than she does. They probably do, but for her height, she is quite thin. I think she is headed for trouble. What should I do?"
—Concerned mother

Any middle schooler can tell you that looking good can help when navigating the treacherous waters of early adolescence. Unfortunately, middler bodies, in the throes of puberty, rarely cooperate. A middler boy may dream of looking like a strong man, but can barely produce a bicep muscle. At the same time, a middler girl may become embarrassed over her thickening waist, realizing that she will never be reed thin like the fashion models she so admires.

A perfect body is an elusive goal. But young adolescents haven't learned that very adult lesson and many adults haven't either. Young people are the targets of numerous advertising campaigns where everyone is "buff" and "diesel," two current terms used to describe svelte silhouettes. The lure proves irresistible and, in some cases, dangerous:

- According to the American Anorexia/Bulimia Association, 1 percent of teens will develop anorexia, 10 percent of whom will diet themselves to death.
- The average age of girls suffering from anorexia, bulimia, or binge eating has dropped from sixteen or seventeen to fourteen, with some children as young as ten years old being di-

agnosed with one of these disorders. (One doctor in Brooklyn reported a six-year-old patient who was eating and purging.)

- By age thirteen, 53 percent of girls are unhappy with their bodies. This number jumps to 78 percent by age seventeen, according to *The Right Moves: A Girl's Guide to Getting Fit and Feeling Good,* by Tina Schwager, Michele Schuerger, Elizabeth Verdick, and Mike Gordon.
- Experts estimate that more than 230,000 high school girl athletes may suffer from eating disorders.
- A 1998 survey by the University of Massachusetts found that 2.7 percent of 965 students questioned at four Massachusetts middle schools were taking illegal steroids to build up their bodies and do better in sports.

In this chapter we will examine the war that middlers wage against their own bodies, oftentimes endangering their lives in the process. We will talk about how the seeds of discontent are planted. Besides the propaganda from the media, peer pressure and even parental demands may leave a young adolescent with a negative self-image. What can parents do to make sure these feelings of insecurity never take root? What happens when your child's preoccupation with body image turns into obsession? What are the signs of an eating disorder? Should you attempt to alter your child's behavior on your own, or will professional intervention be necessary? We will give strategies.

While much attention has been focused on girls and their appearance anxieties, boys are at risk, too. Movies, TV shows, and music videos that showcase strapping young men with trim waists and broad shoulders have set a new standard that young adolescent boys hope to meet. Many are pursuing body-building regimens that are ill-conceived and dangerous. At what point does exercise cross over from healthy to unhealthy? Are substances like creatine harmless or harmful?

We will encourage you to reexamine your attitude toward your own body and food, a process which could be painful. Do you admonish your child not to skip meals and then run out of the house without breakfast, the most important meal of the day? Are you constantly obsessing about being overweight, trying every diet that comes down the pike? Your actions speak louder than words and could sabotage any plan you have to get your children to eat healthful foods.

The habits our children learn now will stay with them for a long time. Knowing how to inculcate in our children a respectful attitude toward their bodies will nourish their spirits for a long time to come.

HEAVENLY BODIES

As far back as the ancient Greeks, those who were worshipped as gods were revered not only for their special powers but also for their splendid physical attributes. Hercules was admired for his strength. Aphrodite's loveliness caused both mortals and gods to swoon. Perseus, a son of Zeus, was a great athlete who slew the monster Medusa. Helen of Troy was so beautiful that the Greeks and Trojans fought a war over her.

We may no longer have Greek gods, but we have modern-day versions in the form of movie and TV stars, recording artists, professional athletes, and fashion models. "I want to be an actress like Sandra Bullock," said one sixth grader from Nebraska. Another enthused, "I love Drew Barrymore because she's so pretty." Look around at the posters decorating your child's walls. Do you find any overweight movie stars up there? How about puny athletes? Any models with acne on their faces? Thought not. More than likely, the images you spied looked like they stepped right off Mt. Olympus. And for most of our children, the crusade to look like one of these entertainers will be as unobtainable as a mortal ascending to the home of the gods.

The quest to look younger and trim has permeated our society. Americans spend $24,200 per minute on cosmetics and skin care products. In 1997, plastic surgeons performed an estimated 2.1 million cosmetic procedures, including nose jobs, liposuction, face lifts, tummy tucks, and collagen injections—a 50 percent increase since 1992. The American Society for Aesthetic Plastic Surgery reports that they are doing triple the number of breast enlargements, despite all the publicity over the dangers of silicone implants.

In the past, young adolescents who underwent plastic surgery did so most frequently to reshape their noses. Now, however, middlers want to reshape their bodies. From 1992 to 1996, the number of adolescents having nose jobs dropped from 5,519 to 4,313, while those seeking to augment

Hurting to Feel Better

"I know someone who has cut herself. She said sometimes she's so angry at simple things, like her mom telling her what to do, that cutting eases her anger and frustration."
    —Fourteen-year-old girl

It seems incredible that young adolescents, hypersensitive to their appearance, would actually inflict injury upon themselves that could result in lasting scars. But that's just what they are doing, in epidemic numbers, according to the experts.

An estimated two million people, mostly young adolescent girls, engage in self-mutilation, intentionally cutting, burning, plucking hairs from their scalp, or rubbing their skin until it is raw. Why? To vent their feelings of depression, helplessness, frustration, and anger. In the words of one sufferer: "It felt good to see the blood coming out, like that was my other pain leaving, too."

Self-mutilation is not new. But in the past the disorder was associated mostly with psychotic behavior. More recently, public admissions by Princess Diana and the actor Johnny Depp that they had suffered self-inflicted wounds has focused public attention on the problem.

Besides the danger from scarring, "cutters" run the risk of infection, including HIV, blood loss, and, if the sharp instrument strikes a large blood vessel, death. Those dangers increase because the person seldom stops after one cutting incident. Rather, the behavior becomes habitual, something done time and time again to relieve the suffering. Many victims have experienced physical or sexual abuse. Some young adolescent girls have fallen into a cycle of self-loathing after being sexually harassed at school.

Because cutting is often done on areas of the body hidden by clothes, some parents don't learn of their child's behavior until she is taken to the local emergency room after a particularly violent episode. Plastic surgery can sometimes repair the physical scars, but it will often take a longer treatment time—involving psychotherapy and medication—to heal the internal ones.

their breasts increased from 978 to 1,172. In 1992, collagen injections, eyelid surgery, and tummy tucks were unheard of for adolescents. By 1996, 135 adolescents had collagen injections, 267 had eyelid surgery, and 130 had tummy tucks. From 1992 to 1996, the number of young people undergoing liposuction went from 471 to 788.

Men have jumped on the "body beautiful" bandwagon, too. And besides coloring their hair and going under the knife, many men are working to keep their bodies well toned. In the human jungle, a tight "butt," or defined "pecs," has the same effect on females as colorful plumage or a large mane in the wild. Young adolescent boys may tune into the TV show "Baywatch," to ogle the girls in skimpy swimsuits. But soon they notice that the young men in tight briefs are the ones garnering admiring glances on the beach.

Of course, staying physically fit is an admirable goal. A young person who incorporates regular exercise into his daily schedule will benefit physically and mentally and, hopefully, maintain that attitude throughout his life. What's out of whack here is that young adolescents are attempting to short-circuit the process and, in so doing, may actually harm themselves. A young adolescent girl is supposed to be gaining weight during puberty. That doesn't necessarily mean she will always have heavy thighs. But when she sees the pounds pile on, she panics. Thus begins the dieting and a lifelong struggle with weight.

Similarly, a middler boy doesn't want to wait years before he can build up his muscles. He wants to attract the girls now. So he visits the sports shop and buys weights, and the health food store to stock up on creatine and other supplements that will help him maximize his workouts. Without proper supervision, he may tear muscles with the barbells and upset his digestive system with the pills. But he will see his muscles grow, and that progress will spur him on.

Body image is about more than dieting and exercise, however. It's about control. Young adolescents have little say in managing their lives. But they soon learn that they can regulate their eating and exercise, thus determining what their bodies look like. This is a powerful tool. And the more parents object, the more they rebel. For that reason, most young adolescents who develop eating disorders or exercise obsessions need professional help. Even well-meaning parents may be unable to turn the situation around. In fact, parental attitudes may be part of the problem.

THE PARENT TRAP

"My wife is telling me that our thirteen-year-old daughter should be thinner and losing her baby fat. I believe her body is taking on a more adult look, al-

though her face does appear to be a little round. What kind of bodily changes can we expect, and does my wife's view sound right?"

—Concerned father

Most of us can remember how it felt to hit adolescence and realize that the bodies we were going to be stuck with for life did not fulfill our expectations. In the fifties, teenage girls who wanted to fill out their sweaters like Marilyn Monroe had to resort to stuffing their bras with tissues. Boys, seeking to emulate Marlon Brando in a T-shirt, might have been able to imitate his swagger, but not his bulging biceps. In the seventies, the "waif" look, exemplified by the British fashion model Twiggy, was in, and young girls with breasts and hips started dieting in earnest in order to wear the skinny tops and hip-clinging pants so popular among young adolescent girls. Beginning in the late 1960s, movies would showcase action heroes for their physical power and strength. The muscle-bound man always got the girl, and young boys everywhere got the message.

We carry our weight-obsessed memories around with us, along with the extra pounds we've accumulated over the years. In the throes of menopause and middle-age spread, many parents, battling their own weight demons, find it difficult to send out to their children positive messages about appearance. If we are unhappy with our own condition, how can we admonish our children not to dwell on theirs? If we are ready to try any new diet or exercise regimen we encounter, how can we discourage them when they restrict their food choices or exercise to excess?

We project our fears onto our children. Let's face it, no parent wants a child who is chubby or obviously overweight. It reflects badly on us as parents, we think. We want our children to be attractive because, through our own experiences, we know how it hurts to be unattractive.

Then, before we can help our children with their body issues, we must first deal with our own. Here are some things to think about:

Never talk about dieting. If you need to lose weight, don't announce it to the world. No weighing food at the table or complaining about what you can't eat. Just cut back in a quiet way and present it to anyone who asks as "eating healthier."

Set a good example. A 1998 study done in the Netherlands found that family eating habits influence young people more than those of friends.

The study, which included 347 fifteen-year-olds, revealed that family members overwhelmingly dictate how and what other family members eat. Also, the researchers found that most food conversations occurred at home among family rather than outside among friends.

Love the body you're in. Researchers from the Karolinska Institute now believe that some people may be genetically predisposed toward obesity. Studies of 200 women showed that a particular gene mutation was seven times more common in overweight women than in women of normal weight. So if the needle on your bathroom scale appears to be stuck, accept yourself just the way you are.

YOUNG ADOLESCENT GIRLS—MATURE BEFORE THEIR TIME

From all accounts, girls obsess about their physical appearance more than boys do. And all of this worrying takes its toll. "My eleven-year-old daughter is overwhelmed with her appearance in the morning," said one mother. "She ends up throwing tantrums and missing her bus."

A 1998 study done by Barbara Fredrickson, a social psychologist at the University of Michigan, found that the more women worry about how they look, the less mental energy they have for other things. In the study, a group of men and women were asked to assess the wearability of a garment by going into a dressing room with a full length mirror. While wearing either a sweater or a bathing suit for fifteen minutes, the participants were given a twenty-question math test to complete. The women who wore the bathing suits had lower math scores than women who were wearing the sweaters or the men who were wearing either garment. The researchers concluded that the women were distracted by their images in the mirror.

While the study was not conclusive, the researchers believe that it could begin to explain why girls begin to struggle in school around the same time they become aware of their bodies. "Girls who have poor body images consistently report that it keeps them from focusing on schoolwork and other things," said Joni Johnston, a psychologist and author of *Appearance Obsession.* "It's all that self-consciousness, all that worrying, that really does take energy away from other things."

According to Joan Jacobs Brumberg, a professor at Cornell University, in her book *The Body Project,* teenage girls didn't start to diet until the 1920s, the era of the "flapper," when women tried to slim down in order to wear the popular chemise dress. Fashion still, in large part, dictates our perception of the "perfect" female body. Currently, broad shoulders and slim hips, a physique common among female athletes, appears to be one body type girls strive to achieve. "The body is a consuming project for contemporary girls because it provides an important means of self-definition, a way to visibly announce who you are to the world," said Brumberg.

Girls begin to worry about their bodies at younger ages because they are entering puberty earlier. One study found that by seven years of age, 7 percent of white girls and 27 percent of African American girls showed some signs of enlarged breasts, pubic hairs, or both. Medical experts are continuing to examine why children are maturing sooner. Theories include better nutrition, fewer infectious diseases, and exposure to substances in our environment that act like hormones on the body's system. Despite the cause, the effect is that young girls are developing womanly bodies while psychologically they are still children. Not surprisingly, most have difficulty coping.

Sex. A middler girl with an hourglass figure will begin to attract the interested glances of older boys. "My fourteen-year-old daughter wears a C-cup bra and might be in a D-cup by graduation," said a single father. "She is already getting her share of attention from boys who are just interested in getting under her shirt. It is really getting her down." Flattered and intimidated by this attention, she may find it difficult, if not impossible, to turn back their advances.

Illegal substances. Because she looks older, this fourteen-year-old may begin to hang out with an older crowd of girls with whom she feels more comfortable. She may be exposed to cigarettes, alcohol, and drugs before many of her classmates.

Eating disorders. Girls who mature earlier—breast development or menstruation before age eleven—experience three times the risk of depression, behavioral problems, and eating disorders, according to Dr. Jean Brooks-Gunn, a professor of child development and education at Columbia University who has been studying adolescence for more than

20 years. While putting on weight in the hips and thighs is perfectly normal for young adolescents, many girls begin to think of themselves as "fat," and they begin to work to take off those pounds.

DANGEROUS EATING DISORDERS

"Our seven-year-old frequently bolts from the table and vomits in the bathroom. Usually it's because the food disagrees with her—too cold, burnt, just doesn't like it. Are there any warning signs for eating disorders?"
—Worried mother

When Calista Flockhart, Fox TV's Ally McBeal, showed up for the 1998 Emmy awards in a backless dress, everyone was aghast. The dress revealed more than skin: Flockhart's backbone protruded, making her look more like a starvation victim from Ethiopia than a million-dollar TV star from Beverly Hills.

Immediately the tabloids kicked in with the rumors that Flockhart was suffering from anorexia. The episode is telling because Flockhart was the "it" girl for 1997 and 1998, the TV star young adolescent boys lusted after. Girls imitated her short skirts and her breezy haircut. How many of them tried to achieve her waif-like appearance?

"I think it will be an ongoing battle for all of us with our daughters until Hollywood gets the message that skin and bones is not the ideal we should all strive for," an aggravated mother typed into cyberspace. "My daughter is five feet two inches, and weighs ninety pounds. Most days she complains she's too fat!"

More than eight million young adults are believed to be suffering from eating disorders: anorexia nervosa, its companion illness bulimia nervosa, and binge eating. An eating disorder is a clinical, psychiatric illness that has serious physical effects. Here are some specific details on the three types of eating disorders:

Anorexia Nervosa

Often called "the pursuit of thinness," an anorexic begins to diet and then can't seem to stop. While some boys do suffer from anorexia, 90 percent of the patients are female, with the peak age of onset between twelve and seventeen. Weight gain looms as an overriding fear, powerful enough to prevent the person from consuming anything substantial. The typical anorexic exhibits an inordinate interest in food and may even do the family shopping and food preparation. Yet, she will consume little of what she offers to others. "My daughter eats yogurt for breakfast, no lunch and picks at dinner," said one father.

The anorexic obsesses over her appearance and, no matter how thin she becomes, will always believe she is not yet thin enough. "My fourteen-year-old daughter, five feet four, weighs 101 pounds fully clothed," said one mother. "Size zero is baggy on her! She thinks she is fat and takes a full-length mirror into the bathroom with her each morning. Do you think she is seeing how fat she is?" Another mother added, "My daughter even thinks her fingers are fat!"

To be diagnosed as anorexic, the victim must be 15 percent thinner than the normal weight for her age and height. Besides weight loss, an anorexic exhibits other signs: weakness, dull and brittle hair that begins to fall out, cessation of the menstrual cycle, slowed metabolism and slower reflexes, and the growth of furlike hair on the arms (lanugo), the body's attempt to hold in heat in the absence of body fat.

Anorexia is a life-threatening condition. At the least, the condition can slow a young adolescent's growth and bone development. But anorexia can affect the heart, rendering it smaller and weaker, and the kidneys. Unless medical intervention is aggressive and swift, the person could die. Celebrities who have succumbed to the disease include the singer Karen Carpenter, the world-class gymnast Christy Henrich, who weighed only 47 pounds when she died at age twenty-one in 1994, and Heidi Guenther, a dancer with the Boston Ballet.

Bulimia Nervosa

This condition, far more common than anorexia, involves a cycle of binge eating and then purging through vomiting, excessive exercise, or the overuse of laxatives. As with anorexia, 90 percent of the victims are female. While a bulimic is also concerned about her shape, she often doesn't appear to be emaciated, but her weight may fluctuate. Princess Diana suffered from bulimia, and we can well remember how the press liked to zero in whenever she appeared noticeably thin.

During mealtimes, the bulimic may consume a normal amount of food. The tip-off comes afterward with a quick trip to the bathroom to purge. A parent also might notice a daughter fasting for twenty-four hours after a binge episode or exercising vigorously for an hour or more. The sufferer may develop "chipmunk cheeks," due to swelling of the parotid glands, which are found above the jaw near the ear.

As with anorexia, bulimia can threaten a young adolescent girl's health. She will probably suffer heartburn, abdominal pain, and may vomit blood. An electrolyte imbalance, caused by depletion of the body's water supply, can lead to weakness and even cardiac arrest.

Ironically, peer pressure may increase rather than halt bulimic behavior. "Fad bulimia," where a group of girls gets together to first binge and then purge, turns an eating disorder into a social event. Health experts compare the ritual to drinking or doing drugs with friends. These binges are usually planned, and an invitation is often tied to a girl's status in the social group. Mounds of foodstuffs are consumed and then the girls take turns purging.

Binge Eating Disorder

This condition is similar to bulimia, but without the purging aspect. Instead, the sufferer will frequently eat large amounts of food while feeling a loss of control over her eating. There is no weight loss. In fact, more than 20 percent of those with a binge eating disorder are categorized as obese, specifically, they exceed a healthy body weight by 20 percent.

A person with this problem will eat abnormally large amounts of food rapidly and past the point of satiety. Eating alone, to avoid embarrassment at the quantity of food being consumed, is a pattern. Afterward, the person will feel disgust, depression, or guilt for overeating.

The health risks for someone with this disorder include the diseases that often accompany obesity: diabetes, high blood pressure, high cholesterol levels, gallbladder disease, heart disease, and certain types of cancer. While most of the sufferers of this condition are adults, experts say some young adolescents experience this syndrome, too.

Eating disorders are most often triggered during periods of stress. And for many ten- to fifteen-year-olds, adolescence is a stressful time. Many victims, whose families have a history of depression, alcoholism, or drug abuse, may have a genetic predisposition for these diseases.

Psychiatrists now believe that some people have personality traits—perfectionism, anxiety, self-doubt, and insecurity—that also may open them to risk.

But external factors cannot be ignored. Females who aspire to careers in entertainment, media, beauty, and fashion will be under pressure to remain svelte. Every now and then there is the exceptional model or star who manages to beat the system. Camryn Manheim, for example, the full-figured actress from *The Practice,* won an Emmy and dedicated it to "the fat girls everywhere." But no one expects that young girls will now attempt to emulate her lead by piling on the pounds.

WORKING TO PREVENT EATING DISORDERS IN GIRLS

It is rare for an anorexic or bulimic to recover without professional intervention. Why? Because the issue is one of control, she isn't going to readily concede to your desire to have her eat more. Telling her she looks fine and doesn't need to diet won't work either. She believes she is too heavy and no matter how many people argue with her, she will not be convinced. What you see and what she sees when she looks into the mirror are two different things.

So what can you do?

Make your daughter a doctor's appointment. Tell her it's for her regular check-up (it might be). Beforehand, confide in the doctor about your suspicions. He will thus be prepared to talk with your daughter and may even have a treatment plan or therapist in mind to suggest during her meeting.

Be prepared for resistance. Eating disorder victims often believe there is nothing wrong with them until they are too weak to stand up. You don't want to wait until that point. Don't accept her word that there is nothing wrong. Trust your parental instincts.

Don't blame yourself. Medical experts now believe that certain personality types are more susceptible to eating disorders. Often, a parent could not have prevented the situation. So stop blaming yourself and focus on getting your daughter the help she needs to become healthy.

Avoid commenting on appearance. If your daughter has recently lost weight and you tell her she looks good, this will merely fuel her need to

Body Image and Special Needs Children

"My daughter has cerebral palsy, but has always been in a mainstream school where she has had lots of friends. Recently, the school psychologist told me to expect a dry spell with regard to her social life. How do I prepare her for this?"
    —Mother of an eleven-year-old

Young adolescents want nothing more than to be like their friends. But for many middlers with a disability or a chronic illness their physical appearance or special needs will always set them apart from their friends. During middle school, when the social scene kicks in, many of these children face the sting of rejection. "My eleven-year-old daughter has Down's syndrome," one mother said. "I have noticed that she is no longer being invited to birthday parties and sleepovers. She's trying to be brave about this, but every time it happens, I feel so hurt for her."

You may not be able to deflect every arrow, but there are some things you can do to help your child adjust:

Talk with her openly about the problem. A young adolescent is intelligent enough to suspect why she has been excluded from a party. Chances are she has spent many years dealing with how others react to her disability or illness. Inventing excuses will just add to her hurt.

Do small things that can make a difference. A new pair of jeans or an attractive hairstyle can help your child appear—and feel—less different.

Make sure she has other friends who share her predicament. As a young adolescent adjusts to a new social order, she should have others her age to talk with. Check out local organizations that might hold group counseling sessions to discuss these concerns. These groups might also have their own social get-togethers that your daughter could participate in.

Get her teacher on your team. Often teachers can help a child gain social acceptance by providing a positive example. One teacher, for instance, has a child whose physical limitations require assistance unpacking his bookbag and spreading out his papers before class begins. The teacher assists him with minimal fuss and comment, thus not calling attention to his disability.

diet some more. Instead, make innocuous comments, such as "That blouse is a pretty color," that cannot be misconstrued.

Be a positive female role model. Girls with eating disorders often feel helpless and hopeless about their future living in a world they regard as dominated by men. The weight loss is viewed as a self-fulfilling prophecy. An eating disorder victim appears frail and unable to fend for herself, thus she is dependent upon the men in her life to protect her. Mothers who exhibit strength of character, independence, resiliency, and the drive to survive send positive messages to their daughters.

Get fathers involved. Margo Maine, former director of the Eating Disorders Program at the Institute of Living in Hartford, Connecticut, says her experience suggests a link between girls who develop unhealthy eating behaviors and fathers. If fathers are emotionally unavailable, or suddenly withdraw as a girl enters preadolescence, these daughters have a "father hunger" that they try to fill with food. They binge, yo-yo diet, or develop anorexia.

Be particularly sensitive if your daughter is an athlete. Many younger athletes, particularly those in middle school, are at risk.

WOMEN ATHLETES—LOSING TO WIN

"One of my daughter's friends is a swimmer and I think she has an eating disorder. She had to lose some weight for swimming. Do you think that triggered her disease?"
—Concerned parent

Female athletes are at particular risk for developing eating disorders. Competitive sports attract women who are intense and driven—high-risk characteristics for developing an eating problem. The nature of certain sports—swimming, gymnastics, figure skating—demands a certain body weight and shape to be successful. Add to those two factors the physical demands of staying in top shape, and you have a recipe for disaster.

Recently attention has been focused on the three problems female athletes encounter: eating disorders, either anorexia or bulimia; amenorrhea, the cessation of the menstrual cycle when body fat falls below 17 percent to 18 percent; and osteoporosis, the loss of bone density which results in fragile bones and increases the risk of fractures. Dubbed the Triad, these three conditions are viewed as red flags to signal that a female athlete is in imminent danger. An education campaign, launched in 1992 by the American College of Sports Medicine, that focused primarily on school athletics coaches, has been credited with saving the lives of many of these young girls.

In the past, coaches were viewed as a large part of the problem. Former athletes like the gymnast Cathy Rigby have talked quite openly about how they were pressured by their coaches to lose weight. Rigby's case is quite typical. As a young adolescent competing during the 1970s, she had the prepubescent body that coaches believed gave athletes an edge in the sport. However, when she turned sixteen, she added height and bulk to her frame and gained thirteen pounds. Told by her coach to lose weight, she fell into a twelve-year cycle with bulimia that left her near death's door on two occasions.

By 1992, the American College of Sports Medicine had identified the Triad and listed the sports where athletes were at risk: gymnastics, running, swimming, ice skating, and diving. The ACSM cautioned that young women were most at risk during adolescence when intensified training for a sport and bodily changes intersect. A task force was put together at USA Gymnastics, and the results have been encouraging. In the 1996 Summer Olympic Games in Atlanta, the U.S. gymnastics team nabbed the gold medal in team competition. While most attention was focused on Kerri Strug completing her vault on a badly sprained ankle, what was truly amazing was the size and weight of the "Magnificent Seven." The U.S. squad averaged 4 feet 11.5 inches, and 92.3 pounds, significantly outweighing the second-place Russians (4 feet 10.75 inches, 84.1 pounds), and the fourth-place Chinese (4 feet 7.25 inches, 78.5 pounds).

"The United States' team is changing the paradigm in the sport," said Dan Benardot, nutritionist for the national team and codirector for Elite Athlete Performance in Atlanta. "If you put our team next to any other team in the world, we not only looked good, we looked fantastic. The other teams looked cadaverous. They looked drawn."

As heartening as these developments are, no one believes that female athletes are safe from the Triad. There is more understanding of the dangers at the top echelons of athletics. In gymnastics, for example, one study showed that 62 percent of college gymnasts had a serious eating disorder. It will take time for the new attitudes to trickle down and, until that time comes, many younger athletes, particularly those in middle school, are at risk. So a parent whose daughter is athletically inclined should work to combat eating disorders. Here's how:

Know which sports are risky. Approximately 80 percent of cheerleaders, for example, from middle school through the professionals, use some form of bulimia to stay thin. Among swimmers, 70 percent between the ages of nine and eighteen were foregoing meals to lose weight. Divers, runners, figure skaters, and tennis players are also viewed by experts as being at risk.

Discourage sport-specific training at an early age. Doctors believe that girls who choose to train for a particular sport before puberty may select a sport that will ultimately prove inappropriate for their body size, thus ensuring an eating disorder problem.

Keep a balance in your daughter's life. A young middler's life should not be all sport and no play. Factor in plenty of time for schoolwork, friends, and leisuretime activities.

Ask that weighing by coaches be eliminated. Fighters, wrestlers, and jockeys are just about the only athletes who are weighed for a purpose. Weighing of young girls is unnecessary and only ensures eating problems.

Make sure the coach will not make comments about weight. Be blunt and make sure the coach understands that even one comment to any of the girls about weight could trigger an eating disorder. In the event you find out that such a comment has been made, report the incident to the school's administration.

Request that ample snacks and water be available. Young adolescent girls need to refuel when working out. If the coach isn't planning to supply snacks and water, ask if the parents can provide them. Besides helping the girls to stay strong, the food will deliver a message that eating is essential for competing.

Find out how performances will be rated. At the Olympics level in gymnastics, judges are being encouraged to focus less on appearance and more on skill. This goal is a tough one because many people, judges included, have a particular body type in mind as the ideal for a certain sport. But articulating your concerns to the coaches may help to facilitate this understanding.

Ask what will happen if one of the team suffers from an eating disorder. Experts say without reservation that the girl should be immediately barred from competing. Some girls who have an eating disorder also are compulsive about exercising. Professionals say that withholding the sport is the first step in treating this obsession.

Focus on female athletes who are positive role models. Gabrielle Reece, a professional volleyball star who stands six feet three inches, encourages girls to celebrate their own personal style. "I can't be five foot five; I passed that a long time ago," she told *Parade* magazine. "If you have big hips, that's what you have. Certainly you can find ways to enhance yourself. But work from your canvas." She added: "Not eating is counterproductive. You can't build muscle without food."

STEROIDS AND CREATINE—MUSCLE MADNESS

When St. Louis slugger Mark McGwire finished the 1998 baseball season with seventy home runs, thus obliterating Roger Maris' previous record of sixty-one, baseball fans everywhere cheered. Yet many parents of young adolescent boys felt a sense of disquiet, not over McGwire's accomplishments, but in the way he achieved his goal.

McGwire had been taking the testosterone-boosting drug androstenedione (pronounced andro-STEEN-die-own), legal in professional baseball, but illegal just about everywhere else. The substance, which supporters say helps build muscle tissue, has been banned by the International Olympic Committee, the National Football League, and the National Collegiate Athletic Association. These organizations believe that androstenedione may give users an unfair advantage in competition. But also, because this substance has never been tested for long-term health effects, it may present a health risk to anyone who uses it.

And therein lies the rub. McGwire has become a hero to hoards of young adolescent boys who will now be attempting to imitate his flourish of a swing whenever they step into the batter's box. Will these same young men imitate him in other ways, by trying to find quick and easy ways to increase muscle mass and endurance? Besides androstenedione, young adolescents have been gobbling up capsules of creatine, an amino acid, as well as a whole host of vitamins and dietary supplements. One herbal stimulant, ephedra, a natural alternative to the street drug Ecstasy, has been blamed for the death of a Long Island college student. "The use of performance-enhancing substances is a threat to an athlete's health," said Dr. Joseph Snyder, of the Family Practice Resident Program of the Lutheran Hospital in Des Moines.

All of these substances are legal to use and most can be purchased over the counter at your nearest health foods store. One chain, GNC, has eagerly gone after the young adolescent market, issuing "gold card" identification to buyers that they can use for special discounts. Most parents remain unaware of what their middlers are buying and swallowing. At the least, these substances can cause minor health problems like gastrointestinal distress, at the worst they can stunt growth, damage growing muscles and tissues, and even cause death. "With the number of young drug abusers now consuming these agents, and their documented potential for serious harm and even death, it is now time for a federal and/or state agency to take a hard look at their continued sale," Dr. Ronald Dougherty, a family physician and specialist in addiction illness, told a 1998 meeting of the Scientific Assembly of the American Academy of Family Physicians.

What are the substances young adolescents are using most often? They include:

Steroids

Anabolic steroids mimic the effects of the male sex hormone testosterone. First developed in the 1930s, steroids can be legitimately prescribed by a physician for certain kinds of anemia, severe burns, and some types of breast cancer. But many athletes use steroids illegally, claiming these drugs, used in combination with exercise and diet, can help increase body weight and strength. Adverse side effects are numerous, however. In males, steroids can cause withered testicles and sterility. In females, irreversible masculine traits, such as body hair and breast reduction, can occur. There are also psychological side effects, such as depression and an increase in aggressive behavior. Prolonged use of steroids can cause strokes, heart attacks, and liver and prostate cancers. In young adults, steroid abuse can interfere with bone growth and lead to permanently stunted growth.

Steroid use also has been linked to a psychological phenomenon called "roid rage." According to Iowa's Dr. Snyder, steroid users "may have a violent streak . . . while they're using them," and "get into trouble."

While no sport is immune to steroid use, Dr. Snyder said that "power sports," such as weightlifting or football, are where players are most likely to use them. And while steroid use is typically associated with boys, Dr. Snyder said that use among female athletes is on the rise. "With the female NBA and things like that, there are a lot more females using the drugs."

In the Massachusetts study that discovered that 2.7 percent of 965 students at four middle schools were taking steroids, authorities placed the blame on adults. "A cycle of steroids costs a few hundred dollars," said Avery Faigenbaum, who did the study. "I don't know a lot of ten-year-olds who have a couple of hundred dollars. I think we have to look at brothers and sisters, I think we have to look at parents and at youth coaches."

Androstenedione

Opinion is divided on androstenedione. One camp believes that androstenedione converts to testosterone in the body, and so is a steroid. The National Collegiate Athletic Association and the National Football League consider it a steroid and have banned the substance. Proponents say that androstenedione does not seem to boost testosterone levels all that much. Major league baseball has not banned androstenedione so McGwire was free to use the substance openly.

Creatine

Sales of creatine in 1997 surpassed $25 million, according to the *Nutrition Business Journal*. An amino acid, creatine is found naturally in foods such as meats, milk, and some fish. A half-pound of meat contains about one gram of creatine, half the amount needed to maintain the muscles of a 154-pound person. Because creatine is manufactured by the body's liver and kidneys, it is unlikely the substance will be banned by any sporting organization.

How does creatine work? The substance is stored in muscles as the compound phosphocreatine, used by the body to release energy. The higher the level of phosphocreatine in a muscle cell, the more energy that cell can release. Creatine also adds to the water content of muscles, increasing their size and enhancing their function.

Experts believe that creatine is more effective for athletes who need quick bursts of energy to succeed. These activities would include weight lifting or sprinting. Athletes who need greater endurance—long-distance runners and cyclists, for example—may actually be slowed down by the additional weight gain of muscle mass that creatine causes.

While the long-term side effects are not known, short-term ones have been documented. These include gastrointestinal distress, nausea, headaches, dizziness, and muscle cramping. Creatine is categorized as a dietary supplement rather than a drug, helping it to avoid scrutiny by the Food and Drug Administration.

If you discover your son is taking creatine, should you be concerned? Probably. "There are too many unanswered questions for us to even begin getting behind the product," said David Lightsey, of the National Council Against Health Fraud, a consumer advocacy group. "We're concerned about what's going to happen a year or two from now to these kids who are taking this product, especially to the ones who are going through their major growth changes."

Talk with your son about what he hopes to accomplish by taking creatine. Many professionals believe that good nutrition and sensible exercise can come close to mimicking the effects achieved through using creatine. And, in the long run, those benefits will come without any risks.

THE SHAPE OF THINGS TO COME

Middlers are preoccupied with their appearance, and while that is so, parents will worry, too. Many times we will be frustrated and feel helpless. Eating disorders and exercise obsessions are serious problems that do not lend themselves to the quick fix. But if we educate ourselves beforehand, sharpen our powers of observation so that we won't overlook warning signs, and seek out the appropriate people to help us, then our children will receive the help they need to survive and adjust through these tumultuous times.

Strategies: Raising a Healthy Eater

Most children don't have daily physical education activities in school. And by late middle school, many of them drop out of organized athletic activities. (More on this in Chapter Seven.) Often these physical endeavors are replaced with TV watching and snacking. No surprise, then, that our children are gaining weight. About 25 percent of American children—one in four—are considered overweight, that's 20 percent over the desired weight on the standard height-weight–ratio chart used by doctors. According to the Centers for Disease Control, this represents a 15 percent increase from twenty years ago.

But how do you encourage your child to achieve the proper body proportions without causing an eating disorder? Here are some tips:

Commit your entire family to eating more healthful foods. Most families could survive eating fewer fatty foods and sweets. Cooking in rather than ordering out may be less convenient, but if you select simple menus, the preparation will probably take less time than waiting in line for your order to be filled.

Involve your child in selecting and preparing the menus. Giving him a say in what he will be eating will encourage him to sign on to a more healthful regimen at home and may help him resist less healthful snacks when he is with his friends.

Include the whole family, not just your weight-challenged child, even siblings who may not have weight problems. Forbidding one child to eat potato chips and then keeping them in the cupboard for the rest of the family will send conflicting messages.

Don't skip breakfast, the most important meal of the day. A 1996 Gallup poll of 410 kids, ages nine to fifteen, found that 51 percent skipped breakfast at least once a week; 15 percent missed it four times or more. Trouble is, skipping breakfast often means your child won't make up the nutrients later in the day. And without anything in the stomach, the head may have trouble operating, which means less concentration for your child.

Never use food as a reward or punishment. We send our children conflicting messages by labeling food as something they get when they are "good." A child with low self-esteem may begin denying herself food because she has been "bad."

Don't push your child to eat everything on the plate. The stomach signals when it is full. To push our children to eat after reaching that point risks overriding the body's own message system. The child who loses touch with her own satiety signals may develop eating problems.

Promote three meals a day and two healthful snacks. Getting into this routine will discourage constant snacking.

Limit TV watching. A study of 4,063 kids ages eight to sixteen published in the *Journal of the American Medical Association* found that those who watched more than four hours of TV a day were heavier than those who watched two hours.

Monitor your child's media viewing. A young person is bound to get a skewed view of the human body after watching television. Young actresses are thinner than average and the actors do have enviable physiques. But these professionals often work very hard at maintaining their bodies, sometimes at great psychological cost. Eating disorders and steroid use run rampant in the entertainment and sporting world. Talk with your children about these issues.

Eavesdrop on "food" conversations. Do you drive the soccer carpool? Then tune in whenever your daughter and her friends talk about their bodies and food. One mother of a ten-year-old was shocked to hear comments about "thunder thighs." While you may not want to interject your thoughts on the spot, you can discuss the issue later on with your daughter.

Call for a reality check. There are some good books written for middler girls and boys about what bodily changes they will experience. (Check the resource section.) These books can help your child understand that middler bodies are "in development."

Eat dinner together. Besides being a great time to talk, dinnertime provides you with a nonintrusive way to monitor your child's eating habits. If you suspect your daughter has an eating disorder, sharing a meal will give you the chance to observe her firsthand.

Discuss body image with your child. Don't ignore comments your child makes about her body. Patronizing her with "You look beautiful," when she is worried about being too heavy, will merely increase her anxieties. Instead, find out why she feels that way. If you agree that she needs to tone up, find ways where she can be proactive, joining an exercise club or changing her diet.

Watch where your children go online. Unfortunately some online message boards and chat rooms that purport to offer support to those with body obsessions merely feed their fears. Worse yet, your children may find new ways to deal with their bodies in negative ways. For example, some message boards have posts about health supplements, while chat rooms on eating disorders often give ideas for other ways to purge.

Watch for changes in eating and exercise. Smoking is a danger sign, since many young adolescents (girls in particular) believe that smoking will help them eat less and therefore lose weight. Also, if your son seems to be spending an inordinate amount of time at the gym working out, he's probably overdoing it.

CHAPTER FIVE

Drugs, Alcohol, and Cigarettes

*

*"I'm a counselor at a substance abuse treatment clinic. I found myself be-
ing interviewed about ways to keep your teen drug-free. I found out
that my own daughter had been smoking pot at the
exact moment I'm giving other parents advice!"*
—Mother of a thirteen-year-old

At younger ages, children are getting high. Abusing substances starts
after the move from the elementary grades into middle school according to PRIDE (National Parents' Resource Institute for Drug Education), the National Institute on Drug Abuse, and the Monitoring the Future 1997 survey. Thirteen is a turning point, reports The National
Center on Addiction and Substance Abuse. This is when perception, attitude, and opportunity change. A thirteen-year-old is three times as likely
to know a drug user and not snitch. A thirteen-year-old is less afraid of
consequences, more willing to follow friends, and twice as likely to have
no adult supervision after school.

Good middlers raised by conscientious, law-abiding parents, not
negligent crack addicts, abuse substances. Why is that and what can you
do to ensure that your middler doesn't become another statistic? In this
chapter, we'll deliver strategies that can prevent your child from experimenting in the first place. The substance abuse epidemic wafts across our
culture and there are no magic solutions to offer. However, there are
turnaround tactics that work.

UNDERSTANDING ADDICTION

Young adolescents who experiment with drugs court disaster. They don't comprehend that. A middler's mindset is "in the now." He isn't thinking about getting addicted to cigarettes or alcohol or drugs. Middlers want to try something forbidden, to experience a sensation, to act cool. "I am young and I have tried smoking cigarettes, cigars, and alcohol because I want to know what it's like," confessed a fourteen-year-old boy. The consequences of such adventures rarely cross young minds. All young adolescents have what's called "poor risk assessment." In layman's language, they are naive, shortsighted, daring, and foolish.

Drugs hijack the brain and capture the will. Any experimentation by your middler is a call to action. With the specter of addiction hovering over our unsuspecting youth, parents have to grasp what addiction really is and how best to battle the lure of substances.

Americans think about substance abuse in the context of war and willpower. Our resources, $16 billion a year, finance criminal investigations and jail construction. The goals are to locate the drug dealers, stop the traffic, incarcerate the offenders. It's a win or lose battle pitting good against the evil sellers and users. Our approach has not won the war.

Far from the frontlines, scientists working in labs have learned exactly where and how addiction occurs in the brain. A substance called dopamine, a feel-good molecule, is key. The more your brain releases, the better you feel. All substances—heroin, alcohol, marijuana, cocaine, and nicotine—figure into this dopamine connection. Heroin and nicotine release more; cocaine prevents the brain from mopping up the supply.

Dopamine does more than squirt euphoria. Like a raging river overflowing its banks and carving out new tributaries, dopamine changes the brain. It etches new circuits and motivates actions. It sets up patterns: the smoker reaches for that cigarette after a meal. It defines rituals—linking that sip or swallow to certain people or places.

The dopamine brainwash feels so great, you want it again. Once that feel-good highway is constructed, it is cemented into the brain. At first a user craves the dopamine flood, but eventually he craves the substance to recover from a drought. An addict snorts or drinks not to feel good, but to stop feeling bad. Addiction interferes with the brain's sound judgment and logic.

That's why alcoholics and substance abusers behave dangerously (drunk driving, stealing, breaking the law) and self-destructively (overdosing).

How your genes deploy, disperse, or inhibit the dopamine connection makes you more or less vulnerable to addiction. There appears to be a genetic reason why some smokers just can't quit while others can.

Comprehending the neurotransmitter pyrotechnics of brain chemistry is complex. What's simple is that drug abuse is not about morality. For years, the drug addict and alcoholic were cast as moral failures. Saying "no," or "not ever again," to cigarettes, a vodka and tonic, a joint, or a heroin fix is not a matter of virtue. Dr. Mark Wielgus, a New York alcohol and drug treatment clinic director, recommends looking at substance abuse as "an illness used by some to cope with the stress and strain in their lives."

Warning Signs: What to Watch For

To prevent your child from becoming addicted to substances, learn to recognize the signals of experimentation. Here is a list from drug treatment specialists, researchers, psychologists, educators, other parents, and middlers. Use all your senses including your sixth sense, the intuition that lies deep in the heart of parents.

- *Changes in school performance.* Is there a drop in grades, an attendance problem? Has motivation slipped dramatically?
- *A different group of friends.* Has your middler traded the old friends (the ones you knew) for a new set (you don't know at all)?
- *Avoidance and isolation.* Is your middler withdrawing? Have teachers, coaches, mentors expressed this? When you look him in the eye, is he uncomfortable? Does he avoid hugs? (You might pick up the smell of alcohol or smoke on his breath.)
- *Physical appearance cues.* Is your child's appetite irregular? Marijuana leads to excessive hunger, called having "the munchies." Has she gone from clothes-conscious to slovenly? Watch for a staggering gait, hyperactive movements, or excessive energy.
- *Emotional extremes.* Is your child nasty, angry, hostile, sad,

giddy, super-confident? Cocaine users feel all-powerful. Amphetamines create edgy, hypermanic moods.

- *Susceptibility to illness.* Is she catching frequent colds, throwing up, dizzy, groggy? Have you thought: *My child doesn't look well?*
- *Defiance.* Has your relationship deteriorated? He refuses to do chores, or virtually anything you request; you punish. He turns defiant and seems *possessed.*
- *Resistance to curfews and checks.* Does she resist your attempts to know her whereabouts? Is she often late, full of excuses?
- *Deliberate attempts to keep you in the dark about school.* Has your child kept information from you? Have teachers sent home warnings, letters, e-mails you've never seen?
- *New problems—lying, stealing.* Drugs cost money. Finding funds can lead to your middler stealing from your pocketbook, wallet, or from siblings.
- *Fascination with (or evidence of) drug paraphernalia.* Does he wear T-shirts with drug slogans or marijuana leaf logos? Are icons (Marilyn Manson, Kurt Cobain, Jim Morrison) of drug and alcohol abuse plastered on walls? Have you found eye droppers, small decongestant bottles, small butane torches, small glass vials, oddly wrapped paper resembling origami?

Any *yes* is cause to look further. Education is your best defense. Attend drug and alcohol lectures in your community. Drug nicknames, packaging, and the forms substances come in vary so much that you need local expertise. Community experts know which drugs are popular and how they are sold in your neighborhood. Talk to other parents. Do research online at the site for Drug Free America: http://www.drugfreeamerica.org/map.html.

Why Do Middlers Take Drugs?

Surely you know the answer: peer pressure, right? The D.A.R.E. (Drug Abuse Resistance Education) program turns on the assumption that middlers are pressured by their circle of peers to smoke, drink, or use illegal substances. It teaches refusal skills—"just say no"—to a generation that hasn't said no. Peer influence is powerful but only one of the explanations.

A thorough review and analysis of drug studies was done in 1998 by Drs. Harolyn Belcher and Harold Shinitzky and published in *Archives of Pediatrics and Adolescent Medicine.* Here are reasons that recurred in the research:

- *Gender.* Boys are *more* likely than girls to experiment. William Pollack, Ph.D., codirector of the Center for Men at McLean Hospital/Harvard Medical School, says in *Real Boys,* "Many boys use drugs to numb the pain of their emotions—the disconnection they feel from their parents, their low self-esteem, their problems at school, with peers, or their budding sexuality."
- *Genetics.* Some children have a predisposition for drug dependence.
- *Personality traits.* Conduct disorder, attention deficit hyperactivity disorder, aggressiveness, moodiness, and a negative attitude increase vulnerability, as do lack of self-control and difficulty coping with adversity. Thrill seekers are at risk, too.
- *Poor parenting.* Children abused or neglected are more likely to become alcohol and drug abusers.

Finally, factor in being a middler. "I feel like I'm having a midlife crisis and I'm only fourteen!" a New York girl remarked. Early adolescence often feels bad. Stress is a constant companion. When we asked in our survey what would be helpful in handling schoolwork, 50 percent checked, "Finding a way to reduce the stress I feel that is always distracting me." Self-image is a troubling chronological challenge, too.

Drugs obliterate those disquieting feelings. "I tried drugs because they feel good," said a Connecticut seventh grade girl. That early adolescence and substance abuse go together isn't hard to understand. Distress goes up in smoke with marijuana, or gets washed away with an ice cold beer. Compounding the psychic weight are development issues. The curiosity that kills cats entices middlers to get high.

Refusal skill training is important, but it is not the sole strategy for combating substance abuse. Understanding your middler's social behavior, personality, and mindset will provide you with a more finely-tuned profile to gauge your middler's liabilities. One by one, let's tackle each category of abuse and how you can campaign against it.

AN ORDINARY "DRUG" WITH EXTRAORDINARY DANGER . . . ALCOHOL

"I'm not saying don't spend time and budget dollars on drug-prevention programs, but in my experience as a principal, it's alcohol that most kids are trying. This is where substance abuse efforts need to start."
—Middle school principal and father of an eleven-year-old girl

This middle school administrator has seen many young adolescents sneaking six-packs behind the bleachers. He warns that we're so busy trying to alert one another to the latest sensation in the cornucopia of drugs out there, we skip over the one that most middlers try first.

In the new ABCs of substance abuse, A for alcohol is the place to begin. Parents need to examine their attitudes toward drinking, their personal experiences, and the history of their entire family. We clink cocktails to christen the New Year. A summer barbecue doesn't sizzle, a sports event doesn't heat up until the beer flows. For every American event there is an alcoholic ritual. Drinking is not only part of life, it's linked to the best parts.

If you have detected the smell of liquor on your young adolescent's breath after a school dance or caught your child giddy at a family party, you are not alone.

- More than half of eighth graders had tried alcohol in the last year, according to a survey by the Commission on Substance Abuse Among America's Adolescents.
- Three-fourths of the thirteen- and fourteen-year-olds polled said it was "easy to get."
- One-fourth admitted getting drunk.
- Binge drinking is on the rise. In 1991, 13 percent downed five or more drinks at one sitting; in 1996, 16 percent.

How do we turn things around? After interviewing a cross section of alcohol abuse counselors and reviewing reams of research, here is a checklist of common mistakes that parents make. The right way to raise an alcohol-free young adolescent (and to turn around a middler who is drinking) is to recognize these errors. Then avoid them.

Mistake #1. Many adults downplay and underestimate the dangers of alcohol. "We keep a case of beer in our garage for parties. My husband

and I don't drink beer. I noticed a handful of cans missing recently. I was annoyed at my stepson. But I admit I was relieved. It's only beer. I could have found syringes."—Stepmother of a fifteen-year-old

If you agree, beware. In the small agricultural town of Columbia, Connecticut (population 4,784), family members returned home one evening to find their son and a friend on the basement floor comatose. The two twelve-year-olds spent their day off from school drinking whiskey. Their evening was spent on an emergency helicopter ride on life support to the Connecticut Children's Medical Center. The Horace Porter School community of parents talked in stunned tones. The boys recovered. The community didn't bounce back from this incident as quickly.

Reevaluate your attitude toward young adolescent drinking. The consequences can be as dire as any drug use.

Mistake #2. Parents dismiss social drinking as a harmless example. Do you always begin a social occasion with a drink? The majority of us do this without giving it a thought. It's time to think again.

Social anxiety and acceptance is the major affliction of early adolescence. If you demonstrate that drinking makes you a better social animal, this message is never more potent than it is to a child between the ages of ten and fifteen.

What about the party animal lesson? "Right after eighth grade, partying with alcohol goes into full swing," says Karen Kirshbaum, CSW, a drug education expert. The transition between middle and high school is marked by "moving up" parties. Make sure your middlers don't pair good times and good friends with alcohol use.

Mistake #3. Parents assume that clear-cut "don't drink" messages are a waste of time. Perhaps too many parents think about the days of Prohibition. Declaring booze illegal spawned a thriving bootleg industry and a legendary mystique of alcoholic flappers and Charleston dancers like Zelda and F. Scott Fitzgerald. Not wanting history to repeat itself, some parents pass on anti-alcohol speeches. According to the experts, fewer than one in three parents of tenth grade students are giving their children firm messages against any use of alcohol.

Here's the message you should be broadcasting: Alcohol is an adult privilege, and not permitted for young preteens. When? Start now. Tenth grade is already too late! In our survey, 33 percent of ten- to fifteen-year-olds told us that among their circle of friends drinking is already an occasional experience.

Highlight the damages that drinking causes, specifically to middlers.

- Tell your child that this is the absolute worst time to douse his brain with alcohol. It's growing in leaps and bounds, busy comprehending and storing information. The ability to plan and formulate complex judgments evolves throughout these years. Drinking damages the brain's capabilities and prevents those skills from fully developing.
- Point out that drinking is a mutually destructive concoction on a date. Research shows that drinking makes adolescent girls more pliant and adolescent boys more aggressive. In one survey, 60 percent of women who drank became targets of a male drinker's sexual aggression. Girls who drink are prone to have earlier sexual experiences. Alcohol is a consistent factor in date rape stories. Drinking washes away inhibitions. So young adolescents are less likely to use contraception, running higher risks of contracting sexually transmitted diseases.
- If your family history contains any members with a drinking dependency, emphasize in capital letters your child is in a higher risk category. Alcoholism runs in families. If there is an alcoholic in yours, your child's risk of dependence is *seven times greater* than a child with no family history. This isn't all genetics, but a combination of nature and nurture.

  The sons of alcoholics, in particular, apparently feel more pleasurable sensations from alcohol. At the same time, they don't become as physically impaired (slurred speech, sensations of stupor). This combination sets them up for more frequent drinking (it feels good and doesn't hurt) and escalates their addiction odds. In fact there is a certain breed of male alcoholic, who starts drinking in adolescence, becomes aggressive, has legal run-ins, and tends to use other drugs. This family pattern is extremely "contagious" to the next generation of boys.

Mistake #4. It's a good idea to let your child try alcohol at home. The rationale is that supervising experimentation will satisfy his curiosity, and prevent him from drinking later on, and in other circumstances. Parents who ascribe to this are the ones likely to host a pre-prom party and serve a toast or two. Or they permit their middler to have a beer because, "I know my son is drinking anyway. At least here I can count his intake."

This strategy backfires bigtime. It whets, not dampens, the appetite. A 1993 Johnson Institute finding explained that when school age children are allowed to partake at home, they are *more likely* to drink outside the home. Even worse, they are *more likely* to develop serious behavioral and health problems associated with their use of alcohol and other drugs.

Mistake #5. Bargaining works. Parents play "Let's make a deal." Usually, it's after they have discovered that their young adolescent has had a drink or two here or there. They offer a middler permission to drink, if the child will promise something in return. The middler pledges to have just one beer, not get drunk, or, most popular later on, not to drink and drive. The deals are contracted in a well-meaning dialect of responsibility and maturity, a better tack than the old commanding obedience mode. Do young adolescents rise to the occasion, exercise restraint and good judgment? Is bartering fruitful? NO!

Mothers Against Drunk Driving (MADD) warns that when parents bargain with young people, such as allowing them to drink so long as they promise not to drive, the children are *more likely* to drive after imbibing. Furthermore, they are also *more* inclined to get into a motor vehicle driven by someone who has had a drink.

Mistake #6. It's no big deal, all young adolescents try drinking. It's just a phase. "I smoked, drank, and dealt drugs, starting in seventh grade. Once I drank the entire contents of my dad's liquor cabinet! At fifteen, I used to tell my mom I was going out to pick up my friends, get some beer, get drunk, ditch the guys, and come home. She'd laugh and say, 'have fun!' Their deliberate ignorance, and mine, almost killed me a couple of times."—Nineteen-year-old girl

Is drinking an adolescent rite of passage? For some, yes. By the end of high school, statistically a full 90 percent have tried a drink. Is alcohol use a harmless phase? No. It's incorrect to assume that drinking is a passing phase, because some will not survive this "phase." More than 40 percent of deaths among sixteen- to twenty-year-olds occur in automobile crashes, with alcohol present in 39 percent. Your middler may not be driving yet, but how often is he riding in a car driven by a friend's older brother or sister?

High school may be the next alcoholic landmine, but after graduation the stakes go up. *Higher* education has taken on new meaning. Forty-two percent of college students admitted to "bingeing in the last two weeks," according to one study. Only 33 percent of noncollege adolescents drank like that. College students typically consume five drinks a week, although 8 percent reported consuming sixteen or more every week. This is not the recipe for scholastic achievement. Academic problems of some 40 percent implicated drinking. A 28 percent dropout rate was correlated to increased use of alcohol. The *Chronicle of Higher Education,* an independent newspaper whose beat is colleges, reported that alcohol arrests rose 10 percent in 1996, the fifth consecutive year for escalating legal troubles.

Look ahead. What your middler drinks or does not drink now is setting a precedent for the future. Be firm. Establish the rules. Enforce the consequences for breaking the rules every time. If he falls off the wagon, your attitudes and behavior will ensure that this won't become habitual.

What to Do if You Suspect Chronic Drinking

For middlers, even one drink can be too many. The National Institutes of Health found that middlers who imbibe before fifteen are four times more likely to develop alcoholic dependence. Emotional reliance happens sooner. How do you know if your middler is on her way to alcoholism?

Look for these warning signs. Remember this acronym, CAGE. The following questions are used in alcohol treatment programs. Review them with your middler. If she won't talk, ask her friends to comment. Problem drinkers are notorious for refusing to acknowledge their dependence.

- Have you tried to **Cut** down on your drinking habit?
- Have you gotten **Annoyed** because others remarked upon your drinking?
- Do you feel **Guilty** about your drinking?
- Do you reach for an **Eye-opener,** a drink to start the day?

If your child is in trouble with alcohol, getting her to a professional is the only course of action. "A diagnosis of alcohol abuse, alcohol dependency, or alcoholism can only truly be made by a health professional trained specifically in addiction. These are very complex medical and psychological states," insist Cynthia Kuhn, Scott Swartzwelder, and Wilkie Wilson, Duke University Medical Center experts and authors of *Buzzed*.

MARIJUANA

"The police stopped our son and found pot seeds. Luckily he was turned over to us, not arrested. We want to set rules against drug use. Yet we are paranoid that if we press too hard our child will retreat further away."
—Father of a thirteen-year-old

- Nearly one-fourth of nine- to twelve-year-old children were offered marijuana last year according to the Partnership for a Drug-Free America Tracking Study.
- Only 7 percent of parents thought their youngsters were on that receiving line.
- 8 percent of sixth graders, 23 percent of seventh graders, and 33 percent of eighth graders interviewed tried marijuana according to the Survey Research Center at the University of Michigan.

Been-there-done-that baby boomer parents are out of step with the drug scene in their children's lives. Today's marijuana (pot, grass, weed, dope, Acapulco Gold) is twenty-five times stronger, containing levels of THC (delta-9-tetrahydrocannabinol) of 5 percent compared to the 0.2 percent in the 1960s. "The perception of this country is that marijuana is safe, that it's a soft drug," says Dr. Donna Shalala, Secretary of Health and Human Services. Beware of dismissing the import and impact of marijuana.

"I missed the signs that my child was smoking pot," parents confess frequently. Are such parents stupid? Not at all. The truth is that middlers dabbling with marijuana can appear normal. The signs of marijuana use are: a change of friends, mood swings, withdrawal, a slip in grades, reckless spending. These experiences typify countless young adolescents. Middle school brings together several elementary school groups. Just because your son brings home a new pack of friends doesn't mean he's consorting with potheads. Emotional, irritable—doesn't that describe nearly all hormonal boys and PMS girls? When a need for privacy emerges at around age twelve, isn't it normal for your middler to hibernate in her room? Perfectly. What about a drop in grades? Middle school is a notch up on the difficulty ladder, academically and socially. Many explanations apply to a struggling student. Middlers ask for, need, and spend money. For all these reasons, parents miss the usual warning signs.

What to Do When You Discover Your Child Is Smoking Marijuana

Avoid rationalizing your middler's behavior. Denial is a huge impasse. Even when evidence is obvious, parents want to believe the child who says, "That joint isn't mine." Other parents want to dismiss pot because they smoked and survived. This is not the sixties. The drug scene is more lethal and middlers are too young and immature to navigate through it unharmed.

Deal with your fury, sense of betrayal, guilt, and remorse first. A melodramatic state of mind is counterproductive. Calm down before you approach your child. "Always sit down while you talk. It is a calming posture," recommends a parent of two girls, ages eight and eleven.

Tackle the marijuana as medicine debate. Some doctors and patients say marijuana reduces anxiety, nausea, and vomiting after chemotherapy; improves appetite, and reduces the muscle spasms and pain afflicting epileptics and multiple sclerosis victims. Meanwhile, the National Institutes of Health examined all existing clinical evidence recently and found *no* scientifically sound proof of these claims. Yet twenty-six states and the District of Columbia have passed various laws and resolutions establishing therapeutic-research programs.

This medical mumbo jumbo and legal wrangling gives young adolescents license to smoke. In 1991, 79 percent of high school students viewed regular marijuana use as harmful. In 1998, it's down to 61 percent. Inform your middler of the facts.

Refute the "marijuana is harmless" argument. Its harmful effects include depressing the immune system, interfering with learning and memory functions, and damage to the lungs. It impairs judgment, concentration, and performing complex tasks like driving. Motivation goes up in smoke.

Investigate the why question. "I smoke because it's something to do with my friends when we hang out," confessed a fifteen-year-old boy in our survey. Ask: "Why did you try the marijuana?" Not: "How could you do this?" It's important to get to know why your child turned to this option.

Was it boredom? Is your daughter feeling badly about herself or her life? Is she distressed over your remarriage or infrequent visitation with her father? Pose the question: "What does it do for you?" Don't interrupt, argue, or lecture. Simply listen.

Find out how often your child gets high. Avoid: "So this is what you've been up to every time you lock yourself in your room?" Tread carefully on where your child is getting his supply. If your middler thinks you are going to round up his friends, call their parents, and search all premises, he will not be forthcoming.

State firmly you cannot permit this behavior to continue. Announce consequences that your child will suffer if caught again. Tell your child that his taking drugs has destroyed the trust between you. As a result, he will be more closely monitored. Make sure he understands that rebuilding that trust is a difficult process. He must realize that this is not prying or invading his privacy. He must cooperate with your questions.

Seek professional guidance. If your child is using habitually, or if you're unsure, talk to your child's teachers. Bring your middler to a therapist. Consult with a pediatrician for adolescents who can test for drug use. You can find out how much marijuana is in your child's system. This lets your middler know his drug use can be monitored. (Clever middlers can tamper with these tests, so be aware.)

Don't give up. If drugs continue to dominate, ask your school social worker to recommend day and away treatment programs (see the resource section). Research treatment programs on the Internet (keyword educational consultants). Can you force your middler to go daily or even away to a drug treatment facility? If your middler is sixteen or under, yes. If you insist, he cannot refuse. However, if your child is seventeen and older, he has the legal right to refuse.

DESIGNER DRUGS . . . THE PUNCH AT THE PARTY

"Over the last few years I have been working harder and coming home exhausted. Rudeness is pretty much my daughter's standard attitude. She went to a 'party' recently. When we got calls from her friends' parents (where the

School Days, School Daze

I was with my friends, and my friend's sister gave pot to us," testified a Connecticut eighth grade girl. Substance abuse begins at home. Older siblings turn on younger ones to avoid getting tattled on. Bathroom medicine chests, liquor cabinets, and the family room bar are bonanzas.

Students sometimes walk into school high.

- In a national survey, 19 percent of middle school teachers and 28 percent of high school teachers admitted recognizing a drunk or stoned student at least once a month.
- A 1997 national survey reported that 41 percent of high school students find drugs readily available at school. Only 36 percent were ready to snitch. Only 14 percent of middle school and high school principals admitted seeing drugs sold on school grounds.
- Marijuana use is four times higher at schools where drug use exists compared to drug-free schools.

Everyone agrees that hallways, locker rooms, playgrounds, and parking lots should be substance-free. Making zero tolerance work is a challenge facing every community. In our survey of middle schoolers, 48 percent said drugs were

party was supposed to be) asking where their daughters were, I knew we were in trouble. None of the girls came home until the next day. They were too strung out to care that the jig was up."

—Mother

Parties down through the years have always tried to be exclusive, away from adults' eyes. The 1920s roared with jazzy young people looking through speakeasy peepholes. In the fifties, bobby soxers sang about parties going on "Behind the Green Door." The Woodstock Generation made history with a rain-soaked psychedelic lovefest. During the eighties, Studio 54 promised nightly glamour gigs, celebs, and cocaine aplenty.

Today's all-night, underground happenings are raves. The location is kept secret, and can be a barn in the middle of an Iowa cornfield or a warehouse in a city like Los Angeles or Tampa. Raves have pulsating electronic music, laser light shows, crowds of dancers, and a pulse-tampering palette of substances called "designer drugs."

available at their middle schools. We asked, "If you were the principal, what would you do to keep the school drug-free?"

> "I'd have drug dogs search and sniff the school every week on Friday" (South Dakota twelve-year-old)
>
> "I'd hire undercover people." (Seventh grade Florida boy)
>
> "Check their pockets and if I find drugs I will tell their parents." (Eleven-year-old Arizona girl)
>
> "Check everybody's locker and see what's in it." (Eleven-year-old Southwest boy)
>
> "Check backpacks and not let them in if they had drugs." (Eighth grader from Florida)
>
> "I would have surprise drug testing." (Principal-for-a-day male sixth grader)
>
> "I'd have people come in who have had experiences with drugs." (South Dakota thirteen-year-old)

Start making your middle school drug-free with this excellent resource: The U.S. Department of Education's *What Works: Schools Without Drugs*. Call (800) 624-0100 or write to Safe and Drug-Free Schools Program, 400 Maryland Avenue SW, Washington D.C. 20202-6123.

Of a 1997 rave which attracted 5,000 from across the entire state, an Orlando, Florida sheriff reacted to what he found in the early hours of a Sunday morning, "I've never seen so much narcotic use in my life. There were people lying everywhere. You could hardly walk without falling over somebody." Before those revelers were dispersed, five were rushed to area hospitals and sixteen were arrested on drug-dealing charges. The month before this fiasco, a rave in nearby Daytona Beach involved the murder of a college student.

Designer drugs are variations on restricted pharmaceutical sedatives, muscle relaxants, and tranquilizers made for human consumption or for animals. These usually stronger potions are mixed up by unlicensed and untrained amateurs. A little chemistry is a dangerous thing.

Ecstasy

Methylenedioxymethamphetamine, or MDMA (XTC, Essence, Adam, E, or Clarity), was patented in the 1930s as an appetite suppressant, but never used. In the 1980s a few psychotherapists resurrected it for their couples' therapy sessions. Its effects include feelings of empathy and a drug-induced willingness to be open. These seemed well-suited for reuniting battling spouses. This experiment was short-lived because of concerns about toxicity and uncontrollable reactions.

Those synthetic sensations of friendly openness are appealing to young people who live with social paranoia and insecurity. Where will I get the courage to ask that girl to dance? How can I risk showing my true colors, my sexual orientation? That thrill of feeling warmhearted and loving toward everyone tweaks every middler's craving to belong. The warm-blooded stimulant effect proves just what the DJ ordered for dancing all night without the need to sleep or rest.

Ecstasy, usually taken in pill form, can cause blurred vision, fainting, anxiety, disorientation, and depression. Frequent use has been proven to cause liver, heart, and brain damage. Ecstasy can be part MDMA combined with any number of items, from decongestants, amphetamines, dog worming medicine, to baking soda, and whatever else an imaginative Dr. Feelgood might want to add. Because you cannot be sure what additives complicate the mix and the effects, multiply the potential danger.

Ketamine

If you think Special K and Product 19 are breakfast cereals, you are out of touch with another rave staple. Ketamine is an anesthetic used in veterinary medicine, hence one nickname—Kat Valium. Ketamine is diverted from legitimate manufacturers by enterprising kitchen chemists. A powder or a pill, it is frequently mixed with other drugs to create special brands. Product 19 is a combo of ketamine and ecstasy. Calvin Klein is a pairing of ketamine and cocaine.

During the Vietnam War surgeons used ketamine while treating battle wounds because it diminished awareness of pain and the warzone environment. Doctors stopped using it because patients reacted with hallucinations and delirium.

Ravers embrace ketamine because its high enhances the experiences from flashing lights, loud music, and manic dancing. It feels like getting drunk, getting an amphetamine hyper jolt, and having hallucinogenic effects (the LSD of the nineties) simultaneously.

Obviously the brain is getting a dangerous multimedia neurotransmitter workout as well. Ketamine can cause slurred speech, dizziness, anxiety, paranoia, insomnia, elevated blood pressure and pulse rate, nausea, and vomiting. In some users convulsions accompanied by rigid muscles occur and others develop psychosis.

Meth
Take a home chemistry set, add ruthless ambition, hold the conscience, and you get a strain of Midwest entrepreneurs setting records. Methamphetamine (meth, synthetic cocaine, crank, ice, crystal meth), has become the biggest mom-and-pop homemade concoction in years according to DEA administrators. It comes as pills, powder, or a smokable clear crystal form. The portable labs that churn out meth often add pulverized diet pills, antifreeze, iodine crystals, drain cleaner, and muriatic acid to it, too.

In 1992, drug enforcers shut down six meth kitchen labs throughout Missouri, Nebraska, Iowa, Kansas, South Dakota, and Illinois. In 1995, the numbers jumped to sixty-six. In 1997, they closed 303.

This middle-America craze can be traced to a California biker—part Johnny Appleseed, part Timothy Leary—who motorcycled across the heartland selling his formula for $1,000 a pop. The meth recipe is only a mouse click away on the Internet.

Meth delivers a stronger and cheaper psychoactive kick than crack. The drug sends the body into the flight-or-fight mode, raising blood pressure, heart rate, and body temperature. After ingesting meth, a person becomes hyper-alert and antsy. A tremendous feeling of superiority, like you can do anything, emerges, along with euphoria. The down side can be violent aggressive actions, paranoia, and psychotic behavior.

GHB
"Georgia Home Boy" is a cutesy translation for gamma hydroxybutyrate (GHB, easy lay), the newest party drug reaching epidemic proportions in Los Angeles, San Francisco, Miami, and New York. This salty liquid, packed in small vials, is sometimes used as an anesthetic in Europe. Health food stores stocked GHB in the 1980s to supplement body building "naturally," trigger weight loss, and induce sleep. No scientific proof backs up the product. Episodes of vomiting, seizures, and

coma linked to GHB resulted in the FDA banning it. However, it's so new that not all states have laws criminalizing it.

Users claim it lowers inhibitions, increases the sex drive (something our hormonal middlers don't need!), and produces an out-of-body high, a lighter LSD feeling. GHB is cheap (less than $10) and easily concocted from mail-order ingredient kits available on the Internet. GHB uses lye as a basis and a bad batch can cancel out your esophagus, at the least, or your life.

Rohypnol

Rohypnol (roofies, the forget pill) is a sedative and the equivalent of "being slipped a Mickey." The drug has neither a taste, odor, nor a coloration. One capsule induces a sleepy relaxed drunken feeling, and obliterates inhibitions. Mixing it with alcohol increases its potency and harm. Male sexual predators use it to prey on unsuspecting females because it creates amnesia, and the prospect of committing the perfect sexual crime since the girl won't remember the rape.

Roofies are ten times stronger than valium. The headlines surrounding roofies have enticed thirteen- and fourteen-year-olds to pop the cheap, available pills. Glenn Levant, president and founder of D.A.R.E., says, "Even smart, high-achieving teenage girls are abusing the drug because it has a sexy, forbidden aura about it and, consequently, some think it makes them attractive to boys." The drug is illegal here but sold in sixty countries to treat anxiety and insomnia.

To prevent your middler from slipping out to raves and protect her or him from designer drugs:

Investigate sleepover plans. Check with her friend's parents to verify when your middler makes overnight party plans.

Warn your middler never to leave a drink unattended.

Research the rave scene in your area. Ask the local law enforcement officials to investigate raves and report the results to parents at a special PTA meeting or community program.

HEROIN AND COCAINE

The number of twelve-year-olds who said they have a friend who has used heroin or cocaine more than doubled between 1996 and 1997, from 11 percent to 24 percent.

Heroin (smack, horse, mud, brown sugar, junk, dope) and cocaine (coke, snow, nose candy, blow, big C) are hard drugs, beyond the realm of possibility for parents when they think about middler drug forays. When today's parents were young in the sixties and seventies, whistling "Everybody Must Get Stoned," only junkies shot up. Crack cocaine (rock, freebase) was for derelicts. Celebrities like Janis Joplin, John Belushi, and Richard Pryor were more like martyrs, scarred by abusive childhood trauma, or sabotaged by celebrity excess. Ordinary kids just didn't try extraordinary drugs.

In the new millennium, heroin and cocaine are no longer confined to ghettos. In fact, John Jay College researchers have concluded that heroin is extinct in black urban areas. Crack use, too, is down since the 1980s, sending the dealers elsewhere. Where? To suburbs like Plano, Texas, a suburb of Dallas with sprawling homes, corporate commuters, and mall-loving young adolescents. Between 1996 and 1997, eleven boys and girls (ages fifteen to twenty-one) overdosed and died from heroin there.

Hard drugs have become familiar from images in movies such as *Pulp Fiction* and fashion layouts where models resemble glazed-eyed, emaciated addicts. When younger children experiment, their reasoning power is so elementary that they are not capable of assessing dire consequences. To them, heroin and cocaine are just another choice on the illegal substance smorgasbord.

Heroin is cheaper and purer so it can be snorted, or put into a capsule and swallowed, or mixed with marijuana and smoked. Hard drugs are extremely addictive. Heroin delivers an intense pleasurable rush, even orgasmic, because it triggers the release of hormones and transmitters regulating sexual behavior. It induces a drowsy, carefree state. Powdered cocaine, extracted from cocoa plant leaves and chemically processed, is snorted or injected. Crack cocaine, which is smoked, is quickly absorbed into the bloodstream, producing euphoria within seconds. Once your middler says yes to a hard drug, *just say no* is an overly simplistic cliché.

Even a one-time user of hard drugs may not live to become addicted. Opiates suppress the body's breathing mechanism. An inaccurate dose can be fatal in minutes. Not even adults can gauge a strain's intensity at times and overdose. Imagine the risk for middlers.

To protect your young adolescent from hard drugs:

Examine yourself for denial. Sue Rusche, cofounder and executive director of National Families in Action, created a video to alert parents. In it she chose to feature a mother reacting to the tragic news her son was dead due to an overdose. This mother was taking notes for a lawsuit against the hospital for even suggesting that her son used heroin.

Give NO second chances. If you learn that your child has used heroin or cocaine even once, get help immediately. Another chance will result in another snort, smoke, or injection. Ignore "I only do it on weekends," or "I'm only taking a capsule not sticking a needle in my arm." A second chance could be a fatal mistake.

Track hard drug use in your community. Invite experts from local or regional drug treatment facilities to lecture parents in your community. They will know how prevalent these drugs are in your neighborhood.

INHALANTS

A 1995 National Institute of Drug Abuse study reported that 22 percent of eighth graders had experimented with inhalants. Experts insist that inhalants are the third most abused substance, topped only by alcohol and cigarettes.

"Huffing," "sniffing," and "bagging" refers to breathing in the fumes from aerosol cans of spray paint, whipped cream, and other items. Gasoline- or paint-soaked rags are put into paper bags and inhaled. Then there are products ("poppers" or "snappers") like amyl nitrite that are used.

Middlers are especially at risk because most of these substances—nail polish remover, paint thinner, hair spray, or cooking spray—are available in any home. Inhalant "highs" cost no money, require no drug dealer. Neither paraphernalia nor a recipe is necessary. No incriminating evidence like vials, seeds, or pipes is left behind.

Inhalants deliver a quick high, rush, or "float" that doesn't last for more than a few minutes. Even though the high is brief, inhalants depress the nervous system and push oxygen out of the lungs, triggering giddy and drowsy sensations. Beware, because even a first-time user can lapse into unconsciousness or suffocate. This phenomenon is called "sudden sniffing death" (SSD). In a British study based on 1,000 deaths resulting from huffing, approximately one-fifth were first-time users. Inhalants are not addictive per se. However, chronic inhaling can injure the brain, lungs, and central nervous system—usually instantly—and sometimes permanently. Chronic abusers can lose their ability to walk, talk, and think.

To protect your child:

Do explain the dangers but don't give out the grocery lists of possibilities. "Media reports about a glue-sniffing epidemic actually educated youth about the intoxicating uses of glue and solvents, and abuse spread rapidly across the country," according to Steven Donsiger, policy director of the Partnership for Responsible Drug Information.

Don't make light of inhalants. A parent who takes a swig of helium while blowing up party balloons to do a Donald Duck impersonation inadvertently gives the wrong message.

Watch for the signs:

- Sores or a rash around the nose or mouth
- Paint marks around the nose or mouth or on clothing
- The odor of chemicals on clothing, in a child's room, or on his or her breath
- Red eyes, runny nose, slurred speech, and poor motor coordination like stumbling

CIGARETTES

"I caught my fourteen-year-old daughter smoking. I bought her a pack of Camels, the strongest brand. I made her smoke the whole pack. She was sick as a dog after that, but she didn't want to smoke again."
—A parent on a radio talk show

"Sounds like a great idea to me. All this other warning stuff, telling us it's not good for our health, that doesn't work. I think if I smoked, being forced to smoke an entire pack would work on me!"
—A teen caller

That exchange sums up parents' frustration and young adolescents' irrational determination to smoke cigarettes despite the well known life-threatening risks.

Smoking causes lung cancer and chronic lung disease. It contributes to diseases of the heart and vascular system, the number one cause of death. Smokers develop thinner skin. Pregnant women who smoke give birth to nicotine-addicted babies who are smaller, weigh less, and have smaller heads. Some studies link these children with diminished verbal and mathematical abilities and hyperactivity. A 1998 study in *Fertility and Sterility* journal found increases of abnormal sperm and genetically defective sperm in smokers. Recent surveys suggest that the way Blacks process nicotine puts them at higher risk for lifelong addiction. Adolescents who smoke are twice as likely to become depressed. A 1997 ten-year study found those exposed regularly to secondhand smoke have double the risk of heart disease.

Yet every day 6,000 young adolescents light up their first cigarette.

- Between 1988 and 1996, The Centers for Disease Control and Prevention reports that the number of daily smokers under eighteen rose 73 percent.
- Youth smoking reached a record nineteen-year high in 1998, with 36 percent of preteens and older teens puffing away.
- In six years since 1991, smoking among Black teens grew by 80 percent, compared to an increase of 34 percent among Hispanic high schoolers. White preteen and teen smoking increased by 40 percent. Apparently many middlers light up a cigarette after a marijuana joint to prolong the high.

Who Is Responsible for the Smoking Epidemic?

"I've been smoking since I was fourteen. It wasn't because I saw one of my friends wearing a Marlboro shirt. Kids start smoking because it looks cool, but that's NOT the only reason. They are also rebelling. I started because I wasn't receiving enough attention from my parents. Okay, so that was stupid. There are healthier ways to go about getting noticed. For a kid, the smart ways aren't always the easiest ones. So before you go out and picket

the advertisers, sue the tobacco companies, look around your home environment. Please. And talk to your children, don't punish them."

—A sixteen-year-old girl

There's plenty of blame to go around. Cigarette manufacturers top the culprit list. Newspapers and magazines detail how tobacco companies connived to hook tomorrow's cigarette market. The key to future profit share was the fourteen- to 24-year-olds. Tobacco executives conspired with advertisers, marketing mavericks, and their chemists. The secret to Philip Morris Marlboro's success wasn't just the macho cowboy image. Adding ammonia to the nicotine also helped as it jump-started the cigarette's "kick." Ammonia converted a portion of the nicotine into a quickly absorbed express train to the brain, highly exhilarating for the inhaler.

Hollywood is being villainized too. Movies of the 1960s showed cigarettes once every five minutes; in the 1990s once every three to five minutes. Smoking protagonists (think Julia Roberts in *My Best Friend's Wedding*) jumped from 19 percent in the sixties to 49 percent in the nineties.

Let's not leave out middlers. "Why smoke? It's cool," explains a seventh grade smoker. A thirteen-year-old girl from Florida told us, "I think that smoking has its risks but I still want to anyway. Why? It's hard to explain." Their stubbornness, know-it-all attitude, and rebellion deliberately puts them in harm's way. Most underestimate the power of nicotine's addictive nature. A middler lives in the present tense of being a social smoker. Few envision themselves as chain smokers. Yet studies show that a full 90 percent of adult nicotine addicts admit they bought that "I can handle this" argument at the start, age thirteen being average.

Top Ten Tactics to Deter Smoking

The truth is that no antismoking magic plan exists. Government analysts have studied the comprehensive approaches taken throughout the country. No one program unhooked smokers after six years of follow-ups. Is there anything that you can do as a parent to prevent your child from smoking, or nip it in the bud? These tactics are based on efforts that had positive effects on smoking rates.

1. *Tally the financial cost of smoking.* When cigarette prices were jacked up in Canada, fewer were bought. Money is a commodity middlers understand. Use it. Explain that the typical nicotine addict spends $700 a year. That could finance a spring break trip to Daytona! The habit costs $55,000 for a pack a day over the next fifty years. That's the price of a luxury Lexus, wheels for Daytona.

2. *Hang up antismoking posters.* California had some success with a massive antismoking advertising campaign. Decorate your refrigerator, family bulletin board, anything, with warnings that will cross his line of vision.

3. *Get into the antismoking action.* Seattle cracked down on cigarette sales to minors, cutting illegal sales from 34 percent to 5 percent in 1989. Community activists all across the country are involved in "sting actions" to thwart the sale of cigarettes to minors. Join up with your child. This is a great way to put middler activism to work. If your town has no such initiative, start one. Need information? Call The National Center for Tobacco-Free Kids at (202) 296-5469.

4. *Enforce consequences.* Ohio fines underage smokers $50. Florida suspends driver's licenses. If you catch your middler smoking, enforce a consequence. Make sure it's one that hurts (no allowance, no video games, whatever your child values). If he's already addicted, it's too late for such tactics. In a moment, we'll offer advice for habitual smokers.

5. *Prohibit apparel that advertises cigarettes.* On any given day, 5 percent of our children are walking cigarette advertisements with their Camel tees or Marlboro Man hats. In a survey of 1,300 students in New Hampshire and Vermont, among younger smokers *all* owned such promotional items. By the end of high school, the smoking rate for those who owned tobacco plugging clothes was 58 percent. None of the sixth-grade nonsmokers had Marlboro Man hats or T-shirts. Don't allow your middler to own this stuff. If your middle school has no such rule, campaign for one.

6. *Teach your middler about the link between stress and smok-*

ing. In fifty New York schools, 6,000 junior high school students took a life-skills curriculum to counter the urge to smoke. The goal was threefold: to teach assertiveness, counter the subliminal pull of advertising and social pressure, and find other ways to handle stress in their lives. By twelfth grade, these life-skills graduates were 25 percent less likely to smoke a pack a day. Help your child find an antidote to stress other than a cigarette.

7. *Visit the sick.* Seeing someone die firsthand is a proven deterrent. "A boy in my school just got diagnosed with mouth cancer from smoking, and that brings kids to reality," offered a thirteen-year-old girl. Have your middler visit someone suffering from a smoke-related illness such as emphysema or lung cancer.

8. *Keep up your antismoking talk.* Believe it or not, research proves that young adolescents listen to parental warnings about tobacco. Even if you smoke, underline what a disgusting, unhealthy addiction it is.

9. *Enlist peer pressure.* Clip articles written by middlers for middlers. An excellent choice: "Kickin' Butt: Smokers Reveal Why the Habit Just Stinks," by Dana Silbiger (*Jump Magazine,* May 1998). If she plays sports, emphasize how smoking impairs her performance as a team player.

10. *Get creative.* A fifth-generation tobacco farmer offers $1,000 to each of his children, payable when they reach twenty-one, if the child remains smoke free. He insists it works. Cajole. Bribe.

Fighting a Nicotine Habit

If your middler is a regular smoker, neither punishing nor propaganda will work. In terms of its addictive power, nicotine scores higher than heroin. It's a stimulant in the morning, a tranquilizer during the day, and a mild antidepressant, too. When a person tries to stop, cravings descend along with a legendary irritability. Desire persists even after the withdrawal symptoms disappear, which they do within a couple of days to two weeks.

Going cold turkey, wearing a patch, chewing nicotine gum, or taking

Wellbutrin, a medication formerly used as an antidepressant, are among the aids smokers employ in their efforts to beat the habit. Willpower alone enables some to quit, but not others. If your preteen is smoking, she must *want to stop*. Once the will is there, do the following:

Take her to a trained professional. Physicians, psychologists, and pharmacists run smoking cessation programs in hospitals, community health clinics, and in private practices. An adolescent group setting is especially appealing to peer-oriented middlers.

Be supportive. Provide transportation if necessary.

Expect relapses. Quitters often wind up smoking again. It takes on average seven attempts to quit. With each commitment to quit, your child ups her odds to get smoke-free.

DON'T CRY OVER SPILT BEER

Don't let the specter of drugs ruin your child's adolescence. Parents have always had to deal with a ready market of illegal and harmful substances. Civil War parents worried about laudanum, a tincture of opium. In the early 1900s tobacco brands like Old Judge and Polar Bear came with baseball cards. Where there are people, there are substances and the lure of abuse. If you remain vigilant and committed, you can safeguard and, if need be, rescue your middler.

STRATEGIES: TEEN-PROOF YOUR HOME

Did you child-proof your home when your child was an infant? Detergents and liquid cleaners were moved from under the sink to higher ground. Electrical switchplates were plugged up. Your toddler is now a young adolescent. It's time for a child-proofing upgrade—if not for your middler, for his friends.

1. Clean out your medicine cabinet. Discard old prescriptions for muscle relaxers, Valium, pain killers, and any other medications that a snooping experimenter might try.
2. If anyone in your family takes Ritalin (or Prozac, or any other medication), never leave the pills on a kitchen windowsill or bedroom bureau.

3. Do an alcohol inventory. Do crystal decanters filled with brandy decorate a side bar at holiday time or year-round? Is your refrigerator (or a spare fridge in the garage) stocked with icy beer during the hot weather? Keep alcohol locked or hidden. Don't forget the kitchen. Cooking sherry, white wines, and burgundy may be recipe ingredients to you, but can be a recipe for experimentation, too.

4. Know that eye-balling how much is in the vodka bottle is ineffective. By adding water to the bottle, replacing what they drank, middlers can trick you.

5. Stop buying aerosol cans whenever an alternative is available.

6. Go through your garage, workshop, and basement for paint supplies, glues, or adhesives that might be "huffed." If you use it, store it where it's not accessible.

7. Store keys discreetly, not on a visible, obvious family key rack. Hide car, boat, and riding lawn mower keys—one reckless middler can wreck the family vehicle in a joyride or sneak into the safe and play with a firearm.

8. Protect your home from intruders. Is it well known that you keep a secret key under the doormat? Your middler's friends may observe this and use your house when you are away.

9. Install a smoke detector in your middler's bedroom. This detects any kind of smoke—cigarette or marijuana. Check often to see that the battery is intact.

10. Get rid of telephones in your middler's room and long cords. These allow middlers to have hushed conversations about drugs. Keep telephones and the use of portables in rooms (kitchen or family room) where you can subtly monitor.

CHAPTER SIX

Young Adolescent Blues and Depression

*

*"My ten-year-old son, who lives with his mother, has been very depressed
lately. Nothing seems to please him. Recently, when my ex-wife told
him he couldn't attend a sleepover party, he became very angry and
told her he would kill himself. I am a little nervous.
Should we take his threats seriously?"*

—Father

While adolescence has its ups and downs, most children are able to weather the bad times and enjoy the good. Yet many middlers are unable to join in. Statistics show that childhood and adolescent depression and suicide are on the rise:

- Nearly six million children under the age of eighteen suffer from clinical depression, according to the National Mental Health Association.
- The prevalence of major depression in prepubertal children is up to 3 percent, and among teenagers it's 8 percent, said Dr. Karen Kennedy, a New York pediatrician, who often lectures on depression. "If a typical grade has one hundred students, three to eight of them will meet the criteria for major depression," she said.
- In a 1998 *USA Weekend* poll of 272,400 teens, half said they occasionally are "really depressed," one in five said they often

feel despondent, and one in three have friends who have talked about or actually tried to commit suicide.

- The suicide rate among adolescents has quadrupled since 1950, now accounting for 12 percent of deaths among young people.
- In our own survey of middlers in the U.S. and Canada, 21 percent said that they had contemplated suicide.

Depression is highly treatable through a regimen of medication and psychotherapy. Unfortunately, most depression in young people goes undiagnosed. Why? Some of the signs of normal adolescence mimic the signs of depression. A child who suddenly drops out of all activities to sit alone in his room on weekends may be depressed. Or he might be a normal young adolescent who has lost interest—temporarily—in old hobbies and friends and is searching for something new to pique his interest.

Also, young adolescents abhor the notion of being depressed, may resist treatment, and act out their feelings in many other ways: anger, fighting, breaking the law, eating disorders, self-mutilation, hyperactivity, failing in school, substance abuse, and sexual promiscuity. Parents who direct their concern toward the child's behavior may actually exacerbate the situation by meting out punishment rather than understanding.

In this chapter we will explore young adolescent depression. Which children are at risk and why? How can parents help? Is medication safe and effective? Does psychotherapy help? When is a child in danger of making a suicide attempt? Are there warning signs? As a society, we throw around the term "depression" so much that it appears to be a disease more pervasive than the common cold. And while, like a cold, we haven't yet discovered a cure for depression, this condition appears to be little more than a temporary nuisance that will evaporate into the mists with the next sunny day.

In some circles, depression still carries with it a stigma. Adults shy away from being labeled as depressed. For a young adolescent, the diagnosis will be even more onerous. Young people aren't supposed to be unhappy. Youth, after all, is full of promise and excitement. In fact, until the mid-1970s, childhood depression was not recognized as a bona fide medical condition that required treatment. Experts felt that children and teens were not mature enough emotionally to become depressed. We now know that interpretation is wrong. Young children and adolescents are as susceptible to depression as adults, more so in some cases because of the stressful lives they lead.

Medical experts rush to assure parents that having a depressed child is not their fault. "Depression is not caused by poor parenting—so don't blame yourself," said Dr. David G. Fassler and Lynne S. Dumas in their book, *Help Me, I'm Sad*. At the same time, there is much that you can do through effective parenting to help your children stay emotionally healthy during the middler years.

WHAT IS CLINICAL DEPRESSION?

What is the difference between sadness or "the blues" and clinical depression? Dr. Kennedy, a New York pediatrician, characterizes clinical depression as a "whole body illness," where a young adolescent cannot reverse the decline alone. The blues, on the other hand, are "temporary and less disabling." Oftentimes the child will recover in a short period of time either through his own efforts or by seeking out a good friend or adult mentor.

Clinical depression can take three forms:

A Major Depressive Episode (MDE)

Often triggered by a specific event like a death in the family, divorce, or a natural disaster, an MDE will produce a noticeable change in your child's behavior and demeanor. These episodes can last anywhere from seven to nine months. "Fifteen to twenty percent of teens will have a major depressive incident at some point during their teen years," said Dr. Karen Kieserman, a Manhattan-based child and adolescent psychiatrist.

Dysthymia

A milder, chronic form of depression, dysthymia may go on for years. Where dysthymia is concerned, there won't be a sudden shift in behavior like with an MDE. Rather, you will slowly begin to recognize that your child never seems to be happy.

An MDE usually produces at least five of the following symptoms, while dysthymia can be present with as few as two (although doctors say that one of the symptoms should always include sadness or diminished interest). The symptoms are as follows:

Depressed mood
Diminished interest or pleasure in all activities

Repeated absences from school or poor performance in school
Significant weight loss (or gain)
Insomnia (or hypersomnia)
Fatigue and loss of energy
Low self-esteem
Frequent complaints of physical illnesses, such as headaches and
    stomachaches
Agitation and irritability
Feelings of worthlessness
Difficulty concentrating
Recurring thoughts of death
High highs and low lows

Manic depression or bipolar mood disorder

Manic depression is called bipolar mood disorder because the patient exhibits behavior that veers widely between the two emotional poles—manic and depressive. According to the American Academy of Child and Adolescent Psychiatry, the manic symptoms may include:

Severe mood changes, unusually happy or silly, or very irritable
Unrealistic highs in self-esteem (for example, a teenager who
    feels specially connected to God)
Great energy and the ability to go days without sleep
Increased talking, with frequent changes in topics and refusal to
    be interrupted
Highly distracted behavior, shifting attention from one thing to
    another constantly
Risk-taking behavior with no fear of being injured

The depressive symptoms may include:

Persistent sadness
Frequent crying
Loss of enjoyment in favorite activities
Frequent complaint of physical illnesses, such as headaches and
    stomachaches
Low energy level, poor concentration, and complaints of boredom
Major change in eating and sleep patterns

RESILIENCY—BOUNCING BACK FROM ADVERSITY

Resiliency is the ability to recover from an adverse change. Much of the information on resiliency has come from concentration camp survivors, people with severe physical handicaps, or those who have come from poor or difficult homes, according to the Harvard Women's Health Watch. These individuals share traits that you can try to foster in your own child:

Authenticity. A resilient person is content in her own skin. She wants to be accepted for herself, not because she wears designer clothes or hangs around with the popular crowd. Help your child get in touch with her original and authentic character.

Responsibility. Teach your child to view even adverse situations as challenges. This tactic helps them to "own" the experience. If your child makes a mistake, he should acknowledge that and learn from the experience.

Flexibility. In our fast-paced world, nothing stays the same for too long. Help your child adjust to these twists and turns by viewing each one as a fresh opportunity.

Congeniality. Teach your child to be friendly and sympathetic to others. Help her to acquire an important trait, such as being a good listener.

Productivity. A resilient person has faith in himself. He doesn't obsess about situations; he takes them on.

Creativity. Teach your child to take positive risks, in sports, academics, whatever. Encourage him to use his entrepreneurial spirit.

Spirituality. "A sense of purpose beyond oneself often produces the unflagging conviction that life is worth living," according to the Harvard Women's Health Watch.

While some young adolescents suffering from manic depressive disorder experience "rapid cycling"—up one day, normal, and then down the next—it is more common for the child to stay in one state for periods lasting anywhere from two weeks to several months. Once bipolar disorder has been diagnosed, the treatment—a combination of medication and psychotherapy—is usually effective.

What Triggers Depression?

Picture your child's mental state as a tower of wooden blocks. What event will it take to cause these blocks to topple over? Let's say your daughter fails to make the girl's field hockey team. That might be equivalent to removing a middle block. There's a slight wobble, but the tower remains stable. She gets a C minus on a science quiz. Remove a top block. No effect. She has a strong average in science and plans to hand in an extra project to bring up her grade.

She is shunned by a group of girls, excluded from a sleepover party. Another middle block and more of a wobble. Coming home from school, she finds out that her younger brother has read her diary. They fight. She comes to you for support. You mildly reprimand your son and tell your daughter to stop getting so upset. She storms out in tears, saying no one ever listens to her. Another block, towards the top.

Back in her bedroom, she looks in the mirror and is dismayed to see her acne has flared up again. Is it because she's premenstrual? This time when a middle block comes out, the tower tilts precariously. She takes out her books and reviews her homework. With a test and paper due tomorrow, she estimates spending at least three hours at her desk and it is already 8:30 P.M. Since she must be at school by 7:30 A.M. for a meeting with her advisor, she knows she'll get less than eight hours of sleep for the third night in a row. Take out another block in the middle and the tower comes crashing down.

Your daughter is depressed. Whether that depression is fleeting or intensifies to become a major depressive episode will depend on your daughter's tolerance level for stress. If we were to measure the above episodes on something called the Holmes and Rahe Stress Scale, your daughter's stress level would have come out to around 175. In general, a person is considered overstressed at 250 or greater, but some people with a low tolerance level for stress may feel the pressure at levels as low as 150.

Of course, we didn't factor in a major life trauma, such as surviving the death of a parent (add 100 points) or living through divorce (add 65 points). Even without such a cataclysmic event, however, you can see that everyday trials and disappointments quickly add up to major mental burdens which can weigh heavily on the mind of your middler.

Who Is at Risk?

While depression may strike any young adolescent anytime, there are certain groups of children who are more at risk than others. Knowing ahead of time whether your child falls into one of these at-risk groups may help you to counteract some of the negative forces at work.

Genetic Link. According to a landmark ten-year study from Columbia University released in 1997, the offspring of depressed parents were three times more likely to suffer from a major depressive disorder, and more than five times as likely to suffer from panic disorders, alcohol dependence, and greater social impairment.

Parents who have suffered from depression should look for signs in their own children, particularly during adolescence when depression statistics edge upward. If you suffer from depression, keep in mind that your illness may, at times, make it difficult for you to be an effective parent. Be sure to seek treatment for your own depression and to reach out to others—your partner, teachers, other parents, physicians, mental health professionals—when you need assistance in parenting your young adolescent.

Minorities. Nearly 40 percent of the youth entering the work force now come from Black, Latino, and Asian families. In order to compete in the workplace of the future, these young people will need the education and skills necessary for getting and keeping well-paying jobs. Unfortunately, beginning in adolescence, many of these young people believe that the door to opportunity will be closed to them. That sense of hopelessness may lead to helplessness and depression.

Immigrant parents often send mixed messages to their first-generation American children. While encouraging their children to work hard in school, these parents often are less helpful supporting their offspring's assimilation into the school community. After two teenage girls (one whose parents were from China, the other from India) killed themselves by lying down on train tracks near their Long Island homes, one father remarked: "We try to pass on our heritage to our children but we sometimes forget they live in a culture that's completely different from what we're used to." Noting that many immigrant parents prefer that their children speak their native language, he concluded: "It is important to have our children talk to us in any language about their problems."

Gay or lesbian young adolescents. Young adolescents, in the throes of discovering their own sexual identity, are, as a group, homophobic. A 1992 Harris poll found that 86 percent of high school students would be very upset if classmates called them gay or lesbian. While there are no comparable statistics for middle school, chances are the findings would be the same. And make no mistake, the gay issue is one that middle schools will increasingly have to deal with. Recent studies show that young people are coming out at earlier ages. In 1993, the mean age for males was 13.1 years, for females, 15.2.

While young adolescents who are gay should be able to count on their parents and teachers for support and understanding, experts say these are the places they are least likely to be helped. Ostracized at home and school, gay children often have no place to turn. No wonder then that studies have found that gay and lesbian youths are three times more likely than their peers to kill themselves.

Young adolescent girls. Sometime around the beginning of puberty, previously confident, talkative, upbeat girls become self-conscious, quiet, and downbeat. How does this happen? Despite all the progress that has been made opening up new opportunities for women in business, sports, and politics, many young girls enter adolescence with an innate awareness that they face an uphill struggle. They look at the world and see that it's still very much a man's world where women can be criticized, traumatized, victimized, and trivialized. Often they need only look as far as their own backyards to view their own mothers, the nearest and dearest role model available, battling society's inequities on a day-to-day level.

Parents and teachers need to be "gender-blind" to correct any imbalance that favors boys and sends a powerful negative message to girls that they will never measure up, no matter how hard they try. Unless that is done, girls adopt an attitude of hopelessness which can lead to serious depression.

Children with learning disabilities and/or Attention Deficit Disorder. A child who must work harder than his peers to compensate for learning problems will be susceptible to depression. It is important that parents and teachers work together to help not hinder the child's efforts. Once a learning problem is suspected, the child should be tested, the specific roadblocks identified, and a program put in place to enable him to work around those obstacles. Such a student will need positive feedback and encouragement, focusing more on his efforts than letter grades (more on learning disabilities and ADD in Chapter Nine).

Traumatic event. Some young adolescents have the internal resources to weather a major life-altering event like parental divorce, death, or serious illness. Others do not and may suffer an MDE. If your family is experiencing a crisis, make sure to keep a watch for signs of depression in your middlers.

Physical Causes

"My daughter's counselor at school called me at work today and said she is very concerned about her. She believes she is suffering from depression. Do you have any advice on how to go about handling this?"
— Mother of a twelve-year-old

If you, or someone who is close to your child, suspects depression, your first step should be to rule out any physical causes. Make an appointment with a physician, preferably an adolescence specialist who will be knowledgeable about the illnesses and problems that plague this age group. (The Society of Adolescent Medicine in Blue Springs, MO, can help you locate a specialist in your area. Check the resource list on page 277.)

Physical causes that might trigger depression include:

Thyroid disease. The thyroid produces two hormones that help regulate metabolism. When the body makes too little of these hormones (hypothyroidism), metabolism slows and a person may feel depressed, tired, lethargic, gain weight, be constipated, have dry, coarse hair, puffy face and eyes, and difficulty shaking a cold. Oftentimes the tip-off comes when the thyroid becomes enlarged (goiter), visibly swelling the neck.

Migraine headache. Serious, recurring migraine headaches, often hereditary, may cause your child to become irritable and have mood swings. If your child is susceptible to these painful headaches, you will want to work with her to minimize stress, which could exacerbate each episode.

Mononucleosis. A viral infection, mononucleosis oftentimes begins with a sore throat and chronic fatigue that won't go away. The lymph glands in the neck begin to swell and your young adolescent may be unable to get out of bed to perform the simplest of tasks. Dubbed "the kissing disease," mono may be transmitted without kissing. Unfortunately, the disease is more contagious in its incubation stage when the carrier is less likely to be limiting contact with others.

Neurotransmitter imbalance. Doctors and scientists have learned a great deal about brain chemistry and what biological factors may cause depression. Chemicals called neurotransmitters send signals from one nerve cell to another. One of these neurotransmitters, called serotonin, is thought to affect a person's moods. Low levels of serotonin can produce depression. This condition can be treated with medication.

Drug reactions and interactions. Your child's doctor also will want to ascertain whether another medication might be responsible for the depression. The Food and Drug Administration, for example, issued a precautionary warning about the medication Accutane, used to treat serious cases of acne, after receiving reports of depression and a few suicides by those taking the drug.

Food allergies. Certain foods which are omnipresent in the lives of young adolescents—sodas high in caffeine and sugar, processed fast foods—may also cause depression. You should talk to your doctor about your child's diet.

Sunlight deprivation. Have you hit a patch during the dark days of winter when your child's not exercising and his exposure to natural sunlight is minimal? Also known as Seasonal Affective Disorder (SAD), depression might be the result. Experiment with changes in physical activity and additional light to see if any of those factors make a difference.

Drug and alcohol abuse. Illegal substances are notorious for triggering mood swings in users, as you learned in Chapter Five. But while drinking alcohol or smoking marijuana may intensify a child's depressed feelings, chances are those substances are not necessarily the cause, but they can be a symptom of the depression. When kids feel bad they look for ways to make themselves feel good. Drinking and drugs sometimes do just that. To find the true causes of your child's depression, you will need to investigate further.

THE MANY MASKS OF DEPRESSION

If all depressed middlers looked sad, diagnosis would be easy. Unfortunately, youthful depression wears many different masks. Here are the ones most frequently worn by middlers:

Raging Bull

"I have a son who is very angry all the time and directs that anger at me, his mother, or one of his siblings."
— Father of a fourteen-year-old

Anger, sometimes intense and violent, is probably the most frequent mask that depressed middlers wear. "As adults, we learn to wallow in sadness," said Thomas Hunter, an associate professor of psychiatry at the University of Miami Hospital. "But kids don't like feeling sad. They won't accept it. For them, it's easier to express depression as anger or irritation." Most of the angry depressed middlers tend to be boys. In general, males act out their feelings, while females turn inward.

Anger is the expression of strong emotions. Your middler is expressing his frustration over a situation that, in his mind, cannot be changed (death or divorce in the family, for example). Without an outlet for those feelings, his behavior may spiral out of control. He may get into trouble at school. Alcohol and drug abuse may follow as he attempts to medicate himself, anything to dull the pain.

Parents viewing this out-of-control behavior will have the most natural of reactions—punishment. Doing so, however, will only ensure that this cycle will continue. Your son already believes you and the world are against him. Being punished just confirms that fact and will make him angrier and more defiant.

What to do: Work with your middler to help him identify his feelings. Tell him it's okay to be angry, but it's not okay for him to be verbally or physically abusive to others. If he feels the need to lash out, buy him a punching bag. If your son's anger lasts longer than two weeks and interferes with his ability to function, you need to seek professional help.

The Goodbye Girl

"My stepdaughter has recently dropped out of all of her activities. She has been very close to her older sister who is leaving for college. She lives with her mother, but I think spends most of her time home alone. I'll do anything to help her, but what?"
— Stepmother of a fourteen-year-old

Young adolescents crave their privacy. But when a middler shuts herself off from family and friends for longer than two weeks, you may be looking at an MDE. If a major trauma has struck a household, she may be thinking that she is responsible for what has transpired. "With a decline in self-concept, teenagers begin to feel that nothing they do ever matters and soon just give up on everything," said Gerald Oster and Sarah S. Montgomery, in their book, *Helping Your Depressed Teenager.*

A young adolescent who is insecure will be an easy mark for being shunned and criticized at school. Becoming extremely sensitive to rejection, she will soon avoid placing herself in situations where she knows she will be ostracized. The situation becomes a vicious cycle. The middler becomes depressed after being shunned, and, not feeling confident socially, will not make any move to get back into a circle of friends. Under the circumstances, it becomes easier to stay at home, shut up in her room.

What to do: It's rare for a middler to remain bottled up twenty-four hours a day. Look for windows of opportunity when you can engage her in conversation. If she won't talk with you, seeing you perhaps as part of the problem, find an adult you trust to approach her.

The Year of Living Dangerously

"Our daughter has changed from a shy, 4.0, college-bound kid to a drug using, D–F student who will not obey rules or accept the consequences we give her."
—Mother of a fifteen-year-old

Sometimes a young adolescent's outrageous behavior is a ploy to be noticed. Whatever has happened, the middler feels unloved and unwanted and looks for a way to shift the focus back to her. If her parents are on the verge of divorce, she may feel that her behavior will distract them and hold off, maybe indefinitely, the inevitable breakup of the family.

Granted, when they discover their daughter's grades have dropped and she is doing drugs, any attention she gets is bound to be negative. But in her view, even a reprimand is better than being ignored, which would probably happen if she continued as a shy, dutiful student.

On her social front, she may be seeing that the girls who are popular with boys are not the best students. She may think, "Why should I be good and work hard? I'll still have a hard time making it in a man's world." With that mindset, she could be easily persuaded to neglect her studies in favor of drugs and partying.

What to do: If your family is caught up in a crisis, don't let your middler fall between the cracks. Spend positive time with your daughter so that she won't be tempted to invite your negative attention. Keep your standards high with regard to schoolwork and give her the praise she may not be receiving from her peers.

The Miracle Worker

"My daughter has always cared about helping others, but lately she has been talking about the world's problems with such a sense of hopelessness that I worry about her. I've tried telling her that these situations are beyond her control, but she doesn't seem to hear me."
—Father of a fourteen-year-old

During the middler years, activism emerges and many develop empathy for the less fortunate of the world. Some are unable to separate themselves from the problems of others. Soon, a feeling of helplessness can take over a young adolescent's life. She sees that many world problems are beyond her control, and soon even her own problems seem insurmountable. It's easy to move from the global picture to the local picture with the feelings of doom and gloom transferred. Soon, your daughter finds it impossible to solve even simple problems. An attitude of, "Why bother?" emerges and you find it impossible to reverse the decline.

We want to encourage our children's empathy for others, but make sure that these feelings don't slip over into depression.

What to do: Talk with your daughter about her concerns. Help her make a difference in a small way. She may not be able to solve world hunger, but she can volunteer in a soup kitchen.

The Accused

"My son, a good student and athlete, was recently caught shoplifting several CDs in a music store. Thankfully, the store decided not to press charges, but I'm concerned about his behavior."
—Father of a thirteen-year-old

Tempting fate by breaking the law is another way that young adolescents express their depression. Shoplifting produces an adrenaline high that can temporarily relieve feelings of anger, frustration, and depression. In addition, performing such a bold act is bound to increase your son's stature within his peer group, thus bolstering his self-esteem.

When a child begins acting out in this manner, the last thing a parent might think of is depression. Instead, the focus will be on his rebellious behavior. Parents will need to separate the behavior from the child. According to Shoplifters Anonymous, few of the people who shoplift actually need or couldn't afford the items they stole. The act is a cry for help. (See Chapter Eleven for more on the topic of young adolescents breaking the law.)

What to do: Don't try to handle this situation on your own. Seek out the advice of a professional therapist. He may suggest individual counseling for your son or group counseling for your entire family.

Rain Man

"These days my son always seems to be walking around with a cloud around his head. Nothing pleases him or excites him. He gets good grades and isn't a behavior problem at home or at school. What goes? Should I be worried?"
—Father of a twelve-year-old

The child who seems continually downbeat is probably suffering from dysthymia. Trouble is, with a child who gets good grades and doesn't have behavioral problems at home or at school, it becomes easy to overlook the fact that he might be depressed. If there are other children in the family who express their feelings more vocally, this quiet child is even more apt to be lost in the shuffle. If a crisis erupts, however, he may be pushed over the edge and seriously harm himself.

Try to react before that time. These situations are ones where you need to be hypersensitive to your child's state of mind. It isn't normal for a young adolescent to be downbeat most of the time. If your child never expresses excitement or enthusiasm over anything, something is seriously wrong. Look over the list at the beginning of the chapter detailing the symptoms of depression and see if your son exhibits any of them.

What to do: Investigate physical causes of depression first. If your son's doctor can't find a physical reason for the depression, you will have to look elsewhere. Is it possible he is being bothered at school by a bully? Involve the school psychologist and ask her to talk with your son.

Running on Empty

"Our daughter is overly focused on her appearance and obsessed with her weight. Recently she told me that she should be thinner, worried that she hasn't lost her baby fat. Now I've noticed that she doesn't seem to be eating."
—Mother of thirteen-year-old

There is a high correlation between depression and eating disorders, such as bulimia and anorexia nervosa. When a middler feels that her world is out of control, she looks to one thing she can control: what she eats. Often these girls do very well in school, too well, in fact, since their behavior often borders on perfectionism.

What to do: Eating disorders require professional intervention. (See Chapter Four for more help.)

(Over) Working Girl

"My daughter is a straight A student, a star soccer player, plays the piano, is captain of the debating team, and still finds time to volunteer at our local shelter for the homeless. I'm thrilled with her achievements, but lately—and I know this seems crazy—she seems so unhappy. Is this just a phase, or is she spreading herself too thin?"
—Mother of a fifteen-year-old

While some adolescents react to stress by halting activities, other young adolescents shift into overdrive. Sometimes parents may unwittingly send out the message that the child must excel at all costs. This pressure often comes from parents who have seen their jobs downsized or their retirement funds evaporate and are worried about their children's future. That concern translates into intense pressure on their children to achieve in school.

With some young adolescents, the overactivity may be a catharsis. "If I just keep busy, the pain will stop." Or, striving to achieve may be an attempt to secure parental love and approval. "If I get all As, maybe Mom will notice." "If I make all-state track, maybe Dad will come to my meet." But no matter how much the child achieves, it is never enough to make the situation right and to make her feel better.

Ironically, some young adolescents who commit suicide have been described as "perfect" students who excelled at everything. However, at the first disappointment, such a child often feels overwhelming loss and depression, never having had to deal with such a crisis.

What to do: Examine the messages you may have been sending out. Could you be part of the problem? Talk with your daughter about cutting back.

Choosing a Therapist

Your child's physician should be able to refer you to a qualified therapist. If not, you must find someone on your own. What are your choices? They include:

Psychiatrist. Because psychiatrists have completed medical school (in addition to many years of post-graduate training) these professionals are able to prescribe medication and deal with your child's total health and well-being.

Psychologist. Most psychologists have a doctorate, while others have a master's degree. They are unable to prescribe medication but usually work in close concert with a medical professional who will be able to do so if necessary.

Social worker. These mental health professionals usually have a master's degree in social work (MSW) and will be licensed and certified by the state. The advantage of using social workers is that their fees are usually lower and many are affiliated with social service agencies which often operate on a sliding scale.

Make sure you validate the person's credentials and qualifications. Check the resource list on pages 276–277 for agencies, organizations, and websites that could be helpful. You will also want to note a therapist's particular expertise. If your daughter has an eating disorder, for example, you will want to find someone who has had success treating young adolescents with this problem.

Beyond qualifications, the most important factor is whether your child will feel comfortable talking with this professional. Meet with the person beforehand and trust your instincts. After all, you know your child best. Do you feel she would open up to this person?

Talk with others who have used a therapist for their child. This may be tricky because many parents are relatively close-mouthed in talking about their child's therapy. You may want to ask your child's physician to put you in touch with some people who would talk with you honestly and openly about their experiences.

Cost will be a factor, so be up front asking anyone and everyone along the way what the dollar amount will be. Of course, if you have a health plan, you will want to talk with someone there about whether your child's therapy will be covered.

One tip: If your child has been tested by his school and has been found to have a learning problem that is interfering with his schoolwork, the therapy he receives may be covered under any Individual Education Plan (IEP) developed by his school.

Treatment—What to Expect

Once your child has entered treatment, it may take a long time for her to sort out what is bothering her and to begin to deal with that trauma. There will be setbacks and more trying times ahead. But the knowledge that you have taken an important step toward helping her should give you some peace of mind.

If, after a reasonable length of time in treatment, you sense that her depression isn't lifting, begin to ask questions. Perhaps the chemistry between your daughter and her therapist is not right. The therapist may feel that your child could be helped by having the entire family enter therapy together. Often, a young adolescent's problems do not exist in a vacuum, but reflect what is happening within the family. This suggestion may be threatening to certain members of your family, so you will want to keep an open mind and focus on your ultimate goal—to help your middler conquer her depression.

One approach in therapy is to help young adolescents change the way they think about their problems. Called cognitive therapy, it can best be summed up as "accentuate the positive, eliminate the negative." Many depressed children blame themselves whenever anything goes wrong and tend to wallow in their misery. Cognitive therapy encourages them to put things in perspective. For example, failing a test isn't the end of the world. There's always another chance to improve performance. Parents can actively participate in this therapy by following the same philosophy at home.

These are times that will test your communication skills. Even if you no longer feel close to your child, probably that wasn't always the case. Try to find quiet moments when you can discuss what's going on. Express your love and concern. Listen more than talk. When it comes time for you to express your feelings, empathize with her. Don't expect miracles overnight. But keep following up and stay close to her.

Should Your Child Be Medicated?

Serotonin selective reuptake inhibitors, or SSRIs, such as Prozac, Zoloft, or Serzone, allow the brain chemical serotonin to work better in the brain. Doctors prescribed or recommended Prozac and similar drugs like Zoloft and Paxil 1.27 million times in 1995 for children ages ten to nineteen, an increase from the 696,000 prescriptions written in 1993, according to IMS America Ltd., a research firm. Because the long-term effects of these drugs have not been determined, many people question viewing these medications as a panacea. There is concern that antidepressants for young adolescents could become as widely prescribed as Ritalin. Prescriptions for that drug, used to treat Attention Deficit Hyperactivity Disorder (ADHD) and attention deficit disorder (ADD), reached 12.1 million in 1996, up from 6.5 million in 1993.

Yet for many parents whose children suffer from serious depression, these drugs have been viewed, quite literally, as lifesavers, preventing young adolescent suicides. The April 4, 1997 edition of the *Wall Street Journal* profiled a family whose four children were taking Zoloft or another medication. Before taking the medication, at least two of the children had considered suicide.

If you are considering medication for your child, here are some precautions to take:

Find the right professional. Your child's diagnosis should be made by a physician who is knowledgeable about depression and has had experience with SSRIs. Be aware that many prescriptions are being written by general practitioners, internists, osteopaths, and other medical professionals without giving the child a full psychiatric evaluation.

Ask the right questions. Why did your doctor select a certain medication? What results does he hope for? How long will the medicine take to work? Are there any serious side effects? Are there dangers if used with other drugs? How have his other patients benefited from this medication? Can you talk with any of the parents?

Evaluate the recommendation for medication carefully. Some doctors believe that patients are more apt to be reimbursed by a health care provider if drugs are viewed as part of the whole treatment package. Make sure that's not the primary reason your child is being medicated. If therapy without medication would be as effective, opt for that and work out another strategy for covering treatment costs.

Watch for side effects. Improper dosages may result in serious side effects. There have been few clinical trials, and even the *Physician's Desk Reference* cautions that "safety and effectiveness for use in children has not been established" for these antidepressants. In most cases, medications to treat childhood depression are not addictive. But side effects can include dry mouth, constipation, headache, and weight gain or loss.

SUICIDAL TENDENCIES

"Why do I feel no one cares about me?"
   —Thirteen-year-old girl

When the anguish of depression becomes too much to bear, young adolescents look for a way to stop the pain. "Kids who attempt suicide are really saying, 'I can't see a way out of this problem,' " said Margie O'Reilly, a child and family crisis clinician at the Monmouth Medical Center, Long Branch, New Jersey. "They don't really want to die; they want to solve the problem."

Middlers, however, are not yet skilled at developing alternatives. They need adults to help them evaluate other options. Managed care has exacerbated the problem. It takes time to detect depression. Physicians who are under considerable time pressure may not see the young adolescent for a long enough interval to make the proper diagnosis and prescribe treatment.

People have many misconceptions about young adolescent suicide which may impede their attempts to help. What are these myths? They include:

Suicide isn't a threat to my child because very few young adolescents kill themselves.
False. Your child is at risk, because suicide is the number two cause of death for young people. In 1995, the suicide rate among young Whites, ages ten to nineteen, was six deaths per 100,000; in 1980, it was five, according to the Centers for Disease Control and Prevention. Among young Blacks, the suicide rate went from two deaths per 100,000 in 1980 to 4.5 deaths per 100,000 in 1995—an increase of 114 percent.

Once a young person attempts suicide, he will not try again.
False. Four of every five people who have committed suicide made previous attempts. Three times as many girls as boys try to kill themselves, but five times as many boys between the ages of fifteen and nineteen succeed, according to the American Foundation for Suicide Prevention in New York.

We should avoid the topic, because talking about suicide will encourage young people to try it.
False. Talking with a young person contemplating suicide may help to defuse feelings of pain and alienation, and therefore, thwart the suicide attempt. Any family living through a natural disaster should be particularly watchful for signs of depression in their children. The CDC has found that earthquakes, severe floods, and hurricanes significantly increase suicide rates for as long as four years after such a natural disaster. The CDC traced disasters that affected 19.4 million people in 377 counties nationwide that had qualified for disaster relief assistance. In one area after an earthquake, the suicide rate increased 62.9 percent.

Young people who resort to suicide really hope to die.
False. What a young person hopes to do is stop the pain. A suicide attempt is often a cry for help before that pain can be stopped by another means. Experts agree that the increased use of alcohol and drugs, which reduces a person's inhibitions, coupled with the ready access to firearms in many communities, contributes to the fact that an impulse to kill oneself may be fulfilled.

Talkers aren't doers. Young people who talk about suicide aren't serious about killing themselves.
False. Eight out of ten people who kill themselves have told someone beforehand what they intended to do. Parents and other adults frequently fail to pick up on these clues. Having a parent ignore such a blatant cry for help is, for many young adolescents, the final straw that breaks any resolve to hold on. "When parents don't have a clue about what is going on, it just increases the child's sense of hopelessness," said O'Reilly.

Reading the Signs

Obviously if your child has been depressed, you will want to be sensitive and look for signs that he is contemplating suicide. Some of the warning signals that a child is suicidal are similar to those for depression—change in eating and sleeping habits, withdrawal from friends and family, difficulty concentrating, and a decline in school performance. According to the American Academy of Child and Adolescent Psychiatry, some of the signs that a child is contemplating suicide are overt. The child may:

Make statements that hint of suicide. He may tell a classmate, "I won't see you again," or advise a parent, "You won't have my problems to deal with ever again."

Put his affairs in order. He may give his treasured baseball collection to a friend and a favorite video game to his brother.

Become a chronic truant or report for school late. After all, if he is going to kill himself, why worry about grades?

Collect information on suicide methods. He will also develop a preoccupation with famous people who have killed themselves.

Be grieving over a recent loss. That loss could be the death of a relative, friend, or even a pet, or the loss of a stable family situation because of divorce or unemployment.

Become cheerful after a period of depression. This is not a good sign! It doesn't mean that the child has shed his depression. Rather, it signals he is now at peace with his decision to kill himself.

Become an Active Listener

Professionals who deal regularly with suicidal youths recommend that parents become active listeners. Your goal is threefold:

Validate feelings. Your daughter may be upset because her boyfriend has broken up with her. To your mind it's just another young adolescent fling, but to her it's very important. Rather than say, "There are other fish in the sea. You'll get over it," empathize with her pain. "I can see that you are really hurting." You are affirming her feelings and encouraging her to talk.

Assess the risk. If she tells you, "I feel like I want to die," try to determine if she is really at risk for hurting herself. "Wow, you really don't want to live? Do you really think about hurting yourself?" If she says yes, probe for more details. In the event you feel she really might hurt herself, ask, "Can you promise you will come to me and talk before you do anything?" If she says she can't, you need to be very concerned for her safety.

Restore hope. Young adolescents kill themselves because they feel hopeless. So your task is to help your daughter see that, whatever has happened, there is still hope for the future. "I know you are in pain now, but the pain will pass." Try to get her to focus on something in the future, an upcoming sporting event or receiving a new computer. Throughout this dialogue, trust your instincts. If you feel the child is in serious danger, seek professional help *immediately.*

COPYCATS AND CLUSTERS

Once a young person sees a friend commit suicide or hears about a famous person who has killed himself, what might have been a seemingly unthinkable alternative becomes less of a taboo. Professionals have documented many instances of copycat and cluster suicides:

- In 1987, four Bergenfield, New Jersey, teens killed themselves from carbon monoxide poisoning. They were found dead in the car with its motor running in a garage at an apartment complex. A week later, another boy killed himself using the same method and the police intervened just in time to prevent two other teens from following suit.
- Shortly after those events, suicide experts from New Jersey attending a national convention discovered that there had been other copycat suicides in other parts of the county. Victims had been found holding articles about the New Jersey deaths.
- In 1997, two adolescents in France, one twelve, the other thirteen, shot and killed themselves, emulating Kurt Cobain, the lead singer of the rock group Nirvana, who shot himself in 1994 at the age of twenty-seven.
- Pierre, a Midwestern town with a population of 13,000, was rocked by a series of cluster suicides from 1994 to 1997. Eleven people from thirteen to twenty-three committed suicide, thirteen times the national rate of thirteen per 100,000 population. Eight of those victims were teenagers.
- Besides Bergenfield and Pierre, other cluster suicides have occurred in disparate parts of the country—Westchester county, Plano, and South Boston.

Parents need to be vigilant for signs of depression and suicide in their own children whenever a celebrity or adolescent suicide is publicized. Rather than ignore the news stories, use them as an opportunity to talk with your children about the decisions these people made to end their lives. Stress that nothing is ever hopeless and that they may come to you to talk whenever they are feeling down.

STRATEGIES: SURROUND YOUR CHILD WITH HELPERS

Surround your child with adults who are accessible, easy to talk with, and ready to help:

Make sure your child has a mentor at school. Advisory Programs pairing a few students with a teacher abound in many middle schools. Your child should be meeting with this teacher at regular intervals. Ensure these meetings are happening and keep in touch with this individual.

Arrange for your child to have other adult mentors. If your child has a special interest—rocks and minerals, for example—find someone knowledgeable about the subject that he can talk to and correspond with. As he moves on in school, this adult could become a valued advisor and friend.

Seek out a pediatrician who is knowledgeable about adolescents. Encourage your child to have a one-on-one relationship with his doctor. This professional will become another adult who is involved and who your child can talk to.

Meet the parents of your children's friends. Establishing these bonds will help you learn what your child and her peers are up to.

Talk about your own feelings. Young adolescents often feel they are alone in experiencing depression. Tell your children when you feel down and let them see how you come out of it.

Emphasize your availability. Tell your child he can always come to you in the event he is feeling down.

Have a family time once a week. Even the withdrawn young adolescent must resurface for a meal or an event, like viewing a family movie.

CHAPTER SEVEN

Taking Good Risks
with Extreme Sports

*

*"My son's favorite sport has always been baseball. This month, however,
he announced that he wanted to become an aggressive skater.
I have to be honest: This sport scares me. I'm afraid my son
will break a bone or, worse yet, sustain a serious head injury.
Is there such a thing as 'safe' aggressive skating?"*
—Mother of a thirteen-year-old

A generation raised on violent video games is attacking sports with a vengeance. These young people are defying their parents—and gravity—as they engage in daredevil extreme games. Their pursuits include downhill in-line skating (at speeds clocked at fifty mph), skateboarding, snowboarding, stunt bicycling, street luge, rock climbing, and kayaking. Believing themselves to be invincible, these middlers often take risks that make parents quake. Some young people refuse to wear protective equipment, thus increasing the potential for debilitating injuries.

Athletics—extreme and traditional—are important elements in the care and nurturing of middlers. "Sports offer both boys and girls a wonderful opportunity to participate in positive risk-taking," said Lynn E. Ponton, in her book, *The Romance of Risk: Why Teenagers Do the Things They Do.* "They can challenge themselves by taking chances, learning about winning and losing, giving their bodies a full workout, and, at least in group sports, learning how to work together."

Yet many parents are concerned that even traditional sports—baseball, basketball, hockey, football, soccer, lacrosse, and gymnastics—have become edgier and more dangerous. In our survey, two-thirds of the students responding said they had been injured playing a sport. "When I was in gymnastics, I broke both of my legs," said a sixth grader from Georgia. A seventh grade Connecticut girl said: "I've had a lot of gymnastics injuries—pulled muscles, ligaments, broken finger, knee problems, sprained ankles and wrists." A seventh grade boy from Florida told us: "I was paralyzed for two hours when a baseball hit me in the head," while an eighth grader from Idaho lamented, "I have too many injuries to list!"

While half of the parents in our survey believe that students still pursue the traditional sports and take necessary precautions, more than one-quarter thought that children today pursue traditional sports more aggressively, and a small fraction said their children were forsaking traditional sports for the more extreme versions. "We as parents tend to make our children aggressively competitive when we encourage them to play sports at an early age," said a parent from Minnesota. "Coaches don't help. They want a winning record."

Many factors besides aggressive coaches, however, are responsible not only for elevating traditional sports to a faster, more dangerous level, but also for increasing the attractiveness of extreme sports:

Stronger bodies. Athletes are bigger, stronger, and more powerful, able to leap tall obstacles (if not tall buildings) in a single bound.

Better technology. New materials and innovative designs have helped invent new games (street luge, for example) and made it possible for athletes to go farther faster.

Women athletes. No longer on the sidelines, girls now want in on the action. And they are playing as hard and fast as the boys.

Wider media coverage. Cable TV and specialized publications have broadcast even fringe sports to a wider, more diverse audience, thus creating new followings.

Star athletes. The "free agent" system, now a standard in professional sports, has trickled down to the amateur level, pushing each athlete to achieve his or her "personal best," which often means going to extremes.

In this chapter we will explore the sports movement, the extreme games and the traditional ones with an edge. How do we, as parents, encourage our children to pursue sports and compete safely?

Tackling and taming an extreme sport or excelling in a traditional one can give an adolescent a real thrill ride and an extra boost of confidence, as well as the admiration and adoration of peers. All of these ego-gratifiers are important sources of self-esteem during the shaky middler years.

THE FITNESS MOVEMENT

We can't talk about adolescents and sports without first talking about how the entire sports landscape has been altered in the past twenty years. A fitness craze has swept our country carrying away even the most determined couch potatoes. According to a 1996 report from the National Survey on Recreation and the Environment, nearly 95 percent of all adults participate in some form of outdoor recreation at least once during the year. While some prefer less taxing activities like walking and bird-watching, many more are looking for adventure. Where will you find these thrill-seekers? How about hiking the Appalachian Trail from Georgia to Maine? Too tame? Then try whitewater rafting on the Potomac River through Harpers Ferry, West Virginia, scaling the 3,000-foot face of El Capitan in Yosemite National Park, or mountain biking on the Slick Rock Trail in Moab, Utah.

Still not exciting enough? Then why not climb Mt. Everest, at 29,028 feet the highest peak in the world. So many people clamor to scale Everest that Jon Krakauer's best-selling book, *Into Thin Air*, describes a 1996 traffic jam he encountered at the peak. The Everest phenomenon might be dismissed as a fluke, if there were not further evidence that many people, seeking adventure, are going all out to find it. Tourists are flocking to Gloucester, Massachusetts, begging fishermen to take them out into "the perfect storm," so that they can experience the turbulent seas depicted in Sebastian Junger's best-selling book by the same name (six people died during that nor'easter). It's not just current books that are providing fodder for people's imaginations. Travelers are following paths blazed by Odysseus, Leif Erickson, Lewis and Clark, and Robert Peary, to name a few.

And there is no age limit attached to this quest for novelty and excitement. Senior citizen groups eschew Atlantic City and Las Vegas and now travel to Alaska to trek across the frozen tundra, sleep on wooden beds they construct themselves, and clean and cook their own fish dinner over an open fire.

What's going on? Are we living in a mad, mad, mad, mad world?

No, we live in a society that has looked around and asked, "Is that all there is?" Automation and safety standards have tamed many occupations that used to be dangerous or, if not risky, at least exciting. Bluntly stated, many people find their jobs sedentary, boring, repetitive, and predictable. After staring at four walls or a computer screen for forty hours a week, there is a desire to test ourselves by confronting bigger challenges.

Couple that adventurous spirit with the fact that we are living in a health-conscious, body-aware society where people expect to live longer and work to keep in shape. We are seeing more people testing their limits because they are physically able to do so.

But aside from the health aspects and the thrills involved, there are other motivations for those who prefer their sports with a large dose of adventure. While all sports are stress busters, the intensity of extreme sports makes them the biggest stress busters around. "I skate, not only for fun, but to clear my thoughts and help me think," said Mark Abramowitz, a twenty-three-year-old aggressive skater from Ft. Lauderdale, Florida. He noted that aggressive skating has helped him to overcome fears in other parts of his life. "You must admit, if you're not afraid to step into a ten vert ramp [a ten-foot U-shaped ramp], little else will scare you," he said.

Others agree with his assessment. "I'm so focused on what I'm doing when I'm climbing that I'm not thinking about anything else but getting up," said Toni Apgar, vice president, group publishing director, PRIMEMEDIA Enthusiast Publications, whose magazines include *Climbing, Canoe,* and *Kayak.* "I don't find that true with tennis anymore or with any other sport not considered extreme." In 1998, Apgar, her husband, and their two children, Christopher, fifteen, and Sarah, eleven, climbed New Hampshire's Mt. Washington. Next on the agenda? Washington's Mt. Rainier. Can Everest be far behind?

MARKETING EXTREME SPORTS

Many children don't need their parents to introduce them to extreme sports. Advertising campaigns for many products, everything from cars and electronics to clothing and cosmetics, celebrate the adrenaline rush one gets from conquering physical milestones. Ralph Lauren was one of the first designers to capitalize on the public's thirst for adventure with tight-fitting Lycra sports clothing. Ads for his men's cologne, Extreme Polo Sport, showed an attractive young man jumping out of an airplane, and riding the air waves on a surfboard. Other designers—Calvin Klein, Tommy Hilfiger, Nautica, Donna Karan—have imitated Lauren with similar lines of sports clothing and colognes. The message being delivered is that extreme sports are cool, and our children are listening. Is it any coincidence that Lauren, Klein, Hilfiger, Nautica, and Karan have such huge followings among adolescents?

Perhaps the most powerful catalyst for change, however, has been the media. There are now publications for many extreme sports, such as snowboarding and in-line skating. And other publications aimed at adolescents devote more space to covering these athletic challenges. *Jump Magazine,* "for girls who dare to be real," runs regular features on extreme sports, including one, "Natural Born Thrillers," which spotlighted eight adolescent girls. A diver from Florida, who without using oxygen routinely goes down to depths of 165 feet and then races to the surface, described why she does it. "It takes you into a zone," she gushed. "After 100 feet, I'm flying. Wow! What a rush!"

A fifteen-year-old from Alaska, who climbed Mt. McKinley when she was twelve, described what it felt like to slip. "You just drop like you're on a roller coaster," the young mountaineer explained. "Your stomach goes in your mouth. I love that feeling. I love the excitement."

Cable TV, with its wealth of new offerings, has several services—ESPN, ESPN2, for example—devoted exclusively to sports. With so much air time to fill up, these cable services must reach beyond the traditional to showcase sports such as aggressive skating, skateboarding, skydiving, jet skiing, and mountain biking, to name a few. ESPN's X Games have become the extreme games counterpart to the Olympics, providing a showcase for many previously unknown sports, elevating the respectability and stature of the athletes. The 1998 winner of the aggressive in-line skating competition, for example, went home with a $20,000 purse.

A record fifteen million people watched the X Games in June 1998. That large audience has manufacturers of sports equipment salivating. After Mike Nick, a junior from the State University of New York at Plattsburg, won the skiboarding competition at the 1998 X Games, he was suddenly sought after by equipment manufacturers, movie makers, and others eager to cash in on this new sport's popularity. Lee Dancie, a street luge star, was paid more than $100,000 to endorse a sneaker bearing his name. Aggressive skaters, rock climbers, skysurfers, and skateboarders also are signing lucrative endorsement contracts.

Extreme sports athletes, income from competition and ancillary sources assured, now have the financial freedom to devote themselves full-time to pursuing their sports, thus taking these disciplines another step closer to becoming part of the sports establishment. Snowboarding is now a bona fide event in the Winter Olympic Games. Many aggressive skaters and climbers are now "stars" with their own fan clubs and followings. One eleven-year-old snowboarder has his own publicist. All that adoration breeds imitation.

EXTREME CHOICES

The dream of becoming a media star might pull some children into trying extreme games. But there are other reasons that a middler, even one who excels in organized sports, would choose to pursue an extreme one instead.

According to one recent study, 80 percent of all children stop playing organized youth sports—team and individual—by the time they are twelve. Even in Canada, where passion for hockey runs high, a poll taken by the Canadian Amateur Hockey Association found that by fifteen, only one in ten middlers still plays organized youth hockey.

Why? Two main reasons: they are not having enough fun and they feel under too much pressure from teammates, coaches, friends, siblings, and, of course, parents. Unfortunately, many well-meaning parents are driving their children away from organized sports. In fact, a *USA Today* poll found that children five through twelve were so affected by parental involvement in sports that 37 percent wished their parents didn't watch their games. Other children were troubled by the competition factor, with 71 percent saying they would prefer no score be kept.

Once you consider these percentages, it's easier to understand why a young adolescent, feeling pressured at home and school, would welcome the freedom of pursuing athletics away from the watchful eye of parents and teachers.

Another attraction? To paraphrase a popular commercial, "These aren't your parents' sports." Adolescents have long rejected adult choices in music, dress, and food. Now these young people have alternatives to adult mainstream sports. Why ski when you can snowboard? Hiking? No way! Rock climbing is more challenging.

This list of extreme sports is not complete because new ones are emerging every day, composites of several other activities. Be cautious, but don't discourage your child. Learn something about the sport, talk with instructors, and assess the risks.

Bicycle Stunts

In 1982, with the release of Steven Spielberg's *E.T.*, record numbers of movie-goers watched kids, accompanied by an alien creature, do tricks on their bikes. By the following year, bike manufacturers had geared up to cash in on the craze, producing bikes with freestyle frames (costing as much as $700) that could twist and turn while being airborne. While your middler may not get to compete in the X Games on his bike, he could attempt to duplicate some of the tricks on his own, so safety equipment is a must.

Bungee Jumping

Born on the Pentecost Island in the South Pacific, bungee jumping has now been attempted by more than one million Americans, thanks to numerous facilities around the U.S. Bungee jumpers are like balls on a rubber band. An elasticized cord is tied to the feet and the person dives from a tower. The elastic cord pulls the jumper back before hitting the ground and propels him back into the air. In competition, bungee jumpers are scored based on the height of their rebounds.

In-Line Skating

The original modern in-line skate was produced back in 1960. In 1980, a hockey player from Minnesota found one of these old versions, and hit on the idea of adding urethane wheels, making for a faster, smoother ride. By 1996, more than 31 million Americans enjoyed in-line skating, compared to 9.4 million in 1992. The largest group of in-line skaters is under twelve (38.7 percent), while the second largest group is between twelve and seventeen years old (25.8 percent). Most people, including middlers, skate for recreational purposes. Roller hockey (like ice hockey on wheels) accounts for 15 percent of the in-line skating market, aggressive skating 10 percent, and speed skating 5 percent. Aggressive skaters do many of the same tricks as skateboarders, also on the half pipe or obstacle courses. Downhill racers zoom down steep, curvy hills at speeds clocked in excess of fifty miles per hour.

Mountain (or Dirt) Biking

Using bikes with fat tires, lightweight frames, and a single gear, dirt bikers, now estimated at more than two million nationwide, careen at breathtaking speeds down rocky hills and mountains. While tens of thousands of young boys are heading for dirt track competition sites in various parts of the country, many more pursue the sport at the nearest mountain. When even a mountain is scarce, dirt bikers have been known to substitute steps and rails, often infuriating residents. Some understanding adults, however, recognizing that dirt biking is here to stay and grow, and seeing it as a positive activity for middlers, particularly boys, are helping to raise funds to construct dirt bike facilities. BMX, the largest manufacturer of dirt bikes, said its sales hit 700,000 in 1997, a third of all bicycle sales.

Mountain Skating

Described as "mountain bikes on your legs," mountain skates look like giant in-line skates. Extreme skaters use them to go over grass, dirt, and ski slopes. Rollerblade, the in-line skating giant that is manufacturing the skate, introduced another version for navigating on rough pavement.

Rock Climbing and Sport Climbing

According to *Climbing* magazine, there are now 300,000 climbers in the U.S. While many climbers pursue the sport outdoors, others prefer indoor facilities, which have increased from one in 1988 to more than 400 in 1998. Climbers scale sheer and overhanging cliffs using only ropes, often with metal hand- and footholds nailed into rock crevices. Rock climbing is one extreme sport where you don't have to be big to be good, an attraction for many middlers. Katie Brown, who at five feet has dominated women's sports climbing, says her size is an advantage because she can get into smaller places.

Skateboarding

In 1997, skateboarding bypassed mountain biking and golf to become the fastest growing activity for which you need sports equipment, according to the National Sporting Goods Association. There are an estimated 9.3 million skateboarders, mostly boys under eighteen. Skateboarding, first invented when someone broke the pushbar off a scooter, has had many reincarnations during its lifetime. During the late 1950s, proponents, recognizing the similarity with surfing, designed boards that could recreate that feeling of riding a wave. The sport fell out of favor during the 1960s because of safety concerns, but bounced back in the 1970s after the invention of the urethane wheel, which provided much better traction and speed. The extreme version of skateboarding requires athletes to perform tricks over obstacles or more dangerous maneuvers on a U-shaped wall called a half-pipe.

Skysurfing

Think of this sport as skydiving on a surfboard. The skysurfer, with a surfboard strapped to his feet, jumps out of an airplane and, before opening his parachute, completes a series of tricks—somersaults, backflips, and so on. In competitions, the skysurfer is graded for the exactness and completeness of the moves (to say nothing of making a safe landing).

Snowboarding

Snowboarding is like surfing on snow. Unlike skateboarding, where the feet are free to move around, a snowboarder's boots are firmly attached to the snowboard with bindings similar to those on skis. No poles are used, and because the snowboarder keeps his body closer to the ground, many people believe that snowboarding actually is safer than skiing. This sport, however, is one where the novice needs the proper equipment and good instruction.

Street Luge

Originally street luge was performed by lying down on a skateboard. Now, however, special boards have been designed with lighter materials for speed, and a wider wheel base for safety. Like its winter counterpart, which is a recognized sport in the Winter Olympics, the idea behind street luge is to get through the course fast and in one piece. While some events have been staged in actual urban settings, usually the competitors face off in specially designed courses.

Surfing

Surfing, the extreme sport of the 1960s, has enjoyed many waves of popularity in succeeding decades. The most recent craze began after VH1, the music cable service, featured a documentary with former Beach Boy Brian Wilson, and Jan and Dean. Both groups had a string of hits back in the 1960s that glorified surfing and the surfer's way of life. One change is that surfing is now as avidly pursued on the East Coast as it is on the West Coast.

Trampolines

Most trampolines are in backyards, and therein lies the problem. Many parents who purchase this equipment to pursue physical fitness for themselves or provide entertainment for their children, fail to provide the adequate supervision needed for safety. In 1996, the Consumer Product Safety Commission estimated that there were 83,000 hospital emergency room visits associated with trampolines. About 75 percent of the victims were under age fifteen. Experts advise parents to allow only one person on the trampoline at a time (most injuries are caused through collisions), outlaw somersaults or other tricks, cover springs, hooks, and frame with pads, and place the trampoline away from structures and other play areas. Needless to say, children should always be supervised by an adult when using a trampoline.

Wakeboarding

Like so many other extreme sports, wakeboarding is a hybrid—a combination of water skiing, surfing, snowboarding, and skateboarding all rolled into one. The wakeboarder rides a surfboard/snowboard and, holding onto a towrope behind a motorboat like a waterskier, does airborne tricks like a skateboarder. Another variation on water skiing is the barefoot variety with jumps.

Whitewater Rafting and Kayaking

These two water sports are not new, but a new generation is discovering them and pursuing them with energy and determination. The mobility of our population now allows larger numbers of people to travel out West to experience the thrill of being carried downstream at dizzying speeds. Each sport also allows families to build whole vacations around cruises down famous rivers, stopping every so often to take in the sights of nature.

ROUGHER CURRENTS IN MAINSTREAM SPORTS

With all the emphasis on extreme sports, what has happened to the traditional ones? The extreme-ness has rubbed off. While you should still do everything possible to encourage your child to participate in these activities, make sure proper safety precautions are being taken.

Gymnastics, where debilitating injuries have always been a very real possibility, has added power tumbling. Participants do many of the same movements seen in floor exercises—back flips, front flips, and twists, for example. The added element is a spring floor which allows the athletes to soar higher.

Changing technology and environment have created hazardous conditions in some sports. Aluminum bats, for example, cause the baseball to fly faster after being hit, thus posing an injury threat to many pitchers who are often in the pathway. In fact, college officials have been so concerned about these increased injuries that they are working toward restricting the use of such bats.

But more than changing any rules or conditions, what has made traditional sports more extreme is the change in attitude. Nike said it all in its ad, "Life is short. Play hard." The athletes responded. While the rules of the game have remained the same, players are constantly looking for ways to take the competition to another level. That effort may involve breaking a long-standing record, pummeling the opponent, or pushing oneself past the point of endurance. It often means playing through pain, ignoring injuries or psychological stress. Don't complain, don't whine, and don't stop—"just do it."

For many adolescents, not giving in to the pain means that many have incurred injuries, most painful, many avoidable, and some lifelong. It also means that our children are taking undue risks, often with the encouragement of coaches and other adults who have bought into the philosophy that winning is the only thing that matters.

Boys in Sports—Going to Extremes?

Team sports like football, hockey, and basketball have become notorious for their violence. Some of the violence is part of the game, with players encouraged to hit hard and even injure opposing players, all in the name of victory. Increasingly, however, the violence is an adjunct, explosions of aggressive behavior that occur when players choose to work out their differences with their fists rather than with words.

Ironically, rather than condemn these displays of violence in sports, the coaches, press, and spectators applaud it. For one thing, it's great theater. The audience comes to watch a hockey game and, as a bonus, gets to see the players hit each other with their sticks. For another, these fights settle the score in a manly way. Real men fight their own battles, and stand up for themselves. The outcome proves who is king of the mountain.

While organized sports for boys in middle school are not violent, they set the stage for high school athletics where rough physical contact begins. In order to play violently, boys must learn to repress empathy. "When boys have to hide all feelings of fear and vulnerability in order to be accepted as 'real men,' they are learning to take unnecessary risks that will endanger their and others' health and lives," said Myriam Miedzian, in her book, *Boys Will Be Boys*. While adults may be able to compartmentalize these attitudes (being violent on the field, nonviolent away from the field) young adolescents have more difficulty isolating aggressive behavior.

Extreme sports may actually be a more positive choice for young boys because these sports rarely, if ever, pit one person against another directly. In most cases, the athlete is battling nature (rock climbing), time (street luge), or himself. Can he go higher next time, do the trick better, stay up longer? At the professional level, there are winners and losers, but for amateurs, the game's the thing. Young boys doing tricks on their in-line skates imitate one another's moves, but there's no score, no trophies, no parents to disappoint.

Girls in Sports—On the Sidelines No More

A rushing torrent of women—aided by Title IX of the Civil Rights Act, which mandated equal opportunities for women in high school and college athletics—has swept away formidable barriers. Women now have access to many sports whose past stance was "no women allowed."

Professional women's basketball is now a reality. All-female hockey teams competed in the 1996 Winter Olympic Games. And in 1998, for the first time ever, a woman pitched in the men's professional league, for a minor league baseball team in Duluth.

Women are invading extreme sports, too. According to American Sports Data, as of 1996, one fourth of the 6.75 million skateboarders in this country were girls. Women used to go to the beach to be seen in their bikinis. Now they go to surf, wakeboard, or barefoot waterski. Women now make up 15 percent of surfers.

All of this activity is good news for middler girls. Unlike their mothers, they are growing up with many talented women athletes as role models. Because many women are now succeeding in traditionally all-male sports, adolescent girls feel empowered. Excelling in a sport can be a terrific source of self-esteem for a girl, causing her to focus not on her body's imperfections, but rather on how well her various body parts can work together to achieve positive results.

Of course, not all the battles have been won. There are still many sports where women face an uphill battle to compete. On the local level, a scarcity of field space in some parts of the country means that girls' soccer, baseball, lacrosse, and field hockey teams often lose fights with boys' teams for access.

Yet there is much that we can do, as parents, to encourage our girls to get in the game rather than sit on the sidelines:

Examine your biases. Before you tell your daughter she can't pursue a certain extreme sport, stop and ask yourself, would you discourage your son in the same way? "One of the important role transitions that mothers have to make as their daughters become older is to encourage and promote positive risk-taking," said Ponton, in her book *The Romance of Risk.* Many mothers, according to Ponton, are stymied in this effort, not only by cultural bias, but by their own histories of being too cautious.

Give a nudge. For many girls, trying a sport, extreme or otherwise, represents a huge step into the unknown. If your daughter is worried about being embarrassed in front of her friends, enroll her in a sport she can do one-on-one with a coach. Boxing, for example, has emerged as a terrific workout sport for girls that delivers a powerful "I can do this!" message.

Consider changing bodies. As middler girls begin to mature, their bodies change dramatically. Suddenly your lithe daughter becomes top heavy and can no longer complete those graceful gymnastic moves. Work with her to find new ways to channel her athletic talents without delivering negative messages about her body.

Watch for eating disorders. As many as one-third of all female athletes suffer from eating disorders (refer back to Chapter Four for more on this topic). Make sure your daughter eats healthful foods and does not skip meals.

Get in the game yourself. If you feel up to it, tackle an extreme sport with your middler. One mother who began skiing with her daughter was thrilled, not only with her own progress, but with the boost she gave her ten-year-old daughter. "She was hesitant to ski at first, but when she saw I was willing to take a chance, too, she was game," the mother observed. "We both did well and had a great time to boot."

Coaches—Extreme and Otherwise

Coaches, rather than being part of the solution, are often part of the problem associated with traditional sports, encouraging young athletes to play rougher and win at all costs. The wise parent will watch from the sidelines and get involved if necessary.

The United States is the only country in the sporting world that does not have a national coaching education program. According to the National Youth Sports Safety Foundation, less than 10 percent of the two and a half million volunteer coaches, and less than one-third of the interscholastic coaches, have had any type of coaching education.

At the middle school level, coaches may be trained in the fundamentals of the game, but unskilled when it comes to dealing with the fragile psyche of young adolescents. Often male coaches fall back on stereotypes, treating boys as men, using profane language and encouraging unnecessary aggressiveness and violence.

More often than not, parents must deal with situations like the following described by a mother venting in cyberspace: "My son, who is playing soccer, was paddled by his coach for leaving his socks outside his locker following a game. When I complained, the coach mocked him in front of the team. Now the boys are teasing him and I feel like it's my fault. He says he hates soccer and doesn't want to go to school."

It's true that parental intervention in any situation can backfire. But that doesn't mean you shouldn't speak up and voice your concerns. Look at it this way, if your child was having a problem in math, would you call the teacher? Of course. Sports should be treated no differently.

Away from school, your child's coach is apt to be a volunteer, often a parent like yourself. While youth leagues produce many wonderful coaches, some adults are attracted to coaching for all the wrong reasons.

In *The Training Camp Guide to Sports Parenting*, Rick Wolff noted that Larry Csonka, a fullback at Syracuse University and later with the National Football League's Miami Dolphins, refused to let his own two sons play youth league football. "The coaches didn't know much about what they were doing," Csonka said. "They just yelled a lot. They acted like they imagined (Vince) Lombardi and (Don) Shula would act." Csonka said he didn't want to sour his boys on the game by having them play under those conditions.

If you have your choice of leagues, you can shop around. But if you feel you can successfully intervene with the coach, or, particularly, if you have to deal with one at your child's school, here's how to do it:

Make sure you know the rules. Some coaches educate parents before the start of the season, going over the rules, philosophy, and what each child should get from the game. If such a session is planned for your child's school, attend. If not, ask the coach if he would schedule one.

Be assured that honesty and good sportsmanship are part of the program. Children should be learning proper etiquette on the playing field (which, hopefully, will carry over off the field). Winning is important, but not at the price of cheating.

Make sure safety is observed. Christine Schrodt, whose sixteen-year-old daughter, Sarah, has been pursuing power tumbling for eight years, says the coach is a "stickler for spotting." She noted: "She doesn't let anyone distract her. I've never seen her out of position. Her hands are always there."

Never approach the coach during or immediately after the game or match. Instead, advised Wolff in *Sports Parenting*, ask if you can call the coach at home.

Avoid confrontation. Instead enlist the coach's help dealing with your child's problem. "It's my experience that 99 percent of these youth league coaches are much more sympathetic to your concerns if you voice them properly," said Wolff.

Don't forget that many youth coaches are volunteers. They are giving up their time and devoting their energies to coaching your child. They deserve your support, not your criticism.

Volunteer yourself. If you feel the level of coaching is that poor, step up to the plate and offer to coach a team yourself.

SPORTS INJURIES—ON THE RISE

Back in the 1980s, Jane Fonda rose to fitness fame with the mantra, "Feel the burn." Unless you felt the pain, "no gain." Adults now know that exercise doesn't have to hurt to achieve results. But to extreme sports aficionados, particularly younger ones, pain and gain go hand in hand. During the 1996 Olympics in Atlanta, the image of gymnast Kerri Strug, completing her vault on a badly sprained right ankle, endured long afterward and made her the celebrity of the moment. The message was clear: win at all costs. To rise above the crowd, these professionals, and now younger athletes, are pushing themselves to the limit. And with many extreme sports that, by their nature, are inherently risky, participants prepare and expect to be hurt. That attitude is partly responsible for a skyrocketing increase in sports injuries among young people:

- From 1993 to 1998 the U.S. Consumer Product Safety Commission (CPSC) noted a 184 percent increase in the number of injuries involving in-line skaters—rising from 37,000 to 105,000. In 1996, 71,888 children were treated for in-line injuries, CPSC said.
- About 300,000 people a year in the U.S. suffer brain injuries from sports, according to the Centers for Disease Control and Prevention in Atlanta. Athletes who suffer head injuries often return to play too soon, leaving them vulnerable to a second blow, which could prove devastating.
- Seventy-five percent of all baseball injuries occurred to children ages ten to fourteen, according to CPSC, with the

highest number of injuries among eleven- and twelve-year-olds.

- Approximately 30 percent of eye injuries among children under sixteen are sports related. According to the National Youth Sports Safety Foundation, 90 percent of these injuries are preventable, mostly through wearing proper protective equipment.

Peer pressure plays a role in injuries. Many young athletes are afraid to admit they are hurt or tired. But overdoing can often lead to injuries.

Some injuries don't happen overnight. Tendinitis, for example, often caused when a group of muscles is overworked for a long period of time, is an inflammation of tendons, or the tissues that connect the muscles to the bone. Many times these chronic injuries require surgery. Too many times, such surgery may bring a promising athletic career to an abrupt end.

What are the types of injuries an athlete could sustain? They include:

Concussion. The most common and the most potentially serious of injuries, concussions are caused by a blow to the head and can range from mild to severe. A mild concussion can cause the victim to "see stars," and become dizzy for a time, but usually has no serious or lasting effects. With a more serious concussion, the victim is unconscious for a prolonged period of time, has problems speaking, may vomit or feel nauseous, and may feel weak or drowsy. Oftentimes the doctor may see that the child's pupils are dilated and that there is blood or clear fluid in the ear canals.

Ankle and wrist injuries. Prevalent among gymnasts (73 percent in one recent study) and in-line skaters, wrist injuries take many forms. A fracture is a broken bone, while muscle strain is a tearing of the muscle fiber. When your child sprains an ankle or wrist, she has torn the ligaments that hold the bones together. While preventing wrist injuries for gymnasts is more tricky, wearing protective wrist guards can help with in-line skating.

Knee injuries. The National Youth Sports Safety Foundation estimates that 40,000 knee injuries are incurred each year. Half of these injuries have some lasting residual effect which impacts the quality of life, the group says.

Anterior cruciate ligament (ACL) knee injuries are on the rise among girls. Experts believe that several factors have come together to place girls at risk for ACL, including: a higher ratio of body fat, differences in strength between hamstring and quadricep muscles, lack of emphasis on conditioning, and differences in ligaments and pelvic width.

To prevent knee injuries, experts recommend wearing protective equipment, avoiding repetitive movements that can damage muscles and ligaments, strengthening leg muscles through exercise, and warming up properly before any exercise.

Dehydration. Before, during, and after strenuous exercise (and most extreme sports are strenuous) an athlete needs to drink prodigious amounts in order to stay hydrated. Telling your young athlete to drink may be greeted with the claim, "I'm not thirsty." Tell her that the body's thirst mechanism doesn't kick in until well after dehydration has begun. Not only can dehydration impede an athlete's performance, but it can be life-threatening. Runners have had to be hospitalized and placed in ice baths in order to bring down their body temperature, raised because of dehydration.

How much should your child drink? The International Sports Medical Institution offers this suggestion: Half an ounce of water per pound of body weight if one is inactive (roughly, for a 160-pound person, that translates to ten eight-ounce glasses per day), and $2/3$ ounce per pound of body weight for those who are athletic (thirteen to fourteen eight-ounce glasses for the same size person).

Workout Before Playing

Whether your child is playing a traditional sport or taking up an extreme one, do all you can beforehand to minimize the risk of injury. A thorough physical is essential, particularly if your child suffers from any condition (a heart problem or asthma, for example) that might place her at risk. With proper precautions, your child can still participate.

Getting in good physical shape, particularly after a sedentary period, should be a prerequisite. At many middle schools, students find that gym class is too infrequent and not strenuous enough to get the serious athlete into shape. So it's a good idea to supplement your child's school program with one at a local fitness center. Capitalizing on this new market, facilities nationwide are launching youth fitness curriculums for children ages eight to fifteen. "Children are wanting to increase their performance," said Marijo Sorrell, a fitness instructor for CBK's Cross Training Studio in Saratoga Springs, New York, as well as fitness director for the General Electric Company in Selkirk, New York. "They see athletes on TV and want to be just like them."

While it might be possible for an adolescent to work out at home, either alone or with a videotape, the experts advise against it. With middlers, the tendency is to overdo, running the risk of damaging bones, muscles, and skin. Lifting too heavy weights, for example, can break the skin and leave behind stretch marks.

Sorrell, who often works with young adolescents, said that most students begin their training in the off-season. Basketball players, therefore, would launch their workouts in the summer. The regimen she designs, Sorrell said, focuses on exercises to increase an athlete's endurance and strength. "The name of the game has changed," observed Sorrell, who played both basketball and tennis herself throughout high school and college. "In the past, performance was based more on talent and skills. Now, an athlete needs strength and quickness."

Different extreme sports call for toning different parts of the body. Here are some things to consider as you work with your middler to get in shape:

Kayaking. Because a child's upper body will be paddling, strengthening arm and shoulder muscles is vital. But, also work to strengthen the hips and lower back to avoid injuries and lower back pain.

Mountain biking. Obviously if your son is going to be pedaling up a mountain, he needs to strengthen his legs. But doctors warn that upper body strength is important, too. Many biking injuries occur when bikers fall over the handlebars. Strong arm and chest muscles might help your child stabilize himself.

Mountaineering. Respiratory fitness is necessary if your daughter will climb a mountain. A good way to accomplish that is by swimming.

Rock climbing. This is one sport that works literally every square inch of the body. But pay particular attention to the hands. Experts suggest using a squeeze ball to strengthen grip.

Snowboarding. Concentrate on strengthening your child's legs. If he has access to a gym, he can use the Stairmaster or treadmill. If not, biking will give him the same results.

Besides long-term conditioning, it is essential that athletes warm up before each activity. Sorrell recommends a five- or ten-minute jog ("nothing too strenuous") and ten minutes of stretching. "Muscles get tight," she said. "The more you stretch, the more your muscles are flexible." Someone who begins to play without warming up runs a greater risk of injury.

EQUIPMENT—THE BEST THAT YOUR MONEY CAN BUY

The March 1998 issue of *Backpacker* magazine included reviews of more than 1,300 pieces of equipment that hikers could tote along on their next hike. There are now hundreds of types of sporting shoes on the market, one for every sport, season, weather, and terrain. The choices are mind-boggling and can easily confuse even an experienced sportster. For a parent, who may not know anything about the sport a child is taking up, shopping for equipment can quickly become a daunting task. How—and where—do you begin?

Do your homework. There is endless information available on virtually every sport imaginable either at the newsstand or online (we give some sources in the back of the book). Read up on the one your child has selected.

Visit a specialty store. Make your first visit without your child so that you can ask questions and make your own evaluations. Oftentimes middlers are swayed by advertising campaigns or designer labels. The most expensive or best known piece of equipment is not always the best one for your child.

Make sure the salesperson actually has experience with the sport. You don't want to buy a snowboard from someone who has never been on the slopes. Also, don't be rushed into making a purchase. A good sporting goods salesperson will understand that you need time to assimilate what you have learned. Take any literature the salesperson offers.

Consider renting first. Many sporting goods stores rent equipment, oftentimes crediting that amount toward whatever you purchase later on.

Avoid cheap equipment. You may save money in the short term, but you might be sacrificing your child's safety. Less expensive equipment often uses less durable materials which may break more easily under heavy use and lead to injuries.

Don't improvise. Dirt bikes, for example, are made to withstand the shock of going down a rocky slope. Attempting such a ride on a regular bike will increase the possibility of injuries.

Dress in layers. When buying clothes for a winter sport, remember that it's best to dress in layers. That way, your child will be able to shed clothes as he needs to in order to stay comfortable.

Don't forget a helmet. So many of the extreme sports run the risk of a head injury that a well-made, properly fitted helmet is a must. CPSC estimates that three million head injuries related to consumer products are treated in hospital emergency rooms each year. Nearly half a million were concussions and skull fractures—injuries that might have been prevented if the person had been wearing a helmet.

Include other safety equipment. Depending upon the sport, you will want to make sure your child is wearing other necessary safety equipment. Wrist guards, knee pads, and elbow pads, for example, are necessary for in-line skating.

LEARNING THE ROPES

Your child has selected his sport, you've bought the equipment. Now what? Time for some instruction. You may run into some resistance from your middler who has watched athletes on ESPN and thinks he will have no trouble duplicating their moves. These extreme sports are never as easy as the athletes pictured on TV make them look. So make sure your child learns the basics of the sport—what to do and not to do:

Enroll him in a class. Talk with the instructor beforehand to get a sense of what your child will be doing. Make sure that the program emphasizes safety and discourages reckless moves.

If your child's chosen sport is more on the fringe (you can't exactly look "street luge" up in the Yellow Pages), you may have to work harder to find a qualified instructor. Your best bet is to ask where you have bought your child's equipment. Oftentimes the salespeople know the pros in the sport and will gladly pass on their names.

Evaluate the instructor's expertise, not appearance. As one parent observed, many extreme sports enthusiasts "are not the clean country club types." Their lifestyle may be offbeat. "They shave when they want," she noted. And dress to suit themselves, not others. But the ones this mother has met have been skilled, polite, and eager to help middlers learn a sport.

Inspect any facilities your child will use. If your son will be skateboarding at a skate park, make sure the equipment is in good repair and that there is adequate supervision.

Investigate alternatives. Climbing man-made walls in an indoor gym is safer than attempting to climb Mt. Everest. While your child may prefer mountain biking in dangerous terrain, suggest he start on flatter, wider trails.

Make sure your child will stay within his skill level. Ski patrols frequently rescue skiers and snowboarders who venture onto black diamond (difficult) trails after one or two lessons. It's worth paying for that extra lesson, then having the instructor evaluate your child's capabilities and match him with a trail that will be appropriate for his abilities.

THE THRILL OF VICTORY

Toni Apgar vividly remembers the time she went mountain climbing with her then thirteen-year-old son. He set the top rope for her, securing it with carabiners, loop-shaped metal fasteners that he hammered into the rocks. "I had to rappel down and I'm thinking, 'I have this thirteen-year-old setting up ropes for me,' " she recalled. "But, I couldn't think of anyone I trusted more. It was real cool for me to show I trusted him."

Pursuing an extreme sport with your middler may result in a subtle shifting of roles. Suddenly, the adult is the student, the child the teacher. Most middlers will relish the opportunity to show their parents a thing or two. Watch the confidence soar!

Because many of these sports are pursued off the beaten track, accompanying your middler will also give you the opportunity to be alone, without the day-to-day distractions that may be interfering with your ability to communicate. Standing on the top of a mountain or paddling together down a river can serve as the quiet backdrop to some pretty stimulating conversations. Even if you sit in silence, enjoying the scenery, you can bask in the extreme pleasure of your middler's company.

STRATEGIES: PLAY FOR SPORTS, PLAY FOR LIFE

The sports metaphor is often employed off the playing field to convey advice on how to succeed in other areas of life. Trite or overused as some of these phrases may seem, they can have great resonance with middlers because they deliver a simple message readily understood. Use them as a way to bring your middler's sports experience full circle.

Keep your eye on the ball. Whether your child is playing baseball, tennis, or studying for an exam, a focus on what is important will win out every time.

"It ain't over 'til it's over." This phrase, courtesy of Yankees great Yogi Berra, can gently remind your middler that there's always a reason to keep on trying.

Go for the gold. Aiming for an Olympic gold medal is less about crushing opponents than it is about setting personal goals and a plan for achieving them.

CHAPTER EIGHT

Virtual Reality vs. the Real World

*

*"The really bad part of this whole situation is not that Billy is skipping
school, but that he has been accessing pornographic websites.
So what do I do now?"*
—Mother of a fourteen-year-old

There is a "cybergap" between generations. As cyberspace unfolds,
parents are entering a new world where their children far outdis-
tance them in knowledge and skill. Fear of the unknown is a major
theme running through parental reaction to this new technology. Where
middlers see excitement and opportunities, parents spy dangers and
temptations. "What is my son really doing on the Net?" "Is my daughter having cybersex with strangers?" "What type of people does my
son meet in chat rooms?" "Is it really possible to buy drugs, gamble, or
learn how to assemble a bomb from information on the Net?"

Parents also worry about the amount of time young adolescents
spend on their computers. Is staring at a computer screen any more productive than staring at a TV screen? When does computer literacy cross
over into addiction territory?

In this chapter, we plan to identify and explore the crisis twenty-first–century style and show parents how to cope with the technology that still makes
so many adults uncomfortable. Parents need to scrutinize their reactions to
determine whether their anti-technology attitudes are unfairly prejudicial.

For example, a young male adolescent is naturally curious about the
female anatomy. Is accessing pornography on the Web a more grievous
offense than flipping through a purloined copy of *Playboy* or *Penthouse*?

There are reasons for parents to monitor their children and be cautious. But overreaction on the part of parents will ensure that middlers under-react to their admonitions.

Parents need to save their ammunition for times when a techno-crisis does occur. Yes, there are dangers out there. What happens when kids engage in cybersex, cybergambling, cyberauctions, and other antisocial activities? Once reserved for "red light" districts, these activities are now available in many living rooms.

Technology has changed everything, even the job of parenting. We will help you become more techno-savvy so that you can keep pace with your child in cyberspace.

THE INTERNET—MAD ABOUT YOUTH

"When I was in junior high, I remember coming home from school, getting a snack, and then turning on the TV to relax for a while before tackling homework. My son comes in, gets his snack, then turns on his computer to check his e-mail. Times have changed!"
—Mother of a fifteen-year-old

What TV was to our generation, the computer is to our children's. Middlers prefer the interactivity the Internet offers them:

- America Online reported that AOL homes spend almost 15 percent less time watching TV, an hour less a day, than the U.S. average.
- Jupiter Communications asked kids what was more fun, TV or the Internet. An overwhelming majority—92 percent—opted for the Internet.
- A survey by Simmons TeenAge Research found that teen online usage increased 50 percent from 1996 to 1998. Nearly two-thirds of teens said they had used or subscribed to online services during 1998, and 42 percent said they spend from two to four hours online each day.

Already, marketers are scrambling to meet this group's seemingly insatiable appetite for things novel, exciting, and electronic. Don't spend any time worrying, however, that the computer will render these children less able to read, create, think, or socialize with others. Janine Lopiano-Misdom, a partner in youth consumer research for the firm Sputnik, told *USA Today:* "This is a do-it-yourself generation, right down to 'zines and web pages. They are going to be the most entrepreneurial generation we have seen in a long time."

Each generation puts its own special stamp on genius and creativity. Who knows what Leonardo da Vinci, Benjamin Franklin, or Thomas Edison would have come up with, given the chance to combine their talents with the endless potential presented by today's technologies. Parents need to regard the computer and the Internet as one vast canvas that their children can use to explore and create new ideas. Like outer space, cyberspace is a little scary, certainly overwhelming, ultimately exciting, and, of course, waiting to be explored by those adventurous enough to take risks.

Parents—Lost in Space?

In the 1957 comedy *Desk Set,* efficiency expert Spencer Tracy attempted to automate a television research department, managed by a very capable Katherine Hepburn. As soon as the computer moved in, however, Hepburn and her staff were told to check out. Chaos ensued, as an inept programmer typed in garbled questions and received garbled answers. The all-female staff, dashing for the reference books, saved the day. Technology took a large step backward and everyone lived happily ever after.

Many adults probably share the Hepburn character's fear of the computer. A cybergap exists in many workplaces today, with older workers viewing the computer as an enemy to be avoided at all costs, and younger workers as an ally to be enlisted on all fronts.

How you feel about this technological revolution depends on where you were in your career when computers began to take over. And your point of view will obviously affect how quickly and willingly you turn onto the information highway.

If you just had yourself to think about, you could probably get away with taking a Hepburn-like stance. But with your children to consider, that position is not only unwise but untenable. Like it or not, your children must coexist and thrive with computer technology. Having at the very least an elementary knowledge of the computer and the Internet will enable you to understand and perhaps even aid your child throughout the middle school years.

Following is a list of most commonly used (and overused) parental excuses for avoiding the Internet, along with our arguments for putting your biases aside:

It's too complicated. Au contraire. If you know how to flip a switch and press a button (on a mouse), you can handle it. Start with an easy service like America Online, which lays out the information available to you in a user-friendly grid.

It's too expensive. Prices are falling and there has never been a better time—or reason—to buy. In fact, many families with limited economic resources are putting a computer purchase high on their lists. Forrester Research in Cambridge predicts that in 1999, low-income households, defined as those earning less than $35,000 a year, will become the leading source of first-time home computer buyers.

It's too time-consuming. The computer, like television, will sop up whatever time you want to give it. But if you have a specific goal—attending an hour-long live chat, for example—you can easily limit your time.

It's too isolating. Just the opposite. Not only can you talk with friends and relatives near and far, you can also go online with your son or daughter sitting next to you.

It's too embarrassing. To admit you know less than your child? View it as a golden opportunity to have your child teach you a thing or two.

It's too dangerous. The dangers of the Internet have been well-publicized, and we will be covering those topics in this chapter. But there are tremendous benefits for you and your family to be found on the Internet.

PANDORA'S CYBERBOX

Parents who remain clueless about the Internet practice selective perception when it comes to technology, seizing on any negative story they hear to bolster their contention that the Internet is dangerous, capable of corrupting our youth, and that, therefore, we should take steps to prohibit our children from going online. "The fast growth of the Internet and the even faster spread of the World Wide Web are frightening many parents, teachers, and other adults," said Dan Tapscott, in his book

Growing Up Digital. "They are uneasy about these powerful new tools being in the hands of children, particularly since many of these adults feel they don't really understand the new technology themselves."

If you are a parent who is apprehensive, don't worry. You have lots of company, now and down through history. Virtually every new advance in communications or transportation—from the steam engine to the telephone—has been met with curiosity, skepticism, wariness, and downright hostility. Change is never easy or painless. The older we get, the more difficult and painful it becomes.

But fear can be a great motivator. And if you are truly fearful about your child venturing online, then do something about it. Educate yourself about the Internet.

Surfing for the Beginner

For the novices, we will start at the very beginning with some basic information about computers, the Internet, and the World Wide Web. Chances are you already know how the Internet works. You may even have spent some time "surfing the Web" or "cruising the electronic highway." But oftentimes these terms get thrown around so casually, we forget (or fail to find out) what they really mean. First, the basic definitions:

Internet. A global network that uses phone lines to connect many computers around the world, allowing them to send and receive data. There are now more than one hundred million users worldwide, a number that will continue to escalate. There are more than one hundred countries connected worldwide.

World Wide Web. A vast network of pages that can be readily accessed through the Internet.

HTML is the basic programming language of the World Wide Web. This code conveys to browsers how to display text and graphics.

ISP (Internet service provider), sometimes called online services. The software loaded onto a new computer frequently will include a free trial run on one or several ISPs such as America Online, GTE, AT&T, or Microsoft. After the trial run expires, you would pay a monthly fee. Besides providing a gateway to the Internet, these online services usually offer e-mail.

Modem. An electronic device needed to dial into the network. Most in-home PCs (personal computers) now come equipped with internal modems.

Online Chat. These are live, online exchanges between one or more users where comments are typed in and appear immediately on the screen. Most people in live chats are identified by their on-screen nicknames. With a service like America Online, you would be able to access a user's profile. With other sites, you would not be able to find out anything about the person's true identity.

Parental Controls. These are settings that allow you to automatically block certain online activities or content on the Internet. Parental controls come with online services like America Online, or you can buy a specific package like Net Nanny.

Search engine. Services like Yahoo, Lycos, and Excite provide a systematic way to search the Web for specific topics.

Spam. The electronic equivalent of junkmail, sent to you without your permission.

URL (Universal Resource Locator) is the address used by the browser to find a website. An example would be www.parentsoup.com.

Web browsers connect your PC to the Internet and help you to navigate more easily on the Web. Popular browsers include Netscape Navigator and Microsoft's Internet Explorer.

As you might suspect, outfitting computers beforehand with the necessary equipment for accessing the Internet has helped to bring people on board:

- In 1991, an estimated 1.1 million people used the Internet. By 1994, that figure jumped to 12 million, by 1995 to 30 million, and by 1997, more than doubled again to 62 million.
- Odyssey, a San Francisco research firm that tracks online usage, says that 23 percent of U.S. homes are now on the Internet.
- Homes are racing to get wired. Ten years ago, only 3 percent of households had more than one line. By 1996, according to the Federal Communications Commission, that percentage had jumped to 16.5 percent.

Detractors are fond of pointing out that Internet saturation is far less than television, which exists in virtually every U.S. home, and cable television, which in 1998, had a penetration level estimated at 67 percent. But the proponents of the Internet can as quickly point out several reasons why cyberspace will eventually rule:

Personal computers now exist in 42 percent of U.S. homes. With prices dropping, more families will opt for newer models, and those newer models—you guessed it—will come equipped with hardware and software to connect to the Internet.

The world is getting wired. There are more than 107 million people online worldwide. According to Emarketer, an Internet research organization, users outside the U.S. were expected to surpass those inside the country by 1999. Fastest growing markets are China and India. The Internet has even reached Tristan da Cunha, midway between the southern tip of Africa and South America, considered the most remote inhabited island (population 300) in the world.

Computers and TVs will merge. We are fast approaching the time when the various technologies will be connected—telephone, computers, and TV. So if you have a TV set (and 98 percent of the homes in the U.S. do) you will have the capability of accessing information online.

Computers are interactive. Our children are watching less TV and playing more on their computers. Why? This generation is hands-on and prefers to be part of the action rather than just observe it.

Youth will win out. Ultimately our children will guarantee the success of the Internet. It's here, they want it, and they know how to use it.

WONDERS OF THE WEB

About 80 percent of American schools now have Internet access, according to the U.S. Department of Education. In 1998, about 40,000 of the 140,000 K–12 schools in the U.S. reported access to the Internet. (Nearly all the nation's nursery schools have computers, too.) In the beginning, computers were viewed as little more than toys in the classroom. If a student was good (or bad), he was given more (or less) time to explore games on the computer.

Now that computers are becoming ubiquitous pieces of educational equipment, teachers are focusing more on how to exploit this tool to enhance each child's educational experience. Rather than an end in itself, the computer is increasingly being viewed as a means to an end. Think of the computer as an elaborate pencil or typewriter, and think of the Internet as a sophisticated, compact library with many pages (320 million, at last count) of information. The challenge then becomes learning how to access the correct information in a timely fashion.

Of course, schools vary in their "connectedness." At the high end, schools have equipped not only their classrooms but individual student laptops with access to the Internet. (One pilot project cosponsored by Toshiba and Microsoft provides laptops to students.) At the low end, schools may be equipped with computers, but oftentimes there are not enough in the classrooms, and these computers may not be hooked up to the Internet. NetDay, first launched in 1996, used individual and corporate donations to bring Internet access to the schools.

Another obstacle for schools to clear is training teachers to be savvy in using the Internet. Many experts see this element as key to how quickly and how well students will learn to use the Internet to enhance their education.

The workplace demands that all workers be computer literate. But just as there are different levels of expertise in any profession, there are different levels of adeptness involved with the computer. For some children, the computer will never be more than an elaborate typewriter with an easy way to check for spelling errors. However, for other students, the computer, through the Internet, will open up vast new areas of information, previously unobtainable for a middle schooler.

What are the advantages of using the Internet over, say, the library? Well, the information available is more vast than anything that could be housed in the typical library. Obtaining the information is faster (no searching through dusty stacks). And automatic "links" to other sites will put your child in touch with more research he may not have thought about when he began.

Most of all, the Internet is interactive. Through bulletin boards, chat rooms, forums, and other meeting places, your child can meet others to exchange information. He can access news stories, write a letter to the editor, chat with other young adolescents about any topic, receive help from a teacher, and, if desired, design his own web page to research the matter in greater detail. And all that by sitting in his room typing!

From all indications, we are just beginning to tap the potential of the Internet:

- More than one million students now take college courses on-line. Experts predict that number will triple by 2000. In the future, your child could attend a "virtual university," taking courses from the best and the brightest professors from all over the U.S. or the world.
- By 2000, some people may be voting online in state elections. You could cast your vote in the privacy of your own home or at any special terminal. Imagine being able to call up a candidate's platform before making your decision. The in-home voting, many believe, would dramatically increase voter turnout.
- In one international project, students from 4,000 schools in the U.S. and 1,000 schools in other countries are using the Internet to report their weather observations. This multicultural project, a true example of the "global village," is teaching children hands-on science, math, and geography, as well as a deep understanding of how weather affects everyone, a giant common denominator.
- Starbright World, a computer network for hospitalized children, helps provide hope and friendship for those who are severely ill. Hospital officials say just the thought of talking to someone online is often enough to motivate a sick child to get up, walk down the hall, and log on.
- Online doctors make house calls. There is now a vast amount of information on the Web to help patients research their diseases, evaluate drug treatments, locate specialists, and network with other similarly afflicted patients.
- Local guides tout their services. While the Internet has global reach, much of the activity occurs in your backyard. Local websites listing restaurants, movies, hotels, weather, and tourist attractions have been launched for cities large and small. Advertising revenues continue to grow, from $700 million in 1998, to a projected $1.4 billion in 1999.

SEX ONLINE

The Internet is like a big city, offering excitement, enjoyment, adventure, and, yes, danger. Consider this: Your son is writing a paper on the U.S. presidency and decides to research the topic online. He types in "www.whitehouse.com," the electronic address of the president (he thinks). But when the page comes into view, he realizes he is far from Pennsylvania Avenue. "WHITEHOUSE.COM'S EROTICA: EROTIC STORIES AND AUDIO SEX," reads the headline. "Take a look: Teens, humping housewives, hardcore boys, posing chicks. Cheerleaders in their locker rooms, experimenting with lesbianism, getting their sweet sisters to take their pictures."

If your son decides to venture further, the next page will offer even more explicit explanations of what lies beyond the cyberborder. To enter, just type in your credit card number. Many a young adolescent male, hormones raging, will be unable to resist. Of course, Mom or Dad might notice the charge on next month's bill, but even if they do, he reasons, he can profess ignorance. After all, he was busy with his homework. Right?

This anecdote illustrates how even the innocent can be led astray on the Internet. According to law enforcement officials, many middlers venture purposefully into restricted zones, eager to sample cyberspace's forbidden fruits. But other children, like our hapless young adolescent above, have strayed onto the wrong site purely by accident after typing in an incorrect electronic address.

The issue of pornography, perhaps more than any other, has come to epitomize the inherent distrust many parents have of the Internet and its influence over their children. Actually a very small percentage—3 percent—of the commercial sites on the Internet traffic in adult material. Nearly all these sites post warnings advising minors not to enter and most require the user to type in a credit card number to gain admission. That stipulation, however, oftentimes fails to deter the determined young adolescent. A 1997 survey of 10,000 homes by PC Meter, a research firm in Port Washington, New York, found that about 30 percent of households frequented adult sites, with 8 percent of those visits being made by teenagers.

There are more than 10,000 pornographic sites already on the Web. A 1995 study by Carnegie Mellon University found 917,410 sexually explicit pictures, short stories, and film clips online. As competition has heated up on the Internet, critics maintain that some of the material is becoming more outrageous. Experts say the online pornography market, overwhelmingly made up of men, is fueled by a demand for salacious material that can't be found in magazines. This material includes pedophilia (nude photos of children), hebephilia (youth), and what has been dubbed "paraphilia," a mishmash of what most people would call "deviant" behavior—bondage, sadomasochism, urination, defecation, and sex acts with animals.

Federal laws prohibit the sale of obscene matter, on the Internet or anywhere else. By most community standards, a large portion of what exists on the Internet would be considered obscene. Some material is e-mailed directly to subscribers, bypassing the authorities. Many opportunities exist for the smut-masters to ply their trade and lure in the unsuspecting before being caught.

Sexual Perverts in Cyberspace

We posed a question at the beginning of this chapter, asking whether viewing pornography on the Internet was any more objectionable to a parent than having a child read *Playboy* or *Penthouse*. Many parents would probably say yes. Why?

Parents are uneasy because the Internet is interactive. Sexual perverts can wander into chat rooms online, pretend to be middlers themselves, and prey on the innocence of children. "My thirteen-year-old daughter has been talking with someone online for several months," confessed one mother. "Now he is calling her and wants to meet in person. Is that safe? Should I allow her to do it?" By 1997, the National Center for Missing and Exploited Children (NCMEC) had attributed fifty crimes involving adult offenders known to or believed to have lured young people into face-to-face encounters after meeting online.

Some argue that children face more serious threats of violence or abuse in their own homes or on the playground. Yet there is something insidious for most parents about sexual provocateurs being able to reach into their homes through a screen and tamper with the innocence of their children. Oftentimes the children who succumb to overtures from online stalkers are those who feel alienated from their family and friends. Finding someone who listens and responds, even online, is irresistible.

While the issue of pornography is uppermost in parents' minds, it is just one of many dangers children face on the Internet:

- "If you can use a mouse, you can place a wager," boasts one website for an online gambling service located offshore on the Caribbean isle of Antigua. Gambling on the Internet, illegal in the U.S., has nonetheless exploded into a $600 million a year business.
- A thirteen-year-old Louisiana boy and his friend printed out *The Terrorists' Handbook* from the Internet "for fun," and proceeded to follow the book's directions to construct a pipebomb. The boy was badly burned when the bomb exploded.
- Websites run by *High Times* magazine and other groups that campaign for the legalization of marijuana contain much information that minimizes the dangers of this drug and can encourage young people to smoke.
- Nearly 200 hate groups have web pages to spread their propaganda. "Youths who would have never considered attending a Klan rally are now exposed to . . . hate sites on the Internet . . ." said the Southern Poverty Law Center in Montgomery, Alabama.

PRIVACY—AN INTERNET INVASION

Marketers, eager to cash in on the young adolescent market, have taken to the Internet to peddle their wares. Type in the name of just about any company, and you can pull up on your screen a list of products, with pictures, descriptions, and, of course, an easy way to purchase online.

Even if your daughter doesn't have permission to use your credit card, she may still fill out information asked for on the site. And herein lies the rub: She will have no control over how that information is used in the future. Her name could be sold to other marketers and she could begin to receive solicitations—through regular mail or e-mail—to buy products. She could be placed on e-mail lists and begin to receive unwanted "spam," or junk mail.

A 1998 study by the Federal Trade Commission found that the Internet industry was doing virtually nothing to protect individual privacy online:

- Canvassing 1,400 websites, the FTC found that 85 percent collected personal information but only 14 percent provided any notice to consumers on what would be done with that data. An even smaller percentage—2 percent—provided such notice with a comprehensive privacy policy.

- The FTC surveyed 126 sites catering to children and found that 86 percent were collecting personal identifiable information. According to the agency, most of the sites did not seek parental approval before gathering the data. Even the Clinton-Gore White House was guilty of asking children for personal information without parental consent.

Most people, although not surprised by the 1998 report, nonetheless found the results chilling. Those who use the Internet routinely type in basic information and even personal data. Indeed, many sites won't allow a person to venture beyond an opening page without registering or joining the site, which often means typing in personal information.

Adults may know the risks and take precautions. But what alarmed those who read the FTC report was how vulnerable children are to online marketers. These youthful consumers are an attractive and captive audience. And many companies are designing websites to appeal to their tastes. Some use cartoon characters and many promise free samples.

While companies may be using the information solely for their own use, many people are uncomfortable simply knowing that they have no control over how the information will be used. And when that information involves a young adolescent, parents are concerned that their children may be on the receiving end of unwanted and, perhaps, objectionable information. The courts have struck down, for violating the First Amendment, two laws aimed at shielding children from online pornography.

So do what you can to protect your middler. Here's how:

Warn your children not to type in personal information, even if asked to do so by a friendly cartoon character.

Before your child subscribes to anything online, she should check with you. Those sites that are sensitive to children (Disney, for example) will ask for a parent's e-mail and send a follow-up notice requesting permission before signing up the child.

Bring the topic up at your parents' association meeting at school. Ask other parents what their experiences have been. You may even want to print out some objectionable sites to illustrate your points.

Talk to your child about the pitches and come-ons he encounters on-line. Compare advertising on the Internet to what might be seen on TV or in magazines. Advertising on the Internet is more powerful because a purchase is just a click away.

CYBER-HOLICS—ADDICTED TO THE NET

"My fifteen-year-old son is spending way too much time on AOL. He was on the computer from 10:45 A.M. Saturday until midnight Sunday! He says it's the weekend."
—Concerned mother

Parents who once worried about their children watching too much TV now worry about their children spending too much time online. Can entering a virtual world prove to be so hypnotic and mesmerizing that our children have difficulty withdrawing? Are our children in danger of becoming addicted to the Internet?

Ironically, initial reports had it that the Internet was a better baby-sitter than TV because of its interactivity. Children who became couch potatoes, spending mindless hours in front of the TV screen, couldn't help but exercise their minds when being online. Or so we thought.

It turns out that for some, and this includes adults and children, the Internet can become, like TV, a passive experience. Once you enter a chat room, it isn't necessary to "say" anything. You can sit and watch the type scroll on the screen. What can be more passive than that?

Some children use the Internet to access and download computer games. So rather than engaging in social discourse, doing homework or research, these children might as well be playing video games on their TV set.

The plus side is that children usually interact with others, playing against them online. Unlike adult aficionados of computer games who prefer a one-on-one controlled environment, and therefore pit themselves against the computer, middlers seem to prefer doing battle online where they can face off against as many as thirty opponents. "A death match is so intense, you feel like you're going to have a heart attack," one fan of the Internet game Quake told Long Island's *Newsday*.

Besides computer games, other aspects of the Internet can be mes-merizing and, therefore, addicting. There's always another site to see, another chat room to visit. Without too much trouble, you can always find someone to talk to online, even in the middle of the night.

For a middler who may be having difficulty connecting in the real world talking with parents and peers, living in the virtual world where conversation flows so easily may prove to be more comfortable. After all, no one can see or hear you on the Internet, and this appeals to many a self-conscious middler. In cyberspace, a young adolescent can invent another persona, describe himself any way he chooses, with no one to contradict him. Social intercourse, without the awkwardness of physically meeting someone face to face, may turn even the most reclusive middler into a loquacious one.

Concern has been voiced, however, about the Internet's psychological impact on frequent users. A 1998 report from Carnegie Mellon University found that people who spend even a few hours per day online experience higher levels of depression and loneliness than if they used the Internet less frequently. The researchers said they were surprised at the results, since they had thought that because the Internet was being used socially, it would cause people to feel more connected and less unhappy.

Part of the problem may be that the more people and children use the Internet, the less time and effort they put into developing true flesh-and-blood relationships with those in their household and neighborhood. Psychologist Luanne Flikkema, of the computer firm Gateway 2000, has identified a trend toward greater isolation in homes with computers. "Scattered family syndrome" occurs, she said, when parents and children spend more time on their individual technological pursuits and less time pursuing activities together.

As with any new technology, there are pluses as well as minuses to the Internet. "The issue is one of balance," said Tapscott in *Growing Up Digital.* "If a child becomes involved for a prolonged period of time in something which is causing disequilibrium in his life, we should be concerned." However, he is quick to add that, "experience shows that compulsive use of the new media is fairly rare and that when it occurs it is usually a temporary problem."

We need to help our children discover the good and attempt to minimize the adverse effects that might occur with their use of the Internet. Here's how:

Set limits. When your child isn't using the Internet to do homework, limit his time. What should that time limit be? Each child and household is different, but you may want to use as a guide any restrictions you have for viewing television. You may also need to decide whether Internet time should be regarded in place of or in addition to TV time.

Teach netiquette. Although the virtual world is different from the real world in many respects, the rules of etiquette or "netiquette" still hold. Advise your child that there should be no name-calling, racist comments, or bullying behavior. Many chat areas reserved for children have monitors who will boot someone out for cruel remarks. Nonetheless, make sure your child knows how you feel.

Strive for balance. Be alert for signs that your child is dropping out of real-life activities in order to surf the Web. At the first sign of trouble, call a time out.

Try abstinence. From time to time, take a hiatus from the Internet and encourage your child to pursue other activities instead. Ideally, do something together to reinforce the "people" connection.

GIRLS—IN ELECTRONIC LIMBO?

Before the Internet became accessible for the average household, the children who were often found playing games on the computer were male. Few computer games, like video games, were developed to appeal to girls. It appeared that companies making the software had pretty much written off the younger female market.

Parents of girls didn't protest too loudly because there was an underlying fear that video and computer games weren't all that healthful for children anyway. If your daughter chose not to join her brother in shooting or nuking others, so much the better, right?

However, it soon began to dawn on these same parents that their daughters were missing the opportunity to become computer savvy. Now with the spread of the Internet, that skill has taken on added importance. Just in time, a whole bevy of software companies has jumped on board to develop games and websites tailored to appeal to the taste and sensibilities of girls.

It turns out that girls are interested in computers, just not in quite the same way as boys. Girls tend to shy away from the physical violence so appealing to boys. "The fact is, girls simply find violence-driven games boring and not complex enough to engage their interests," said a report from

Purple Moon Media, a Silicon Valley company that produced software for girls.

The Internet is particularly appealing to girls because they are interested in friendships and relationships. Exploring the Internet, they can find many chat rooms and sites to satisfy those needs (see the resource section on pages 278–279).

Parents need to remove their gender bias when dealing with their daughters and the computer. Here are some thoughts:

Grant equal time. If your children must share a computer, make sure your daughters are given equal time.

Check out your school program. Make sure that girls have the same access to advanced computer classes. Historically, boys have always been more encouraged than girls to pursue math and sciences. Technology runs the same risks unless parents ensure their daughters will be granted the same opportunities as their sons.

Encourage your daughter. Explore sites with her and select software that will help her hone her computer skills. Most girls want the computer to be "useful," so emphasize ways the computer and Internet can help her with schoolwork or hobbies.

Select appealing games. Some of the games that have proven to be popular with girls (Barbie Fashion Designer, for example) seem to exacerbate a parent's worst fears about gender stereotyping. If there are some games you are ideologically opposed to, look for ones that will interest your daughter yet still pass your test. Remember, the important thing is to make sure your daughter is comfortable on the computer.

CAUGHT IN THE WEB

Curiosity and middlers are inseparable. They are learning about themselves and the world. And through the unlimited capability of the Internet, they now have access to mounds of information previously out of their reach. Unfortunately, some of this information, in immature and inexperienced hands, can lead to dangerous consequences.

The following suggestions have been gathered from many sources, experts, government officials, parents (many of whom answered a request from the online service Parent Soup), and the middlers themselves. As you gain more mileage in cyberspace, you may come up with your own ideas. Remember that each child is different. Some may welcome a parent's initiative to set limits; others will rebel against those restrictions. Know your child and work with him to come up with the best methods.

Surf the Web together. If you have just gone online, sit down with your child and take a tour of the Internet. If you have read about interesting sites point them out to your child.

Be specific about what is inappropriate. Don't assume your child knows what objectionable material is and how it may crop up on the Internet. Talk about the issues. State your views on what you consider off limits.

Advise your child never to divulge information online. Your child probably knows she should never give out her address or phone number to a stranger. But after chatting with someone in a chat room, a stranger may seem like a friend. Make it an ironclad rule that she should never type in any personal information and that she should inform you immediately if someone she meets online makes her feel uncomfortable.

Use online controls. America Online offers ways for parents to block children's entrance to chat rooms or websites considered off limits. Yet AOL officials say that only about 25 percent of subscribers take advantage of this safety feature.

Invest in software. Programs like Net Nanny and Cyberwatch are not foolproof, but they can provide some measure of protection, particularly for younger children. KidDesk Internet Safe, from Edmark Corp., has been cited by the *Wall Street Journal* as an effective program. You will need to spend some time customizing the software for your child in order for it to be effective.

Be forewarned, however, that some of these screening programs may blocks sites and words you may deem appropriate for your children. Words like "breast" and "gay" were blocked from e-mail in one such screening program. You may decide you need to monitor the monitor.

Peek over your child's shoulder. Ideally, the computer should be in an open area in your home where you can observe your child without seeming intrusive. However, every now and then, there's nothing wrong with actually looking at your child's screen and asking, "What are you doing online now?" If your child attempts to clear the screen suddenly or prevent you from seeing, your antennae should go up.

Make sure you are home when your kids are online. Treat the Internet as you would a visitor to your home. You want to be there to monitor the goings-on.

Rule out face-to-face meetings. Make sure your children know they should never agree to meet in person someone they have met online. Many children may not understand how easy it is to invent a persona online. One mother went online pretending to be a female fourteen-year-old and no one challenged her. "My children were stunned at how easy it was to become someone you're not," she said.

Investigate "gated communities." Private websites that screen visitors have started to turn up. Their aim is to keep out those who don't follow the rules.

Sign an Internet agreement. Many schools require children to sign a contract promising to adhere to certain rules while on the Internet. If your child has signed such a paper, review it with him and stress that you expect the same observance at home. In the event your school doesn't have a contract, you might suggest it draw up such an agreement.

Limit Internet time. Often it takes time to access various sites. Before your child logs on, inquire what he hopes to do and set a time limit.

Sign up for an adult class. Many community colleges and local libraries now offer computer classes for adults. See if one has classes that you and your child can take together.

BRAVE NEW CYBERWORLD

We are watching a technological revolution unfold before our eyes. Our children have no knowledge of a world before the computer and the Internet. To them, it's not a revolution, merely business as usual. But we know how far society has come, what has been lost, what there is to be gained. Perhaps our children understand the technology better than we do (or ever will) but that technology doesn't exist in a vacuum. Computers and the Internet may bring the world closer together and send information faster to our children. But that world is still the one we know so well, with all its risks, temptations, benefits, and surprises. And the information still needs to be interpreted, digested, and understood for it to be relevant or helpful.

In the end, then, serving as our children's trusted translators and advisors is probably the way we will ultimately close the "cybergap." Just as we fear for their safety when they walk near a busy roadway, so we fear for their welfare as they journey down the electronic highway. We can help prepare them to keep a sharp eye and ear, watch for dangers, and, once their pathway is clear, to relax and have a good time.

STRATEGIES: MAINTAINING CLOSE ELECTRONIC TIES

When we travel around the country giving talks, one complaint we often hear from parents is that their children never talk with them. During the middler years, privacy becomes a major issue. The torrent of information that once poured forth from your talkative child slows to a trickle during adolescence.

But we've discovered a wonderful new vehicle for communicating with your child: the Internet. Remember how we talked earlier in this chapter about how people oftentimes open up during chats online? Well, guess what? Your children open up, too. They may tell you electronically what they would never reveal to you in person.

Why? It is often difficult for a young adolescent to say something face-to-face to a parent. Online, it's a different story. Your son doesn't have to look at you while he's talking. There's no interrupting. Your middler can present his argument in total without fear of being knocked down before he finishes.

The same goes for the parent. Do you have trouble getting your child to sit still long enough to listen? Then type up what you want to say and e-mail him.

E-mail also allows you to face the issue without facing the issue. You can say what you want in the e-mail, but when you see your child, the topic doesn't have to be brought up unless he chooses to bring it up. Your message is getting through, and he can save face without having to admit you told him so.

We never give our children enough positive messages. E-mail allows us to do that. We can send messages from work or when we're on the road. It may sound hokey à la Hallmark, but it works!

CHAPTER NINE

Failing and Succeeding in School

*

*"I'm having an extremely difficult time with my eleven-year-old
regarding schoolwork. Grades of 96, 99, 100, are now 20, 50, 70.
Her teachers and I both feel that she is capable of being a top student.
She is uncommitted, irresponsible, and careless."*
—Mother

Many middlers lose their grip on academics during these years. Parents of (up until now) high achievers are at a loss to fathom a young adolescent's freefall. "My fourteen-year-old is gifted. He's in honors and got all A's on his first quarter report card. Imagine my shock at this quarter's three C's due to an abrupt halt in doing his work. Why would a kid do this?" Parents of students who struggled through the elementary grades become anxious about the rigors of this next educational phase. Others are just plain apoplectic over a habitually poor student who has given up. "My thirteen-year-old won't take school seriously any longer. She is always grounded and still she has a 39 grade average."

Underachievement is *epidemic,* say all experts. Sylvia Rimm, author of *Why Bright Kids Get Poor Grades,* defines it as "a discrepancy between a child's school performance and some index of the child's ability." Mothers of girls have been alerted to their daughters being especially shortchanged in the math and science departments. Increasingly, parents of boys are being warned, too. In a recent University of Michigan study of 9,000 eighth graders, the boys were less academically engaged, had worse study habits and poorer attendance, and were less likely to complete homework.

Adults panic about their children's capability to prosper in a more sophisticated, competitive millennium. To them failing in school looks like a preamble to failing in life. So the question of poor performance becomes an urgent "Who is responsible?" witchhunt. "Bad" teachers, "bad" parents, or a child falling in with "a bad crowd," are the usual suspects.

This chapter is a test . . . for you. Adjust your reading glasses. Sit up straight. Sharpen your pencils. Anticipate lots of required reading. Are you getting nervous? (Good, now you know how your young adolescent feels.) Here's the problem: your son or daughter is not doing well in school. Find out why. Find the correct formula to break the cycle. Failure is not an option.

If you are ready to close this book, don't. We can't write you a quick-fix prescription for academic success. That said, the clues, theories, and strategies presented here can help you break through familiar stalemates. "Having my parents getting on my case *less* would help me handle my workload better," said an eighth grade girl.

A WARM-UP EXERCISE

Did you know that students today are smarter than ever before? (Yes, we are talking about your middler.) James R. Flynn, an American Ph.D, professor emeritus at the University of Otago in New Zealand, stumbled upon this cerebral evolution by accident. Initially, he set out to rebut the stereotype of African Americans as intellectually inferior, reported in the 1994 book *The Bell Curve*. He investigated test results all around the world over several decades from the military and two versions of standard I. Q. tests. The numbers show undisputed improved scholarship skill. If today's children took a 1932 Stanford-Binet test (the standardized academic test), about a quarter would rate very superior, a distinction formerly earned by a tiny 3 percent.

Better nutrition, urbanization, more test-taking experience, smaller families are all possible explanations for this genius trend. Because they make brains more agile, television and even video games get credit, too.

Despite the gains in intellectual ability, why isn't there a similar rise in achievement test scores? That is a conundrum that stumps everyone. So you are in good company sitting at your kitchen table clueless as to why your ten- to fifteen-year-old is underperforming in school.

To help understand and rectify your child's performance problems, we've developed an underachievement map. Navigate, explore, and experiment until you know which spots pinpoint your student's road-blocks and how to break through.

IS YOUNG ADOLESCENT DEVELOPMENT THE PROBLEM?

Yes! "Hey, how are you? I guess I'm ready for the math Regents, but not science. My parents are hoping for me to get in the 90's; I'm hoping 80's. I can't wait for summer to be here either. I'm going to Virginia Beach. I've never been there before. I'm sure Nick will be nice to you when you finally get together. C-ya later" (note written during English class by a fourteen-year-old girl).

Young adolescents go to school to be with their friends, not to learn. The agenda has academics on it somewhere. How they are going to fare on a test is juxtaposed with how they are going to fare at the dance on Saturday, or in the cafeteria at noontime. Grades are a concern that competes with who's going out with whom, upcoming rock concerts, vacations, sports events, and many others that mirror a middler's daydreams.

Some young adolescents manage school, while others can't. It's a parent's task to keep them focused.

MISCALCULATION MOTIVATION

Our ten- to fifteen-year-olds continually exhale "I'm bored." Do they even want to learn? Yes, insists John Lounsbury, a pioneer and renowned expert on education (and namesake of the John Lounsbury School of Education) at Georgia College and State University. "Learning is natural. It is inherent. It's built into the human experience. People seek to grow and learn. Even the children who act like they don't, *want to learn.*"

During the years from ten to fifteen, intellectual machinery grows. Middler minds expand from concrete to abstract concepts. World hunger is as likely to concern them as their own hunger pangs before dinner. They bristle at social injustice, and the ordinary kind, "You gave him more ice cream!" Middlers weigh problems, master skills, sign onto social causes. Expanding consciousness goes hand in hand with the desire to learn. Take this as gospel that you and your child can get over any hump of educational derailment.

You might be thinking: *Then why is my middler turned off to her studies?*

"I sat reading the newspaper recently," one mother remarked, "when

I heard my thirteen-year-old in the next room singing some hip-hop haiku in harmony with MTV. She sang every word in the exact syncopated beat with the singer. With those memorization skills, how can she be struggling with Spanish?"

Lounsbury explains, "We, in the business of education, have a misunderstanding about motivation. We assume that students are not motivated. There's no such thing as 'unmotivated.' The problem arises because students are not always motivated to learn what we decide they should learn."

To close the gap, teachers invent gimmicks, cajole, bribe, and threaten in order to steer young adolescents in the right direction, "right" being what the teacher deems appropriate. Parents do likewise.

The goal of both teachers and parents should be to align natural motivation with the curriculum. Middle schools have restructured themselves to coordinate their agenda with early adolescence. Cooperative learning—students working in groups—is popular and productive as it capitalizes on peer-oriented middlers. Active, hands-on learning replaces the passive teacher lecturing and the student taking notes.

Those on the cutting edge want to take the revolution further. Visionaries like Lounsbury want to give middlers more power to decide what to study and how best to learn. Increasing student involvement jumpstarts motivation. Here's how:

Find out if choice is used by your child's teachers. Are students presented with a list of books and asked to select a few? When a project is assigned, can the child decide the topic or choose from an array of suggested titles?

Use choice at home. Options empower a learner. Ask your child, "Do you want to review for that test now or later?" Skeptics argue that given control, middlers would introduce field trips to the mall, slash sequential math, extend lunch, and ban homework. Park your reservations.

SCHOOL LIFE AND SOCIAL LIFE

We look at test scores to assess success or failure. In our survey we *asked students* how they were doing:

- 62 percent said, "I am doing very well."
- 27 percent confessed, "I am holding my own."

- 11 percent admitted, "I am having a hard time passing two or more subjects."

We asked, in their opinion, what would help?

- 6 percent said having parents help with organization of assignments.
- 16 percent wanted access to extra help from teachers and other students.
- 50 percent thought finding ways to reduce stress seemed the best approach.

Interestingly, many jotted down their own recipes. "I need to find a way to juggle sports and school," admitted a thirteen-year-old girl from Indiana. A seventh grader from Connecticut said, "I need to study more and pay more attention." Another girl quipped, "Getting off the phone would be the best thing for me."

In our efforts, usually the last expert we consult is the student. We focus on teacher competence and training, and parental involvement. Obviously both matter. Yet we forget the third angle in the learning triumvirate: the middle school students.

What role students play in their education fascinated researcher Laurence Steinberg, Ph.D., professor of psychology at Temple University. He headed up a major study of middle and high school students, spanning ten years, studying 20,000 adolescents and their families. The goal: to understand why students were interested or not in their studies. Rather than repeat looking at life in the classroom, his findings, published in *Beyond the Classroom,* concentrate on student life *outside* school.

He found students blasé about learning. School is separate from socializing.

- "Goofing off with their friends" is how one-third summed up the school day.
- Nearly a fifth admitted they didn't try as hard as they could.
- Half don't do homework. Those who do, spend an average of four hours a week. (In other industrialized countries the average is four hours a day.)
- Less than 15 percent read for pleasure five hours a week. A third spend at least five hours "partying."

- Fewer than one in five students said that their friends value getting good grades.
- Less than one-fourth of all students talk about schoolwork with their friends.
- When asked "which crowd would you most like to be part of," a meager one in ten chose the brainy bunch. Nearly one-third wanted to be in the party-hearty crowd. Nearly one-sixth aspired to hang with the druggies.
- 40 percent are in extracurricular activities, mostly school sports, and say they are too tired to study.

Although more high schoolers than middlers offered most of these discouraging statistics, middle school parents can learn from them. For many young adolescents, school is at the bottom of the list. If a middler does not view school as the primary arena of life, if school process and progress is not woven into the social chatter with friends, and if academic standing is a liability, we can't expect student achievement to be a reality.

Middle schoolers need to connect learning with life, outside of school walls and in the company of their companions. Learning has to look like a process that makes life more fulfilling from birth onward or else buzzwords like "integrated learning" and "lifelong learner" will never become real. Help your middler integrate learning with these:

Make scholastics social. Encourage your child to invite a friend over to study. Drop your middler off at a library to meet friends regularly after school or in the evening. When projects arise, ask your daughter what her friends are doing. Have research sessions at your home. Get lots of poster board and markers. Turn up the music, surf the Net, serve up learning along with the pizza and chips.

Show learning as an ongoing process. When did you last take an adult education course to upgrade computer skills or explore genealogy? The best way to teach lifelong learning is to live it. Schedule a project. Get a book on gardening and plant a vegetable patch, even if it's only tomatoes in a container. Get a video on how to rewire a lamp. Show by example how you are willing to learn something new, and that learning equals enjoyment, adventure, and fulfillment.

Locate a peer group where learning happens. Okay, let's get real. Your perfectly cool fourteen-year-old isn't exactly hooked on inviting his pals over for cookies and an impromptu *Jeopardy!* based on Cliff notes. His friends would never let him live that down. If your middler is entrenched in a cadre of anti-intellectuals, find another group. Sign her up for a scuba class or a YMCA lifeguard instruction course. By steering her toward community classes, you link her to a peer group united by learning.

Gauge extracurricular activities. "I'm not sure I'm going to try out for soccer," an eighth grader told her father. "I know you expect me to, but I'm worried that all the work this year will be too much and playing school sports means every afternoon I'm running till 5:30." Parents eyeing college scholarships pressure middlers toward activities. Don't lose sight of the main event—schoolwork.

Postpone working. School is your child's most important job. Convey the message now because high schoolers seek paychecks. A University of Minnesota study of 12,000 students in grades seven to twelve found those working more than twenty hours a week were more likely to be emotionally distressed, drink, smoke, use drugs, and have early sex.

UNLEARNING A LESSON ABOUT ATTITUDE

"I have a son who just turned thirteen. He has not been doing well in school. His self-esteem is very low. The teacher said he can do the work but won't. I can tell when he does well he likes that. Tell me how to improve his attitude about school and himself."
—Mother

Renowned scholar Kenneth B. Clark searched for the answer to why underprivileged students don't succeed in school. In the end, neither geography (the ghetto), nor race, nor biology (genetic inferiority) were to blame. The students suffered from a poverty of spirit and of confidence. Clark coined the term "attitudinal disadvantage," which means the students possessed a self-defeating attitude. They felt like losers. The current educational push for higher standards for all students aims to undo the historical message that held only 20 percent to 25 percent of students to high expectations.

When a student believes that he is dumb or deficient, that self-image thwarts success. The underlying problem is the child has learned too thoroughly he isn't smart. It's written in red ink on test papers, and officially inscribed on report cards. Parents' disappointment and teachers' warnings rei force it. Schools excel at sorting and selecting, identifying winners and losers. Has your child gotten the message that he's incapable?

Failing students are marched off to a back-to-basics camp of skill drills. Instead of turning the student around, these tactics misfire. Why? Being assigned to remedial classes tattoos the failure label. The student feels more convinced that succeeding is impossible.

If your middler has a history of school difficulty, and a laundry list of extra-help scenarios, tackle the loser image. Many of you suspect self-esteem is pivotal. Chances are you're frustrated by this *the-more-I-try-to-help, the-worse-things-get* downward spiral.

To break the cycle of poor performance, to demolish your middler's feelings of incompetence, Clark and others recommend:

Get the arts into your middler's life. A national study of 25,000 students by James Catterall, professor at UCLA Graduate School of Education & Information Studies, proved that those with higher involvement in arts activities did better academically.

Some schools have programs that expose students to the arts or nature. Others don't. (Ironically, it's usually the gifted students who get the more aesthetic educational tour. Those who need it rarely get it.) Take your middler to showings of great artists. Let him sit in the audience to hear fine music from classical to jazz. Get tickets to plays. Have him try his hand at writing poetry or acting, dance or martial arts. Creativity revitalizes.

Look for the can-do approach in remedial effort. Jean Glass of Arizona, a statistician of survey results on tutoring, believes that pairing your child with a knowledgeable person in an individualized setting works. Tutoring is endorsed by 42 percent of Americans according to a *Newsweek* poll.

Extra help *works best* when tutors connect positively and convey to the child that he can make the grade. Think of it as academic therapy. Sylvan Learning Centers, Huntington Learning Centers, and SCORE are companies coaching with a combo of pep, personality, and positivism (see the resource list for information).

Schools are starting up programs. In the blue ribbon Harrison, New York, Louis M. Klein Middle School, principal Dr. Rosemary Brooke implemented S.O.S., selecting underachievers and linking them in small groups with a teacher who hones their study skills. "We looked for a name that wouldn't negatively label the child and devised methods that motivate. Now I've got parents of students of all levels calling, wanting their children in S.O.S.!"

Introduce your middler to admirable adults. At-risk youth are not usually surrounded by adults they admire, Clark learned. Role models are restricted to sports figures or rappers. All middlers need adults in a variety of fields to look up to and imitate. Link your child to coaches, musicians, thespians, youth group leaders. Make sure your child doesn't get the message that the only way to succeed is with a microphone or a basketball. A calculator, a microscope, or a telescope are surefire props to the top, too.

Develop your middler's oral language skills. Put aside reading, writing, and arithmetic momentarily and concentrate on another fundamental—oral ability. When a child feels like a loser, he is silenced. Talk to him. Encourage him to express his ideas and feelings. Get a dialogue going about anything. See that the teachers spend time on oral linguistic development. One easy activity is the fish bowl. Topics are scribbled on pieces of paper. A student selects one and has to talk about it. The topics needn't be academic. The game helps middlers formulate their voices and validates what they have to say.

THE PIECES OF THE LEARNING PUZZLE

When parents are faced with an underachieving middler, is the barrier ability or willpower? It can be both in a *What came first—the chicken or the egg?* riddle.

Middle school is harder than elementary school. The workload is more intense. By fourth grade, most parents have discovered any visual problems, hearing deficiencies, or writing difficulties. Most visual perception problems such as confusing letters disappear by age nine. At the same time, many children with more perplexing learning disabilities squeak through the elementary grades without having a particular roadblock identified. It is during middle school, when parents cannot explain a child's "hitting the wall," that many discover bona fide learning disabilities or a child's different learning style.

Dr. Mel Levine, University of North Carolina Medical School director of The Clinical Center for the Study of Development and Learning, breaks down the *process* of learning itself. Such a step-by-step look based on Dr. Levine's approach will help you pinpoint your child's difficulties. If a question registers, look closer. Talk to your child's teacher.

Have you heard, "Mom, you know how hard I studied for that test, and I still bombed out!"?
Learning is a two-way street. Having trouble getting information into one's head is an input problem. Proving what has been learned by tests or class assignments is output. Figuring out in which direction a child encounters failure is key. It could be simple test anxiety or the more subtle brain glitches of a learning disability.

Does your child have a history of trouble falling asleep? Is she often exhausted after dinner, during the homework hour?
Learning requires an efficient mental machine. To be successful you must be alert and maintain a state of readiness. Our brain tells us to relax before sleep, and to rev up upon awakening. If this rhythm is off, fatigue occurs. Some children have problems falling asleep and waking up due to a faulty mechanism. Oftentimes, with middlers it's that they simply don't get enough sleep. Sleep patterns change during the middler years. Young adolescents morph into night owls, wanting to stay up later and sleep longer in the morning. These emerging adolescent sleep patterns clash with the crack-of-dawn school bells. Assessing your middler's energy level is critical.

Does your child have trouble finishing everything?
Learning entails "previewing" or looking ahead. A sharp learner comprehends what a task involves and knows how to proceed from the beginning to the end. When a student can't preview, he gets lost and can't finish an assignment.

Part of this involves time-management skills. A textbook example is the student who puts off a major report because "it's not due for two months." She doesn't have the capacity to break down the project into steps: researching, writing a first draft, editing, and assembling. A middler with this shortcoming gets bushwhacked in last-minute crash-course work.

To hone previewing skills, have your middler write the last paragraph

COULD YOUR CHILD HAVE A LEARNING DISABILITY OR DISORDER?

The National Institutes of Health estimates that 15 percent of the population have some form of learning disability. Every year 120,000 children are diagnosed. African American children are diagnosed less, so beware of that bias. Learning difficulties often run in families.

A learning disability (LD) is a neurological disorder, not a matter of intelligence. In fact, LD students are as intelligent as anyone yet suffer a gap between their ability and performance. They often excel in art, music, or sports. Their brains are different either in structure or how they function, creating difficulty in how information is stored, processed, or produced. They have trouble with reading, writing, speaking, computing mathematics, and can be impaired building their social relationships. See if your fifth to eighth grader shows any of these warning signs:

- Does he reverse letters, such as writing *left* as *felt?*
- Is he slow to learn spelling strategies, such as prefixes, suffixes, root words?
- Does he avoid reading out loud?
- Does he avoid writing compositions?
- Is handwriting difficult for him or illegible at best?
- Does he grip a pencil awkwardly, fist-like?
- Does he have trouble recalling facts?
- Has he had difficulty making friends?

Answering yes to one or two of these is not reason for concern. However, if your child has more of these characteristics, talk to your middle school teacher.

of a story first. Instruct him to outline a project from beginning to end, and construct a time schedule. Celebrate the finish line of every task. If finishing has been an eternal difficulty, it's more than development.

Does your child know how he's doing?

Previewing entails being able to track progress (or lack of it). A middler who "self-monitors" knows where he is succeeding and where he needs help. He connects input with output. *If I don't study that list of definitions, I'll do miserably on the quiz. If I don't finish those science labs I missed, I*

The most common learning disabilities are:

- Dyslexia, a reading disability, by far the most frequently detected learning disability. Between 15 percent and 45 percent of children with this problem also have Attention Deficit Disorder (ADD).
- Dyscalculia, impaired ability to do mathematical problems.
- Dysgraphia, a writing disorder making it hard to express thoughts on paper.
- Auditory, Memory, and Processing Disability, difficulty understanding and remembering sounds and words.

Attention Deficit Disorder (ADD), or ADHD with added hyperactivity, is not a learning disability. Yet 20 percent of ADD students have learning disabilities. An ADD student is prone to extreme distractibility. He cannot focus. Ritalin, a stimulant, works for many children, but not all. Nine out of ten classified with it are boys.

Follow these steps if you suspect your child may have a learning disability or disorder.

- Talk to your pediatrician, your child's teachers, and the school counselor.
- Request that your child be evaluated at the school, which is your right.
- When your child is diagnosed specifically, by law he is entitled to a customized learning curriculum called an IEP, an Individualized Education Program. This program alerts teachers to give your child special cues or attention, and also equips you with information to assist at home.
- For more information: contact the Learning Disabilities Association of America (412) 341-1515, http://www.ldonline.org, or by e-mail: ldanatl@usaor.net, and see our resource list on page 280.

won't pass for the quarter. A helpful "How are things going?" from you reminds a child to check his progress.

Previewing is a life skill. A boy with a new driver's license needs to self-monitor—*if I continue speeding, I'm more likely to get into an accident or get a ticket.* Work on it.

Can your child concentrate?

Learning means maintaining controls. During class, the brain filters out distractions: whispering classmates, the rainfall hitting the window, her stomach rumbling. When it works properly, it's easy to concentrate. If the filtering mechanism is faulty, the student can't focus. This defines Attention Deficit Disorder (ADD—see the box on pages 204–205). Don't forget that early adolescence itself is a major distraction. Assess your child's history of concentration.

Is your child persistent?
To achieve, a student needs *internal motivation.* In our survey of National Middle School Association (NMSA) teachers, 65 percent believed that the desire to please herself was mainly responsible for a student's achievement. It's effort, not innate ability, that spurred 81 percent to get to the top of their class, according to a study done by Karen Arnold at Boston College.

Has your middler had a career of inconsistency?
A mother told us, "We have a thirteen-year-old whose grades go from A to F since fourth grade. Is there a syndrome to this trend?"

Certain students have a continually uneven record. Test scores are up, then down. This is aggravating to parents and, believe it or not, more frustrating for middlers. Inconsistency can be a faulty valve in the brain or purely motivational.

Inadvertently students get punished when they do well. "See Johnnie, this time you got a B, I knew you could do it, *if you applied yourself.*" A better strategy: compliment or reward for effort, and review mistakes in order to profit from them.

Does your middler hate writing?
Learning demands synchronizing—doing a number of things at the same time. Writing entails formulating ideas or opinions, spelling, and using grammar rules simultaneously. Arithmetic requires that you divide a problem up, and work on parts. Your mind is not unlike a computer. You run one program and then open a box and do another.

Some students can synchronize. Others jump frantically, incapable of performing well in any of the "boxes." If your child hates writing assignments, discuss his synchronizing ability with teachers.

Is memorizing a stressful event?

Learning depends on memory skills. Middle schoolers have to memorize vocabulary and Civil War battles. Fiction requires comprehending characters and plot. Today's young did not cut their educational teeth on memorizing the way we did. Learning multiplication tables by rote has given way to calculators. "Children today are asked to understand more and memorize less," points out Guy Strickland, principal and educational researcher. "This is an improvement, but . . . children who don't practice memorization skills will be less skilled at memorization."

A snowball effect can ensue. When a middler doesn't have good memory skills, he learns fewer vocabulary words. Stumped word after word, reading slows to a snail's pace. Language and thought are intertwined and so a limited vocabulary means a middler has fewer "word tools" to use in analyzing and problem-solving.

Don't confuse bad memory with forgetfulness common among middlers. If memorizing is recently a problem, help develop extra ways to learn material.

Does your child avoid discussion?

Learning requires escalating language skills. Talking "automatic" conversational language is easy. "Literate" talk, defined as the words used during intellectual discussions and arguments, is quite a different skill. Today's young have had more exposure to visual stimulation than to words—television, video games, even the computer.

Learning expert Levine insists, "Kids today are linguistically deprived." And middlers are notorious for being monosyllabic. When a young adolescent doesn't use an intelligent array of words as well as the conversational ones, she is *less likely* to be able to express herself, develop opinions, and even remember things. Your middler needs to elaborate on what she learns to commit it to long-term memory.

Distinguish between conversation and intelligent discussion. If your child rarely verbalizes, ask about her schoolwork. Discuss politics. Solicit her opinions. Listen to her thoughts. Toddlers need parents to label objects in order for them to learn their first vocabulary; young adolescents need parents to entice them to read and talk more, and go for that higher literate conversational flow.

Researchers are standing on the threshold of so much new knowledge about the brain and how students learn. Lucy Jo Palladino, Ph.D., clinical psychologist and author of *The Edison Trait,* says, "As a child, Thomas Edison was a misfit. His mind was constantly wandering and he couldn't sit still. He needed to learn in his own style and at his own pace."

Learn all you can about your child's cognitive strengths and weaknesses until lightbulbs go off in your head. Now you have specifics to work with and discuss with your child's teachers. (If problems go way back, consult our box on learning disabilities.)

ARE YOU SUBTLY UNDERMINING YOUR MIDDLER?

Ten- to fifteen-year-olds recognize hypocrisy. A fourteen-year-old calls you on your little white lies. This "gotcha" antenna is aimed at your attitudes and your behavior with regard to education. You can mouth "school is important," but if your family's culture and environment don't back you up, you'll trigger underachievement. Look for these learning slurs. Rectify them.

You don't need an education to succeed. Our culture's Horatio Alger folklore is rich with tales of self-made men and women such as billionaire computer whiz Bill Gates and superstar Demi Moore who did just fine, thank you, without a college degree or high school diploma. The variations are endless—the Paul McCartneys who cannot read music, athletes who can barely read. Stress that these are the exception and that doing well in school is still one of the best—if not the best—predictors of later success in both occupation and earning power.

Being witless has never been cooler. Sitcoms sketch characters who take pride in their anti-intellectual antics. Intelligent comedies are practically oxymorons. Movies like *Dumb and Dumber* and *There's Something About Mary* solidify the glamour of being stupid. When you regularly relish entertainment that celebrates illiterates, you are setting a standard that undermines the worth of becoming smart.

Many family stories disparage their most learned members: "He may have plenty of degrees but he has no common sense." Your child soaks up your world view, and will entertain second thoughts before following in the footsteps of family brain/moron.

Get good grades, a degree, a job, and get miserable. We labor under intense job pressures. We err weekly, if not daily, when we complain endlessly about our work life. If you lecture your child about the importance of mastering school so he can go to college and land a well-paying job, what good is your advice if your personal satisfaction is nil? Your middler is perceptive enough to figure out that education may secure a job, but not happiness or satisfaction, so why bother. "Being a real model who shows that hard work pays off" is a New England teacher's best tip for parents who want to spur a child upward.

Instead of undermining, parents should:

Raise expectations. In our survey 76 percent of NMSA teachers recommend that parents set high expectations and reinforce small achievements. Raise the bar realistically. Select your middler's favorite subject and focus on improving there. Little steps, taken over time, will lead up the academic ladder.

Promote reading. You've probably heard how reading to a child is the single most influential thing a parent can do to ensure successful learning. You can't sit your fourteen-year-old on your lap anymore. Yet a pro-reading campaign is necessary. Reading boosts vocabulary, comprehension, grammatical finesse, and powers of analysis.

During middle school the workload increases and reading for pleasure decreases. A fourth grader averages thirteen minutes or less reading time per day, and that diminishes during middle school according to reading expert Judi Paul. Select books for your child based on her interests. For a baseball nut try checking *Same Time Next Year* out of the library. For a budding marine biologist, check out *Jaws* or *Meg*. Give magazine subscriptions from *Sports Illustrated* to *YM*. Reading opens the door to achievement.

Nurture your student. What family traits account for high achievers? Freeman A. Hrabowski III, Kenneth Maton, and Geoffrey Greif, authors of *Beating the Odds*, studied African American math and science whiz kids to see what accounted for the stellar success of a group usually not known for this type of achievement. A child who feels loved, whose welfare is central to parents, is destined for greatness. Interacting with teachers proved invaluable as did closely watching a child's progress and pitfalls.

Enforce consequences. Just as you have to set goals, you have to enforce consequences for doing poorly. "Too many parents do not hold their middlers accountable for their assignments," noted a teacher. Our chorus of teachers agrees. Freedom, privileges, and rewards should be tied into doing or not doing well.

THE HOMEWORK REVOLT . . . AND EVOLUTION

The ultimate confrontation between parents and middlers is over homework. Homework is "in" says Harris Cooper, a psychologist who has traced its history. In the 1940s, homework was demoted for taking time away from sports, socializing, and sleep. The 1950s' Russian launching of *Sputnik* scared Americans, prompting more math, science, and homework. The 1960s' personal fulfillment theme sent homework to the bottom of every "me" wish list. The dawning of a new century with higher academic standards and intense competition designates homework as critical again.

For many young adolescents, homework isn't just one four-letter word; it's two. Some middlers stubbornly strike. "When you go home you're supposed to relax!" insisted a twelve-year-old. "My ten-year-old refuses to do any of his homework without a parent coaching him the entire way," confessed an exasperated single mother.

Parents wonder, is homework worth the struggle? The answer is uncertain. During the elementary years, homework has little or no impact on later academic achievement, according to a University of Missouri study. Advocates do maintain it sets up useful lifelong study habits.

During middle school, homework gets mixed reviews. University of California's Julian Betts followed 3,000 seventh graders and found that doing fifteen minutes of math every school night for four years accelerated the students' achievement by one full grade level. And yet many experts in the field of middle school education officially question the effectiveness of some homework that is more "busywork" than building blocks. Assignments that force young adolescents to regurgitate textbook pages (one study reported that 90 percent of homework does just that!) do more harm than good. They turn students off, not on, to learning and turn up the argument meter between middlers and their parents. "Have you done your homework?" becomes a wedge.

Here's what you can do to fend off the homework revolt and maybe even help it evolve:

Explain the logic behind homework. "Homework is necessary because we need assignments to get better," an eleven-year-old acknowledges. *Whose child is this?* If that crossed your mind, you aren't alone. Since homework is a practice so ingrained into our culture that it is not likely to be eliminated, cast it to your middler as an experience that will affect achievement. It enables students to practice developing skills, from mathematics and analytical thinking to reading.

Give your student control. Tell your middler that homework is his "business," to be run his way. In our survey for *The Roller-Coaster Years,* 43 percent of students polled listened to music while doing homework. Only 17 percent did their assignments in silence. Apparently this generation has a higher threshold for noise. Let him decide whether he prefers working at his desk or the kitchen table, alone or with a study partner. Does he prefer right after school or after dinner? Tell him to identify his problems and bring these to you. Respect his methods unless he fails. Then help him decide how to reorganize.

Interact with your child. A new trend, interactive homework, delivers benefits. These assignments are not designed to be done solo, but with a parent. Teachers Involve Parents in Schoolwork (TIPS), developed by Johns Hopkins University scholar Joyce Epstein, works math by focusing on averages. Families discuss averages, from children's heights to baseball hitters' records. In Baltimore, TIPS significantly improved grades and writing scores. Parents praised the program as an opportunity to talk with their middlers. The ultimate compliment—students completed more TIPS assignments than other homework. Co-opt this interactive style by linking schoolwork to family activities and conversations.

Factor in your family style. "Sitting down every day at a set time and helping your child with his schoolwork is one of the most effective things a parent can do to turn around an underachiever," said a Florida middle school teacher. However, two overworked adults (or one single parent) don't want to "play school" at the end of a long day. Children of divorce travel from one household to another. Iron out with your middler and his teacher how your schedules can be aligned. Save projects or questions for weekends if weeknights are hectic. Noncustodial parents can use the visiting time to assist with homework. With effort, all parents can accommodate and send a powerful message that homework matters.

Start a homework revolution with (not against) your middle school teachers. John Lounsbury, on the forefront of progressive reform, is calling for homework to evolve. How? Among his suggestions: Rather than assign everyone to read the text, divide the class up into groups. Have one group design questions based on the material, another scan for new and difficult vocabulary words, and another get the night off. Opt for assignments that send middlers out into the community. Get a task force going among parents, the PTA, and educators to talk about the old and the new forms of homework. Start with John Lounsbury's essay, "Homework—Is a New Direction Needed?" (See our resources list, page 279.)

A final word worth remembering comes from *Wall Street Journal* columnist Sue Shellenbarger: "The time we spent together on homework will be remembered long after the grades they get have been forgotten."

WHEN YOUR MIDDLER'S WORK IS STILL A MYSTERY

A perplexed dad confessed, "My eighth grade son is failing science. All his other grades are great. I'm at a loss why. He does his in-class assignments and labs, but doesn't hand them in. He just shoves them in his desk! Recently he had a project due. He spent hours, then turned in only half."

Our young adolescents can defy logic. Louanne Johnson, former teacher of the year and author of *School Is Not a Four-Letter Word,* insists that there is no single strategy to explain poor performance. If you have an able student who is earning poor grades, Johnson hypothesizes, "What would I do? I have tried many different things, but I've never done the same thing twice, because there is a different reason every time one of my students failed."

She cites an ailing history student. As it turned out, this calculating Casanova wanted to fail one section in order to be transferred into another—his girlfriend's class. Another anecdote stars a perplexing A student whose failing grades turned out to be the only way she could avoid getting beaten up in the girls' bathroom. The theory behind this Agatha Christie meets Miss Marple approach is that there is a reason for everything a child does.

We asked NMSA teachers: What's behind a child faltering in school? Was it being distracted by social activities, boredom, learning roadblocks, laziness, problems at home? "It's all of the above," wrote many. "Every child needs to be handled differently," said a Connecticut educator.

Attaching the right reason to the wrong academic outcome sounds simple, until you play twenty questions. Either your middler cries, storms into her room, or gives you nonanswers. Playing detective is a cognitive crapshoot, but worth a try. Collect information any way you can. Talk to teachers who see your child more than you do and are privy to insider information about what goes on in school. Canvass coaches or any adult who might have a pipeline to your child's secrets. Examine your home life. If there's a theory to be hatched, you and adults who know your middler are the team to invent it.

THE LATEST NEWS

With underachievement on so many minds, new information emerges all the time.

Enlist Dad. The National Center for Education Statistics recently interviewed the parents and guardians of 17,000 kindergarten–twelfth grade students. The report, *Fathers' Involvement in Their Children's Schools,* characterized fathers as a secret scholastic weapon. When fathers got involved in the education of their sons and daughters, the children were more likely to get A's, both in traditional families and in single-parent households. (In the latter, twice the number of A's.) Noncustodial dads' edu-coaching proved even more effective with middle schoolers who not only got better grades, but enjoyed school more. In these post-divorce families, fathers also reduced behavior problems often stemming from angry youngsters. Suspension and expulsions were fewer when they got involved.

Despite this powerful role, who shows up at PTA meetings, who volunteers for class trips, and in the homework helping department? Mothers (56 percent) outdid fathers (27 percent) in actively participating in daily school life by a two to one margin.

Educating fathers on the importance of their role is the first step. If you are divorced, be willing to share this fact with your ex-spouse. Ask your PTA to launch a father-involvement campaign, which could include father-son or father-daughter breakfasts or dances. Actively recruiting male attendance at events will cross over and improve overall participation. Fathers are spending more time with their children than their predecessors did twenty years ago. Spread the word that some of that time should be spent on homework, reading to a child, and gluing science projects together.

Get a computer for your middler in school and at home. Technology is a proven turnaround tactic for underachievement. A ninth grade algebra class in Carrollton City, Georgia went from a 38 percent average failure rate down to 3 percent after putting computers in the classroom. Technology energizes students. In the U.S. Department of Education's report *Getting America's Students Ready for the 21st Century,* technology-rich schools had better attendance records and motivated students toward higher quality work for which they took greater responsibility. These gains held for all students regardless of age, race, or parental income.

Computing excites that "gotcha gene" because young adolescents know they are better at computing than adults. Tutoring their parents electronically enhanced students' levels of competence and self-confidence. In one study of fourth to sixth graders, computers led to middlers spending more time on schoolwork and increased family involvement.

Apple Computer, Inc. ran a ten-year study and noted that technology-rich environments positively affected performance on standardized tests and improved communicating abilities on complex subjects. A by-product is that students become engaged with the learning process itself. The labels *self-starters* and *lifelong learners* are more likely to characterize the Net generation.

If you don't have a computer, stop rationalizing and buy one. Start lobbying your middle school for computers if they are not in place. Make upgrading technology a goal of your PTA if they are still spending their dollars primarily on perks like yearbooks or new sports equipment.

By now your head may be spinning with all the potential causes and possible elixirs for your child's underachievement. A turnaround is going to take longer than the time spent reading this chapter. Consider this your research project.

STRATEGIES: HOMEWORK ASSIGNMENTS FOR YOU

Test Your School Spirit: Are You Part of the Solution or Part of the Problem?
In 1994, Congress put parental involvement on its list of eight recommendations, called the Goals 2000 legislation. Half of the states have enacted thirty-eight laws. Teachers and administrators want parents to become partners, yet admit many parents who come to school sabotage, rather than support, a student's success.

Read each of the situations we've designed below and choose one answer. Proceed to the scoring to see if you are helping or hurting your child's chances for academic success.

1. You receive an announcement in the mail of an upcoming speaker at your child's school. You would

(a) glance at it briefly before automatically pitching it in the garbage (you are pressed for time always); **(b)** read it in order to see if the topic specifically addresses your child's needs; **(c)** read it, commit to attend because you can always learn something new.

1. _____

2. During a recent conference on your child's academic performance, the team of teachers informs you of their suspicions that your child may be using drugs. How would you respond? You would

(a) ask for specific evidence and vow to take action; **(b)** feel your emotions rising in disbelief, but reluctantly agree to ask your child if this is true; **(c)** review your child's recent behavior, question how you may have rationalized any signs, and ask the teachers for their best advice.

2. _____

3. You've heard through the grapevine that one of your child's teachers may be gay. How would you handle the innuendo? You would

(a) call the principal, the superintendent of schools, or the president of the PTA and demand to know the sexual orientation of the teacher in question; **(b)** focus on the teacher's character and ability, and dismiss the need to know intimate details; **(c)** ask your child for details that verify the rumor, and with this ammunition make your case that this teacher is unfit.

3. _____

4. Your PTA is marshaling volunteers for a fundraising effort to finance school repairs or another program. You would

(a) get involved in the effort because any school fundraising initiative deserves your time and effort; **(b)** dismiss it because, in your opinion, you pay high enough property taxes and you are sick and tired of all the fundraising bandwagons; **(c)** volunteer because your child has told you s/he will benefit personally from this.

4. _____

5. When you drive by the school complex, you always see students hanging just outside the gate smoking cigarettes. Who do you blame for this?

(a) The school for not enforcing strictly enough the no-smoking ban on campus; **(b)** yourself, the school, and your entire community for not organizing an effective strategy for combating young adolescent smoking; **(c)** the parents of the cigarette-puffing culprits for not knowing what their children are up to.

5. _____

6. How do you feel about the home-schooling trend?

(a) You feel it is an individual right but a huge responsibility to take on the job of educating your own child; **(b)** you agree there are parents who could do as good a job (if not better) at educating their own children as your school is doing; **(c)** you doubt whether home-schooling parents can deliver the full range of educational, social, and extracurricular advantages that community schools can.

6. _____

7. How would you rate your child's middle school on the effectiveness of their communication with you? My child's school

(a) does an excellent job of keeping me informed of my child's performance and behavior and school events; **(b)** does an inadequate job of keeping me abreast of my child's particular needs and any programs that would be of interest to us; **(c)** only contacts me when there is a problem with my child's behavior, and this negative attitude is disheartening.

7. _____

8. Do you think the teachers in your child's school demonstrate that they care and are committed to their students?

(a) Sometimes the teachers demonstrate that they care, but their attention usually goes to a special elite few students, not the majority; **(b)** honestly, most of the teachers with whom I come into contact treat teaching as a job and resent parents who want extra time or extra help; **(c)** absolutely, yes, because I see them chaperoning, coaching, providing extra help, and going out of their way to go that extra mile.

8. _____

9. Over the years since you were a child, schools have changed. Do you think that teachers have changed?

(a) No. I think that the teaching profession still draws people who care about children and want to work hard to help them succeed in life; **(b)** yes, I think that teachers have become more arrogant, more demanding of higher salaries, and less able to do their job; **(c)** not much. I think there have always been good and really bad teachers because I've had both kinds.

9. _____

10. When a student becomes a behavior problem in public school, and doesn't respond when disciplined, what should be done? The school should

(a) have a strict plan and an alternative school for students who repeatedly misbehave; **(b)** look at what they are doing, because obviously they need to do more if they can't bring a student into line; **(c)** have a comprehensive strategy, bringing the student's parents, school psychologists, and guidance counselor evaluations together to turn around the child.

10. _____

Scoring: List your answers below. Look for the point value in the table provided. Write your points for each answer. Total your score. Proceed to the evaluation to see what your answers mean.

Answers	Point Values			Answers
1. ____	(a) 5	(b) 10	(c) 15	1. ____
2. ____	(a) 10	(b) 5	(c) 15	2. ____
3. ____	(a) 10	(b) 15	(c) 5	3. ____
4. ____	(a) 15	(b) 5	(c) 10	4. ____
5. ____	(a) 5	(b) 15	(c) 10	5. ____
6. ____	(a) 10	(b) 5	(c) 15	6. ____
7. ____	(a) 15	(b) 10	(c) 5	7. ____
8. ____	(a) 10	(b) 5	(c) 15	8. ____
9. ____	(a) 15	(b) 5	(c) 10	9. ____
10. ____	(a) 10	(b) 5	(c) 15	10. ____

Total _____

Evaluation

(50–75 Points) The Critic. If you scored in this range, your attitude harbors resentment and bias toward educators. Chances are you have good reasons behind your beliefs. Growing up, you may have had bad teachers. Or you may have butted heads with teachers your children have had who didn't live up to your expectations. You may, along with many other parents, feel overwhelmed with any number of pressures: high taxes, time constraints, and failed school efforts to curb smoking, drinking, or drug use. The danger of your mindset is that you are sending a negative message to your middler about school and teachers. If you doubt and disparage teachers' intentions, dismiss their evaluations, ignore opportunities to join community events and efforts, and jump at every chance to criticize, you are undermining their influence in the eyes of your child, their student. In so doing, you are part of the problem and not part of the solution.

(80–115 Points) The Advocate. If you scored in this range, you are definitely in your child's corner. The problem is you are shortsighted. You see your middle school and its teachers only in relation to your child and not in the larger context. For example, your decision to attend a speaker's program or join in a fundraising effort is predicated upon what's in it for you and your middler. You approach students smoking in school or mis-

behaving as problems for their parents, and no concern of yours. You may be too inclined to point the finger at teachers, other parents, or students who might hurt your child's chances for success. What you fail to realize is that being an advocate is critical, but a part of that job is to understand that all school issues and problems affect each and every child in the community, yours included. If you are to be the best partner you can be in your child's success, you have to enlarge your viewpoint, contribute your support, and join forces with those who are part of the solution.

(120–150 Points) The Ally. If you scored in this range, congratulations! You are the best kind of partner and your attitude will ensure your middler's success. You have a positive attitude toward teachers and are not likely to be affected by the rumor mill. You understand that teachers today have a difficult job and that, for the most part, they do it well, offering their students academic, social, and recreational opportunities. You are willing to participate in events or efforts because you know your contribution makes the parent-school partnership stronger and better. Knowing that your first responsibility is to your own child doesn't prevent you from being aware of, and active in, a wide range of problems, including young adolescent smoking or drug use, that affect all the middlers in your town. Your faith in educators and your commitment to joining them models to your child how valuable school is. With more parents like you, there would be fewer problems and far more successful solutions.

Schools today push our emotional buttons. We have to understand how our attitudes affect our students so we can change them, or act upon them, to maximize success for our young.

MORE STRATEGIES

Get to the bottom of a learning snag, disability, or disorder. Look at learning about your middler's school performance as a continuing project. Look for articles on education and read them whenever you see them. If you suspect learning problems, keep asking teachers, specialists, and administrators until you are satisfied your child is diagnosed accurately.

Help teachers meet the higher standards climate. Teachers are under greater pressure to graduate smarter students. Your struggling middler is a reflection on them, too. In a New York State United Teachers survey, 73 percent said there weren't enough learning labs or teachers to deliver one-on-one help to needy students. 71 percent said their schools had not reduced class size, a proven way to increase a teacher's effectiveness and decrease student failure. 51 percent had not received staff development to meet higher standards. Work with your teachers to pressure the school district to green-light extra-help programs, more professional development, mentoring programs for new teachers, and any other ideas the educators envision.

Play the race report card. African American parents feel discouraged by the incessant negative stereotype of minority students, especially boys. If your young adolescent needs more evidence that he can make the grade, show him achievers. Dennis Kimbro, professor of entrepreneurship at Clark Atlanta University, chronicles extraordinary black magnates, tycoons, and millionaires in *What Makes the Great Great*. Repeat such stories. Put successful faces and famous quotations around your middler's room.

Offset gender liabilities. A recent University of Virginia poll found middle school girls reluctant to want both motherhood and a challenging career. Does your daughter believe she can be feminine and smart, too? If she cannot reconcile ambition with traits that boys find appealing, beware. If it's boys or books, hormones make it a nonchoice. Show her both sides of being a woman, competence and intelligence as well as nurturing and attractiveness.

Boys have obstacles, too. Four boys drop out of school for every one female. More boys are labeled with learning disabilities and disorders. During the years from ten to fourteen, male self-esteem drops because emotions are suppressed by our he-man straightjacket definitions. If he's pressured to act like a man, can he still ask for extra help? Keep boys' psychological gender handicaps on your radar, too.

Think positively about your middler. Young adolescents can learn and accomplish great things. Emily Rosa's fourth grade science fair project wound up in *The Journal of the American Medical Association*. Her experiment examined the validity of healing touch therapy (an idea she got while watching TV). A new age healer sat behind a screen while Emily placed her hand over the right or left of the practitioner's. She recorded whether the practitioner could feel her human energy field—the basis for touch therapy. The practitioner felt her field 44 percent of the time, too close to random guessing. So the middler wound up creating a controversy with her simple yet valid emperor's new clothes style. It is our children who will save the environment, cure cancer, stumble on an AIDS vaccine, and more that we cannot even imagine.

Unlock your child's potential. Every child, even an underachiever, has a passion, an ability, a skill, or a talent. Keep looking until you find your child's. Tapping into that essence will lead you into your middler's soul and heart, and ignite the mind.

CHAPTER TEN

Dealing with a Violent World

*

"Since my son was mugged and had his new jacket stolen, he has had a dramatic personality change. He spends all his time in his room, playing violent video games. It's been almost six months now. How much more time should we give him before taking him to a therapist?"
—Mother of a thirteen-year-old

A violent act explodes an individual's personal sense of control. For a young adolescent, who already feels powerless, being a victim can be a devastating experience. Nearly one million children ages twelve and up are the victims of violent crime each year. In 1997, about 2,100 murder victims were below the age of eighteen. Ready access to guns has added a deadly element. In 1997, 18 percent of murdered juveniles under age thirteen were killed with a firearm, as were 84 percent of those murdered juveniles thirteen or older.

Crimes involving guns are notable for their horrific nature. On February 2, 1996, Barry Loukaitis, fourteen, calmly walked into his algebra class at Frontier Middle School, Moses Lake, Washington, and shot and killed his teacher and two students. Thereafter would follow at least seven other school shootings. On March 24, 1998 in Jonesboro, Arkansas, two boys, one thirteen and the other only eleven, waited on a grassy knoll and opened fire when teachers and students filed out of school for a fire drill precipitated when the eleven-year-old pulled the alarm. One teacher and four students were killed in that attack and ten were wounded. Thirteen months later in a high school in Littleton, Colorado, two teenagers in a bloody rampage killed thirteen others and then themselves.

These incidents destroyed the notion of school as a protected place for children. But for many children, school has always been a war zone:

- More than 6,000 students were expelled in 1996–97 for bringing a gun to school, 34 percent in middle school.
- In 1997, 20 percent of middle and high schools reported at least one serious crime such as rape or robbery.
- During the 1992–93 school year, school shootings reached their peak when fifty people were killed in school-related violence, according to the School Safety Center.

In this chapter we will examine violence, both real and virtual, for its effect on our children. In our recent survey, 89 percent of parents and 92 percent of teachers said that today's world is far more dangerous than anything they knew as children. But they sounded an encouraging note: 65 percent said it was possible to protect young adolescents "most of the time." How? First off, you must do some soul-searching, examining your own attitudes and behavior with regard to violence. Second, you must educate your child about violence, talking about images in the media and teaching him how to recognize danger. And, third, you must do whatever you can to reassure yourself that your child's environment is as safe as possible.

Headlines focus on the school shootings. "The common denominator when you try to find out what is going on is that all these kids feel disrespected," said John Devine, of New York University's School of Education. "And the youth culture tells kids to retaliate when they feel dissed." The parents we hear from during our talks are more concerned with day-to-day bullying or sexual harassment. "My thirteen-year-old daughter told me that some girls at her school are threatening to beat her up because she talked to a boy one of these young ladies likes," said one mother. "I'm scared to death she is going to be hurt."

We will talk about the effect graphic portrayals of destruction in the electronic media have on middlers. Is there anything we can do to shield our children? We have collected information from child advocates around the country and will give you some guidance.

A scant minority of children receive counseling after being a victim. These are the times when parents need extrasensory parental perception to read the child's mind. Many middlers, embarrassed and humiliated by the experience, will put on a happy face. But underneath that bravado is a child in crisis who needs parental help like never before.

BREAKING THE CYCLE OF VIOLENCE

The threat of becoming a victim weighs heavily on the minds of many middlers:

- Bodily injury is a major middler worry. A seventh grader from Iowa spoke for many of his contemporaries when he said, "I worry about being mugged or jumped."
- KidsPeace polled 1,000 children ages ten to thirteen and found that, besides AIDS, their top concerns were being kidnapped and being physically or sexually abused.
- In 1996, more than 15,000 students wrote to Congress through the Respecteen civics program and listed crime and violence as their top concern.

We deliver contradictory messages about violence to our children. "On one hand we value violence and at times find it entertaining, yet we condemn the violence in our children's behavior when they model and mirror our value system," said Ronald Keith Barrett, a professor of psychology at Loyola Marymount University, who lectures extensively on youth and violence.

If we are to address violence, we need to examine our own behavior and attitude:

We should practice nonviolence in our own lives. Even if we take out our anger on inanimate objects rather than people, we send our children the wrong message.

We should avoid ambivalence. Violence is something to be avoided and used only as a last resort.

We need to teach our children alternatives. There are better ways to deal with anger or to resolve disputes than with brute force.

We must monitor our children's entertainment. At the least, we need to be aware of what they are watching and talk about the messages.

We should be ready to help. Our children may need our aid to deal with the violence in their lives. We should make it clear that we are there for them.

MOVING IMAGES—THE POWER OF VIDEO

Movies, TV programs, and video games are an overwhelming presence in our children's lives. Unfortunately, too much of this entertainment is teaching our children how to be violent. "When mindless killing becomes a staple of family entertainment, when over and over children see cinematic conflicts resolved not with words, but with weapons, we shouldn't be surprised when children, from impulse or design, follow suit," President Clinton told a gathering in Jonesboro, three months after the school shootings.

The Motion Picture Association of America has devised a rating system for shielding children from inappropriate movies. Unless accompanied by an adult, those under seventeen are not allowed to view films labeled "R" for "Restricted." After the R-rated *Scream 2* opened—because of a bevy of young, attractive TV stars this movie was a must-see for most young adolescents—hordes of middlers showed up at a popular Manhattan theater. The theater's management risked riot and loss of business but firmly turned the young crowds away.

Why were young adolescents so eager to see *Scream 2*? Because they had seen the original film, *Scream*, also rated R, on video, probably with their parents in the next room. As you can see, the entertainment industry's safety net has many holes that allow middlers to slip through. There are no restrictions that prevent those under seventeen from renting an R-rated video. Nor are there laws against middlers buying CD's or video games that promote violence.

In many ways, the battle focuses on the small screens in your home—the TV and the computer. The bad news is that there is a lot of objectionable material out there. The good news is that, because the TV set and computer are in your home, you can still exercise some control over what your child watches. In Chapter Eight, we talked about the computer and safety on the Internet. Here, we will focus on television.

TV as a Guide

By the end of seventh grade an average child will have watched 100,000 acts of violence. In April 1998, a three-year study by four universities found that the level of violence on TV had remained about the same for three years, but the number of violent programs appearing in prime time—when most young adolescents are watching—had increased. Overall 61 percent of the programs contained some violence, the same as the year before, and up from

58 percent in 1994–95. But in prime time, the shows with violent content increased from 14 percent to 67 percent of all shows examined, and shows on cable with violent content increased from 10 percent to 64 percent.

More than the percentages, however, what dismayed the researchers was the fact that in 75 percent of violent incidents on TV, the aggressors within the scene showed no remorse, suffered no criticism from others, and were not penalized for their actions. How do we, as parents, then teach our children that actions have consequences?

Critics have amassed a mountain of evidence to show that children who watch violent programming are affected in three different ways:

Imitation. According to the *Harvard Mental Health Letter,* more than fifty field studies over the last twenty years have demonstrated that children who habitually watch more media violence behave more aggressively and accept aggression more readily as the way to solve problems. According to the Center for Adolescent Studies at Indiana University, preteens who rated themselves most aggressive also logged the most hours watching violent TV shows.

Intimidation. Children who watch violent programming overestimate the chance of becoming the victim of a violent crime. Studies by George Gerbner of the University of Pennsylvania's Annenberg School of Communications, have illustrated this phenomenon, not surprising considering that the great majority of characters in TV shows are victims of violence. So even if your child is not prone to violence, watching violent programming may cause her to become overly cautious, paranoid for her safety, and depressed.

Desensitization. Children who watch violent programming become immune to it. Madeline Levine, in her book *Viewing Violence,* notes that in order for a person to react quickly in an emergency situation, he or she must first be sensitized to the dangers. Because constant viewing of media violence causes a person to become less aroused to violence, a person would be less likely to come to another person's aid.

Trash TV Imitated in the Classroom

More meaningful, perhaps, than scientific studies, are the experiences parents and teachers have on a day-to-day basis, witnessing firsthand how middlers imitate what they watch on TV. After a talk we gave to middle school educators at a state convention, one teacher told us that he became concerned with the mob mentality being exhibited in his class-room. Students routinely ganged up on one or two members of the class, taunting them, calling out insults, hoping to force a confrontation.

He asked students what they did after school. The vast majority watched the *Jerry Springer Show,* famous for inflammatory topics. "My daughter is a teen prostitute" and "I'm pregnant by my brother" are two examples. With volatile guests and a studio audience whose thirst for violence fans the flames, cursing, fistfights, and out-and-out brawls ensue. In April 1998, Nielsen ratings, the TV industry's barometer of who is watching what and when, discovered that Springer's largest audience consisted of young adolescents, ages twelve to seventeen, followed by younger children, ages six to eleven.

Television has the power to validate behavior, even when those actions are antisocial. "Television doesn't kill people, but it provides the ideas, the social sanction, and often even the instruction that encourages antisocial behavior," said Levine.

GANGSTA RAP—MESSAGES OF HATE

"How can I review the music of my son and stay objective? I am an older parent."
  —Father of a fifteen-year-old

What feelings does popular music touch off in our children? Well, if they are listening to gangsta rap, they are apt to be filled with thoughts of drug use, racial hatred, misogyny, and violence. "Lyrics that describe violence and drug taking in a positive way both reflect a society which is violent and drug-ridden and help to perpetuate violence and drug abuse," said Myriam Miedzian, in her book *Boys Will Be Boys.* Miedzian is particularly concerned about gangsta rap's vilification of women. "There is a frequent boastfulness in the lyrics that makes it unthinkable that a woman could or should resist a man's advances," she noted.

Ironically, gangsta rap is a mutation of hip-hop, whose syncopated verse emphasized hope and focused on moving young people away from drugs and violence. In his book *Gangsta,* music journalist Ronin Ro recounts how early rap groups like Public Enemy and Boogie Down Productions urged young listeners to improve their communities. "Whereas P.E. and BDP helped wean youth off of the addictive habits of gold jewelry, self-hate, and straightened hair, gangsta rap influenced youth to buy guns and adopt a paranoid victim's worldview," Ro said.

Several events occurred that helped to move rap firmly away from its nonviolent roots. The 1991 beating of Rodney King in Los Angeles, and the riots that followed, convinced many young blacks that they needed to fight back. Several popular movies—Dennis Hopper's *Colors,* John Singleton's *Boyz N the Hood,* and the Hughes brothers' *Menace II Society*—portrayed gang members as modern day Robin Hoods and gave them an international stage. The music, showcased in the movies, quickly captured the attention of a young audience. There were sixty-two million rap albums sold in 1997, compared to country music's seventy-one million. Thus began a rush by West Coast record producers to sign the next up-and-coming gangsta rap group, no matter how repulsive the message. "On the radio, you never used to hear 'I want to do this to you, I want to do that to you' in a distasteful way," said Michael McCary, a member of Boyz II Men, a rock and blues quartet that debuted in 1991. "Now it's blunt, and it'll get worse before it gets better."

Within a short space of time, middlers of all ethnic backgrounds living in safe suburban neighborhoods, whose only contact with the gangs glorified in gangsta rap was through listening to CDs or watching videos on MTV, were effecting the dress, lingo, and philosophy espoused by these urban rappers. In fact, one of the youths charged in the Jonesboro killings bragged that he was a member of the Bloods, one of the most vicious Los Angeles gangs. "That gangsta rap has grown so large may explain why White kids now affect gangbanger fashions and attitudes in Little Rock, Arkansas; it may shed light on why murder figures are rising in low-income areas; antisociality is now the norm, and the gun, and not mediation, is the primary arbiter of social conflict," said Ro.

The music industry operates with a voluntary labeling system that marks certain CDs with "Parental Advisory" notices. *Voluntary* is the operative word, however, because most recording companies and performers use either minuscule labels or none at all. Even if you stop your own child from purchasing an objectionable CD, chances are he can easily obtain a taped copy from a friend.

Most middlers listen to music through earphones hooked up to portable tape or CD players. Unless a parent inquires, a child's musical selections are apt to remain personal and private, making it more difficult for parents to monitor.

PARENTAL CENSORSHIP: WHAT YOU CAN—AND CAN'T—DO

In the movie *The Truman Show,* Truman Burbank, played by Jim Carrey, lived in a world that had been created just for him, a place filled with bright colors and smiling faces, and void of any anger or violence. It should have been a paradise, but instead was a prison. Truman recognized the falseness of his environment and longed to live where he could experience the full range of human emotions.

We might flirt with the idea of creating a Truman-like universe for our children. But in the end, such a strategy would prove not only undoable but unwise. Our children would recognize our subterfuge and rebel. And eventually, they would have to leave their sheltered existence and learn how to cope with a complex and dangerous world. Our efforts to protect them would leave them merely unprepared.

That doesn't mean we should relinquish our authority. We should use anything we can—V-chips on TVs to block out objectionable programming, warning labels, rating systems, reviews—to screen and monitor what our children listen to and watch. But we need to accept that, despite our best efforts, our children will still be exposed to some R- and even X-rated material. Therefore our strategy should include constant communication with our children to counter the information coming at them from other, more hostile sources.

Not all young adolescents who watch violent movies and TV shows and listen to gangsta rap suffer adverse effects. What makes the difference? Like a loathsome weed, violence can only take root in those hearts and minds that are neglected and deprived of love and attention. You—the parent—are the critical player, the gardener so to speak. You must remain vigilant, constantly tending to the care and feeding of your child's mind, making it more difficult for thoughts of violence to take hold. Here are some strategies you can keep in your toolshed:

Keep the TV out of your children's rooms. Fifty percent of children ages six to seventeen have TVs in their rooms. Monitoring your child's viewing will be doubly difficult if the set is on his turf.

Open an account at your local video store and monitor rentals. Many stores will allow you to pay a set amount good for renting a certain number of videos. Once you have done this, ask the store's management not to allow your children to rent R-rated cassettes.

Network with other parents. There's strength in numbers, so get together with other parents and establish some guidelines.

Talk about consequences. Counter what your children are seeing on the screen, where criminals get away scot-free. That seldom happens in real life. Pull an example from the headlines and discuss crime and punishment.

Encourage activism. Is your child dismayed about something she has seen on TV? Show her how to lodge a protest with a local TV station, network, or government agency.

Print out the lyrics to a gangsta rap song. When seen in black and white, these lyrics may be somewhat shocking to your child. Talk about these themes and why you find them objectionable.

Talk about the lives of the gangsta rappers. Many of these entertainers not only sing about violence, but live in a violent world filled with guns and drugs. Several (Tupac Shakur and the Notorious B.I.G.) have met violent deaths.

Watch with a purpose. Select a TV show or video with the idea of sparking a discussion with your adolescent. For example: *Lilies of the Field* or *The Milagro Beanfield War* (cultural diversity), *Gandhi* or *Norma Rae* (activism), *Free Willy* or *Silkwood* (environmental concerns), *Philadelphia* or *In the Gloaming* (AIDS), *Dead Poets Society* or *Good Will Hunting* (integrity), *Miracle Worker* or *Rainman* (handicaps), and *West Side Story* (gangs and violence). Some of these movies have strong language, and may be intense for some younger middlers, so you might want to preview beforehand. But their messages are positive and should help get your child thinking.

Start a movie club. Start a Mother-Daughter, Father-Son, or other variation Movie Club, where you can get together with other parents and children, watch a movie on video, and then have a discussion. Better yet, select a movie based on a book everyone has read. Then talk about books versus movies, bringing literature to the screen, and which format everyone thought did a better job of stirring the emotions and imagination.

Be alert to the danger signs. You will know when a young adolescent has watched too much violent programming. If your normally docile son is suddenly picking fights with a younger sibling, or your previously outgoing daughter is now afraid to be out at night, find out what movies or

TV programs they have been watching. Start the discussion and make some suggestions about future viewing choices.

PEER HARASSMENT—WHERE THE VIOLENCE STARTS

Experts feel that most violence in schools starts with bullying or, the new term, peer harassment. In fact, 58 percent of students reported that they had missed school at least once because they were avoiding a bully.

The new twist is that, in the past, the violent person was the bully. Now, the victims, feeling tormented by their peers and abandoned by the adults in their lives, are lashing out. In Pearl, Mississippi, and Paducah, Kentucky, both shooters were described as having been targets of harassment.

Interestingly enough, experts are finding the most effective way of stopping peer harassment is by focusing on neither the bullies nor their victims, but rather on the "silent majority"—the 85 percent of kids who sit on the sidelines. The goal is to turn these children from spectators into the caring majority.

According to one program developed by Cherry Creek (see resources on page 282 to obtain a copy) if a child sees someone being bullied, he or she should intervene using the CARE strategy. Parents should talk with their children about these steps:

C: Creative problem-solving. "You've been giving Johnny a hard time. Tell me something you actually like about him."

A: Adult help. Find an adult if someone might get hurt. Telling an adult to protect someone is different from tattling to hurt someone.

R: Relate and join. "My clothes never seem to match, either. Some of us just don't have any fashion sense. It's kind of funny. But no matter what, we don't make fun of other people at this school."

E: Empathy. "You shouldn't say that about Jane. I'd be hurt if you said that about me."

The Cherry Creek program also encourages those being bullied to use the strategies that can be remembered by the acronym HA-HA-SO.

H: Help. Get it or give it.

A: Assert. "Stop calling me names. It's mean and unfair."

H: Humor. "Yes, this is an ugly shirt. My grandmother always does this to me."

A: Avoid. Walk away.

S: Self-talk. "I know I'm not really ugly."

O: Own it. "You're right. I am a Native American. Do you want to know what our culture is really like?"

Children must learn to recognize bully behavior, report it to an adult, and be prepared to do something to stop the bully from succeeding. Have conversations with your child. You might even use a TV program (*The Simpsons,* for example) where bullies threaten weaker children. Role play with your child to devise strategies for coping as a victim or an observer.

If your child is the victim, he may not tell you. Watch for changes in behavior—no appetite, stomachaches, excuses to stay home from school—that signal something is amiss. Talk with your child's teacher. Has he noticed your child being bothered by a bully? Unless the school has already begun to deal with the bully, take your concerns to the administration. In the current school climate sensitized to bullies, your fears should be taken seriously.

What if your child is a spectator? As long as your child isn't being targeted, should you do nothing? Again, remember Jonesboro, when many children, and probably some of the parents, knew these boys were being mean and making threats. Yet no one did anything to alert the authorities. The wise parent will talk to other parents and get the school to introduce a bully prevention program.

VIOLENCE AND BOYS—AN UNBREAKABLE COMBINATION?

Nearly everything connected with boyhood—toys, books, movies, even history lessons—teaches boys that violence is manly and desirable. In some neighborhoods, refusing to fight means setting oneself up as a convenient target for every tough guy who comes along. Geoffrey Canada, in his book *FistStickKnifeGun,* reminisces about growing up in Harlem where a young boy couldn't walk on his block until he had proven himself. Canada and his brothers fought. Now, however, as the title of Canada's book suggests, the neighborhood toughs no longer fight just with their fists. "As the number of guns available to young people has increased, so have the odds that they will be shot in a confrontation," he said.

Deprogramming our boys from violence is not an easy task but we can start with the following ideas:

Incorporate conflict resolution at home. Using mediation and critical thinking to solve problems discourages violence. "Boys who have studied conflict resolution have learned to be good listeners, to 'put up' rather than put down, to cooperate, to see things from the other side's perspective," said Miedzian, in *Boys Will Be Boys.*

Seek out nonviolent "manly" role models. Athletes like Michael Jordan, who play hard on the field but abhor violence and remain gentlemen, are worth emulating.

Set them loose against nature. Mountain climbing, kayaking, white water rafting, and other "extreme" sports allow boys to fight nature rather than each other (review Chapter Seven for more on extreme sports).

Rethink war. There is a growing realization that the "John Wayne–Rambo" style of fighting enemies has glorified war and glossed over the human death and suffering. War is truly hell, a sobering fact brought dramatically home through the gruesome battle scenes and emotional turmoil depicted in Steven Spielberg's film *Saving Private Ryan.*

Encourage volunteer work. Signing up to work in a child care or elder care facility will teach your son empathy for others.

Teach anger management. Try a six-step program launched in New Haven, Connecticut, which accomplished an 11 percent decrease in fights in public schools:

1. Stop, calm down, think
2. Say what the problem is and how you feel
3. Set a positive goal
4. Devise solutions
5. Think ahead to consequences
6. Try the best plan

GANGS—VIOLENT GATHERINGS

Young adolescents opt for the gang life for many reasons, as you've read in Chapter Two on friends. What we didn't discuss there was the gang life's link to violence. Most gangs deal drugs, and young people quickly discover that dealing is a fast, easy way to make lots of money. Unfortunately, too many young people also get hooked on drugs or shot in drug battles. Unless they join a gang, some youngsters risk getting beaten up every day. It takes a strong middler, with lots of adult support, to resist.

Gangs are no longer just for boys, either. Increasingly girls, under intense pressure to be popular and sexy, are choosing gangs. There are more than 9,000 girls in gangs, law enforcement officials say. Gang membership may be to blame for the 103 percent increase in the last decade in the number of girls under eighteen arrested and charged with violent crimes.

Soon, however, girls discover that they may have left an abusive home life behind only to enter a life where they are abused by the male gang members. In *Finding Our Way,* Allison Abner and Linda Villarosa share the accounts of several female gang members who ended up either pregnant or shot. "Five days after we were shot, my boyfriend died," recounted one girl, who now steers clear of the gang life. "It cost my boyfriend's life and it almost cost mine."

Reading such accounts may help a middler reject gangs. As a parent, if you have concerns about your child and gangs, look into Gang Prevention Through Targeted Outreach, a national program first implemented in 1991 by the Boys & Girls Clubs of America, which connects local clubs with courts, police departments, schools, social service agencies, and other organizations in the community.

VIOLENCE AGAINST GIRLS—TARGETING OPHELIA

"My girlfriend is being bothered by an older boy at our school. I went to a dance with her and he had some guys watching us all night to make sure we didn't get too affectionate. He is stalking her inside and outside of school. She thinks she can handle him, but I'm afraid for her safety."
—Fifteen-year-old boy

Like Ophelia who pursued Hamlet, girls are becoming more aggressive in their pursuit of boys, often using phone calls, letters, e-mail, intermediaries, and personal appeals to nab a boyfriend. One young man, quoted in the magazine *Maclean's,* said that he often has sex with girls just to get rid of them.

However, these situations are not the norm. Increasingly girls are the quarry not the hunter and oftentimes encounters cross the line into harassment, abuse, and violence. In a survey by the American Association of University Women, four out of five young women in school—an astounding 81 percent—reported being sexually harassed. Twenty-five percent of those women reacted by no longer wanting to go to school or speak up in class, and 16 percent reported their grades dropped.

What is sexual harassment? It's any word or action sexual in nature that is unwelcome and makes the recipient feel embarrassed and degraded. Sexual harassment is less about sex and all about power. The harasser uses intimidation to put down another and make himself feel better. But because these comments or gestures are sexual in nature, a young woman on the receiving end winds up feeling self-conscious about her body. Many young women resort to wearing baggy clothes and avoiding public areas in schools—the playground, cafeteria—where they fear they may be targeted.

Parents need to define exactly what constitutes sexual harassment. Playing "how would you feel if . . ." will help boys understand the hurtful nature of sexual comments. Girls need to grasp that they have done nothing to invite the harassment and should be told how to respond:

Confront the offender. The girl should identify the comment as sexual harassment and tell the boy he will be reported to school authorities if he continues to bother her.

Make a record. Your daughter should write down the time, place, and comment made. Doing this in front of the boy will also bring home that she is serious about reporting him.

Seek out an adult. She should alert a teacher or guidance counselor about the harassment. If the harassment doesn't stop, you and your daughter should follow through. Many schools have procedures for filing a formal complaint.

Date Rape—A Night to Remember

According to the National Victim Center, over twelve million American women have been raped and the majority of them were between the ages of twelve and seventeen. Date or acquaintance rape, where the woman knows the man, accounts for more than two thirds of the sexual assaults reported by adolescent and college-age women.

Any adolescent girl who is in an abusive relationship, where the boyfriend is prone to explosions of anger and jealousy and treats her like his property, is in danger of experiencing date rape. "For a lot of boys, acting abusively toward women is regarded as a rite of passage. It's woven into our culture," said Bernard Lefkowitz, author of *Our Guys,* about a group of high school football players in Glen Ridge, New Jersey, who sexually assaulted a mentally retarded teenage girl with a bat and a stick in 1989.

Boys should understand that they never have the right to force a young woman to have sex. Parental conversations with young girls about sex need to stress the right to say no, loudly and forcefully if necessary. Your daughter should be cautioned about placing herself in situations where she would be unable to escape or seek help. Advise her against accepting a drink from a boy she doesn't know well or at all. Many rape victims are first drugged. She should also know that being with a boy who has been drinking or doing drugs places her at risk. One study of sixty-seven rape cases found that in forty-eight of those the rapist was under the influence of alcohol, marijuana, or both. A young man who, if sober, would heed a girl's refusal, might not if he is high.

VIOLENCE AGAINST GAYS AND LESBIANS— THE UNPROTECTED MINORITY

Between 33 percent and 49 percent of the harassment, threats, and physical violence are estimated to be aimed at students thought to be homosexual. In October 1998, public attention was focused on the plight of homosexuals in the schools when Matthew Shepard, a twenty-one-year-old college student, died after being tied to a fence in Wyoming and severely beaten.

In Wisconsin, a gay student sued his school district in federal court for failing to protect him from harassment—he had been regularly spat upon, subjected to a mock rape, repeatedly kicked in the stomach, urinated upon, and had had his head thrust in a urinal. He accepted a $900,000 settlement. His case brought to light a disquieting fact about the way some schools handle such gay-bashing. While the bully in question had been suspended for harassing his girlfriend, he was never punished for tormenting the gay student.

How schools deal with homosexuality depends a great deal on location. In some large cities that boast large, vocal gay populations, school districts have been responsive. In New York, Los Angeles, and Minneapolis–St. Paul, for example, school districts have counselors and support groups available for gay and lesbian students. New York and Los Angeles have gone even further and established all-gay public high schools as havens for homosexual students who have been tormented in mainstream schools. New York's Harvey Milk High School, named after a gay San Francisco councilman who was gunned down, has attracted widespread attention for its sensitivity toward this group of students.

Some states—Massachusetts was the first—have passed laws protecting the rights of homosexual students. After the Wisconsin decision, gay rights activists hope that other states will follow suit. Such action would be long overdue because many other areas of the country have been unresponsive to the difficulties encountered by gay students, refusing to offer protection and, in some cases, prohibiting gay support groups. Utah, in fact, has passed a law banning all gay student clubs.

In some school districts, teachers are forbidden to mention homosexuality in the classroom, even when discussing famous people who might be gay. What gets forgotten are the many gay and lesbian students in the school population who then have nowhere to turn. Bullies who are looking for convenient targets need look no further. Gay youths are two to three times more likely to attempt suicide than straight students. (Review Chapter Six for more on suicide and depression.)

What can you do if your son or daughter is gay or lesbian and is being harassed? Treat the situation as you would any other involving peer harassment. Why your child is being harassed isn't the issue. The problem is the harassment, and you should put school officials on notice that you want it stopped.

In the resource section, on page 282 we have listed four organizations where you can go for more help and information: the Hetrick-Martin Institute in New York; Parents, Families, and Friends of Lesbians and Gays in Washington, D.C.; Gay and Lesbian Parents Coalition International; and the Lambda Legal Defense and Education Fund.

PRIDE AND PREJUDICE—TEACHING RACIAL TOLERANCE

In our schools and neighborhoods, middlers who are racially different must often suffer the slings and arrows of their classmates. Those who have done research into bias crimes, like anti-Semitic graffiti and Black church burnings, agree on one fact: When a strong voice speaks up condemning such attitudes, others join in. Many middle schools around the country are using this strategy to shut down prejudice. Another method is to force children of different backgrounds to work together on a project. In this situation, conflicts are put aside in order to work for the common good.

Whether or not your child is a member of a minority group, there are some exercises you can do at home to increase her appreciation of different races:

Help your child to appreciate her culture. Language, food, clothing, and holiday celebrations, will give your child reasons to celebrate her heritage. Invite her friends to participate in a ritual and explain some of your family's traditions.

Look for common ground. Despite our different ethnic roots, most people are more alike than they are different. Help your child discover how her likes and dislikes coincide with those of her classmates.

Help your child understand the hurtful nature of prejudice. Many middle schools conduct exercises where children role play to understand what it would be like to be shunned because of eye color, for example. You can role play with your child at home, too.

Start a community response. If a bias crime occurs in your neighborhood, don't wait for another crime to follow. Contact community groups and work to educate and mobilize the residents against such prejudice.

HIGH NOON IN JUNIOR HIGH—READING, WRITING, AND RIFLES

In 1997, a Justice Department survey found that one household in three contained at least one firearm, more than 235 million. While some of these weapons are bought on the street, some, including the ones used in school shootings in Jonesboro, Springfield, and Paducah, came from the child's own home or the home of relatives.

Experts say that soldiers and police officers learn not only how to fire weapons, but also when to refrain from doing so. Yet most children learn about shooting through playing games—laser tag and paint-balling are two current favorites—so they think of guns as toys, not weapons.

Shoot 'em-up video games are another way children interact with guns. Consider the video game "Postal," a $45 video program from Ripcord Games that was reviewed in *Maxim* magazine: "Armed with shotguns, flame-throwers, and napalm, you mow down entertainingly innocent by-standers, ranging from church congregations to high school marching bands. Your maimed and dying victims beg for mercy or run around on fire, screaming for help; every so often a woman shrieks, 'He's going postal.' " The parallels between this game and the events in Jonesboro are chilling.

Calling a Truce

The right to bear arms is a harbinger of disaster to some but still sacred to others. Both of the youths in Jonesboro were reportedly taught to hunt by relatives and had access to guns. There are many young people, of course, who own hunting guns and observe proper safety procedures. But can any parent ever feel totally confident that a gun entrusted to a child won't be used carelessly or fall into the wrong hands? As adults, we need to ensure that the young people in our lives are protected from these arsenals in home and in school.

The Guns-Free Schools Act (GFSA) requires that each state receiving federal funds under the Elementary and Secondary Education Act (ESEA) must have a state law which requires local authorities to expel from school for at least one year any student found bringing a firearm to school. States are required to submit annual reports to the Secretary of Education. The law includes a provision for referring expelled students to alternative programs.

Schools around the country are trying various methods to keep guns out of schools. See-through book bags and eliminating lockers make it more difficult for students to conceal weapons. There is an emphasis on "telling is not tattling" to encourage students to report weapons. One school has a hotline that students can call to anonymously report weapons, as well as drug use, bullying, harassment, or other behavior associated with violence.

If you have guns in your home, here are some precautions to take:

Profiles in Violence

Can you spot the possible killer among your child's classmates? While experts say there is no definitive way of identifying potential shooters, a sample assessment tool for predicting violent juvenile behavior developed by the National School Safety Center at Pepperdine University provides some clues. Caution: These guidelines should just be used to detect whether there is a problem in the making, not for confronting the individual.

A "yes" answer for each category should be assigned five points. The total score determines a youth's predilection for violent behavior.

- Has a history of tantrums and uncontrolled outbursts.
- Characteristically resorts to name calling, cursing, or abusive language.
- Habitually makes violent threats when angry.
- Has brought a weapon to school.
- Has a background of serious disciplinary problems at school and in the community.
- Has a background of drug, alcohol, or other substance abuse or dependency.
- Is on the fringe of his peer group with few or no close friends.
- Is preoccupied with weapons, explosives, or other incendiary devices.
- Has previously been truant, suspended, or expelled from school.
- Displays cruelty to animals.

Make sure all guns are locked up. The keys should be kept in a safe place unknown to your children. A survey from the National Institute of Justice found that more than half of the guns in the U.S. are stored unlocked.

Keep guns separate from ammunition. More shocking: 16 percent of guns are both unlocked and loaded.

Discuss the guns with your children. Stress that the guns are off-limits.

Have discussions with other parents about guns. If your child spends time at other friends' homes, don't be shy asking whether the family keeps guns. Assure yourself that the guns are safely locked away. One

- Has little or no supervision and support from parents or a caring adult.
- Has witnessed or suffered abuse or neglect in the home.
- Bullies or intimidates peers or younger children.
- Tends to blame others for difficulties and problems he causes himself.
- Consistently prefers TV shows, movies, or music expressing violent themes and acts.
- Prefers reading materials dealing with violent themes, rituals, and abuse.
- Reflects anger, frustration, and the dark side of life in school essays or writing projects.
- Is involved with a gang or an antisocial group on the fringe of peer acceptance.
- Is often depressed and/or has significant mood swings.
- Has threatened or attempted suicide.

5–20 points: Youngster is potentially at risk for juvenile misbehavior.

25–50 points: Youngster is at risk and needs a significant amount of positive support, mentoring, role modeling, and skill building.

55 points and above: Youngster is a "ticking time bomb." The child and immediate family are at risk. Seek help from law enforcement, social and health services, or other youth-service professionals.

group organized in Connecticut by the mother of a child slain accidentally by a gun distributes bookmarks with this checklist for an adolescent sleepover: "Pajamas. Toothbrush. Clean socks . . . and most importantly! Are there any guns in the house?"

KEEPING YOUR CHILD SAFE AT SCHOOL

How tight is the security in your child's school? There should be a minimal number of campus entrance and exit options. Besides requiring visitor sign-in, many schools close their buildings during lunch when strangers may sneak in. Others control access to parking lots, gyms, and other buildings.

Of course, keeping out strangers wouldn't have helped in any of the recent school shootings, since the perpetrators were students. For that reason, many schools try to assure the safety of all students by conducting locker checks for weapons and drugs, employing security guards, and using metal detectors.

As a parent you should assure yourself that your child's school is safe. What should you do? Here is a checklist of some procedures implemented at many schools that you can inquire about:

Does the school have a system for recording and tracking crime?
When school administrators know the types of crimes being committed, they can devise appropriate programs to deal with them.

Is there an emergency communications center?
Ronald D. Stephens, executive director of the National School Safety Center, in Westlake, California, said a communications network should link classrooms and schoolyard supervisors with the front office or security staff, as well as with local law enforcement agencies and the fire department. Detention classrooms should have emergency buzzers or call buttons.

Have all posters been removed from windows?
There should be an unobstructed view out of and into each classroom and hallway.

Does the school require picture identification cards for students and staff?
Those without cards must then sign in and receive visitor passes.

Is a dress code enforced?
Whether or not your school requires uniforms, it should at least have a stated dress code and enforce it. Any clothing that could be construed as gang-related should be prohibited.

Is there a peer mediation program?
Offering students an opportunity to sit down and discuss their differences often can head off a violent confrontation.

Is safety a top priority among parents?

See that safety is on the agenda at the school's PTA meetings. Ask that a school administrator and a local law enforcement official come to address the gathering to answer all questions.

Do the children receive safety instructions?

Some schools sponsor safety days when local law enforcement officials come in to talk about keeping safe on the street. See if your school has one scheduled and, if not, offer to help organize one.

Is there a mechanism for spotting troubled students?

While there is no sure way to predict those children who will be prone to violence, your child's school should educate its staff to single out children at risk and refer them for treatment.

Is there sufficient staff to counsel troubled students?

Obviously school budgets dictate how many guidance counselors are available, but oftentimes if enough parents voice their opinion about how funds should be spent, the administrators will respond.

Is there a way to track repeat offenders?

These students need to be closely monitored by experienced staff members.

KEEPING YOUR CHILD SAFE ON THE STREETS

Young adolescents, wrapped up in their own worlds, are often oblivious to the dangers that lurk around every street corner. Two middlers engaged in a lively conversation about what new CD to buy, or a lone middler blocking out with headphones ambient street noise that could signal an approaching stranger, make convenient targets.

While virtually all middlers have sat through classroom discussions about kidnapping and street crime, most don't believe it will ever happen to them. Assailants take advantage of their trusting nature.

Don't assume your child has absorbed the proper safety tips at school. Teach your child some "street smarts" so he can avoid becoming a target. Here are some things to remember:

Dress down. Many young adolescents, particularly boys, are mugged for their designer jackets, hats, backpacks, even shoes. Other times the robber, often another young person, will be after the victim's Walkman, portable CD player, or watch. If you know your son will be out without you, suggest that he wear low-key clothing and leave his electronic gadgets at home.

Know local safe havens. In some cities, certain stores or apartment buildings bear a designated "safe haven" sticker where children know they can go if they fear they are in danger. Point these places out to your child.

Recognize mall dangers. Young adolescents spend an inordinate amount of time in malls, so make sure your children know the danger. Since many of the restrooms are located down long, deserted corridors, advise your children never to go on their own. They should avoid stairwells, particularly those that have no surveillance cameras, and dark parking lots, where assailants may lurk behind cars or trees.

Report the crime. Your child may not have been the first victim targeted by the assailant. If the police can establish a pattern, they may catch him. Also, reporting the crime puts law enforcement officials on notice that the police presence in your neighborhood needs to be beefed up.

AFTER AN ATTACK—DEALING WITH THE TRAUMA

Whether an adolescent has actually been the victim or merely witnessed a violent crime, the emotional impact can be severe. The person may have trouble functioning normally, a condition referred to as post traumatic stress disorder (PTSD). Trauma, a major shock to the system, can last for months or years. Your child may:

> Withdraw from social activities.
> Avoid friends.
> Have difficulty sleeping.
> Lose her appetite.
> Be fearful of going out alone.
> Falter in school.
> Experience flashbacks, particularly when hearing about other attacks.

While only time can truly heal the wounds, that recovery time will be longer if your child attempts to get well on her own. It is critical that your young adolescent get professional help. Your child's physician can suggest a course of action. Often, talking about the event can be cathartic. There are many groups set up for victims of violence where they can share their fears, anger, and frustrations, and help each other to recover.

We live in a violent world and there is no conceivable way that we can protect our children all the time. Yet we can shelter them some of the time, monitoring their media intake, evaluating their friendships, preparing them to be on their own, and heading off some of the dangers that may come their way.

STRATEGIES: RESOLVING CONFLICTS PEACEFULLY

Parents and educators should teach middlers how to resolve conflicts in a nonviolent manner. One program now used in more than 350 schools across the country is the Manhattan-based Resolving Conflict Creatively Program (RCCP). Beginning in kindergarten, children are taught how to mediate their differences.

Many of the strategies used in the RCCP approach are ones you can employ at home with your young adolescent. Here are some suggestions:

Attach words to feelings. Middlers often don't know what they are feeling. Run through the list: "Are you angry, sad, hurt, confused, disappointed . . . ?" Once your child can name his emotions, he will be one step closer to dealing with them.

Identify angry feelings. Physical changes—rapid breathing, flushed skin—often precede an angry outburst. If your child can learn to recognize these changes, he can be better prepared to control his anger.

Employ "build-ups," rather than "put-downs." Negative statements make people feel bad and can lead to anger. Count put-downs on TV sitcoms. Help your adolescent understand the detrimental effects of a put-down and encourage him to bolster friends with positive statements.

Explore the causes of anger. A rude bank clerk triggers anger in some adults. Help your child uncover what sets him off. Then he can learn to avoid these situations or manage his anger better.

Notice what triggers anger in others. If your child makes some of his friends angry, and therefore becomes a target for their feelings, help him to identify what he does wrong so he can break this pattern.

Write in journals. Buy your daughter a journal and have her write down how she is feeling when something positive or negative occurs. In some classrooms, the teachers have children exchange these journals so they can share their feelings.

CHAPTER ELEVEN

When Your Child Breaks the Law

*

"I found two very expensive coats hanging in my daughter's closet. When I asked her where she got them, she told me she bought them off a girlfriend who shoplifted them from a store at the mall. I think my daughter took them herself. What should I do?"
—Mother of a fourteen-year-old

For most parents, the idea that their child could be arrested and charged with a crime seems unthinkable. Yet a juvenile crime wave is washing over the country, and law enforcement agencies are coming down hard on these youthful offenders.

Between 1988 and 1994, the numbers of juveniles arrested for violent crimes—murder, forcible rape, robbery, and aggravated assault—increased more than 60 percent. From 1994 through 1997, those arrest rates declined, but still remain 25 percent above the 1988 level. "We cannot relax. These rates are still far too high," U.S. Attorney General Janet Reno has said. An expected increase in the number of juveniles over the next fifteen years may mean that juvenile arrests will reach a new peak, she added.

According to the Justice Department's Office of Juvenile Justice and Delinquency Prevention (OJJDP), in 1997:

- Juveniles were arrested for 12 percent of all violent crimes—8 percent of murders, 12 percent of forcible rapes, 17 percent of robberies, and 12 percent of aggravated assaults.
- After more than a decade of stability, the juvenile arrest rate

for drug abuse violations increased more than 70 percent between 1993 and 1997.

- The numbers of juveniles arrested for curfew violations nearly doubled between 1993 and 1996, before falling slightly in 1997.

One disquieting fact is that the offenders under age fifteen represent the leading edge of the juvenile crime problem, according to OJJDP. Between 1980 and 1995, crime arrests for youths under age fifteen increased 94 percent, compared with 47 percent for older youth.

In this chapter we will look at the many ways that young adolescents can run afoul of the law. While the headlines focus on the heinous crimes, many more young juveniles are being caught committing smaller, petty offenses that may derail schooling and become a permanent blotch on records. How does a parent handle the situation to protect a child's rights? What steps should parents take to ensure that their son or daughter understands the gravity of the situation and will not be a repeat offender?

What crimes do middlers commit? The list is long and varied. Many of these crimes are nothing new where young adolescents are concerned—shoplifting, vandalism, underage drinking, fare evasion, loitering, curfew violation. Others are more serious and newer territory for an age group so young—drug possession, robbery, assault, rape, computer hacking, and murder.

What fills many parents with terror is that these juvenile criminals often look like the boy or girl next door. "Could my child be next?" many parents wonder. Two fifteen-year-olds, after a night of drugging and drinking, allegedly killed a forty-four-year-old real estate salesman and attempted to gut and sink his body in a Central Park lake in New York. These children were described as being from "good" families. But coming out of a nurturing environment no longer guarantees that a young person won't break the law. What factors are responsible for this moral vacuum that seems to be sucking in today's youth? We will give food for thought along with tactics you can use to weave values into your parental safety net.

HIGH JINX, HIGH RISK

Six mothers gathered in a circle on a cold February morning to discuss issues facing their children. The usual topics were covered—dating, smoking, homework. But then one mother made a confession: Her son, standing outside a house on the New Jersey shore where a party was going on, had been arrested and charged with underage drinking. She cried talking about how humiliating it was to be summoned to a police station in the middle of the night and find her son in handcuffs. Soon, two other mothers empathized. Their sons had been arrested, too, one for evading the fare on a New York City subway, the other for shoplifting.

These three offenses—underage drinking, fare evasion, and shoplifting—are common where young people are concerned. What parent among us can't remember committing one of these infractions, palming a pack of gum at the local candy store, sneaking onto a bus through the back door, or passing around a can of beer behind a neighbor's garage? Why did we do it? Youthful bravado, being goaded on by friends, the thrill of committing an illicit act and getting away with it. For most of us it was a one-time occurrence. "When I was ten my mother dragged me back to the grocery store to return a candy bar I had taken and apologize to the owner," one father recalled. "Boy! I never did that again!"

Fast-forward to present times. Most small, privately owned businesses are gone, replaced with chain stores filled with surveillance cameras, impersonal sales help, and large signs that proclaim, "We prosecute shoplifters." In this new environment, if your son "lifts" some candy, he will receive more than a slap on the wrist. And many parents, if they discover their child has shoplifted, will be afraid to take him back to the store to return the item for fear he will be charged.

Law enforcement officials have a different point of view, too. "I remember being at a party where everyone was drinking," said one mother. "We were all underage and the host's parents weren't home. Someone called the cops and we were all taken down to the police station. It was a small town and the cop knew all our names. He called our parents to come pick us up. We were never charged with anything. That would never happen today and I'm constantly warning my two sons to be careful."

Juvenile justice used to focus on rehabilitation. Now, punishment is the order of the day. How has the public's heart been hardened to youthful offenders? Jonesboro, Paducah, Springfield. Everyday towns where children as young as eleven killed without apparent guilt or remorse. No one could accept that these juveniles, no matter how young, couldn't have understood the gravity of their crimes. Even if it were possible to rehabilitate these young adolescents, many who watched televised recaps of the carnage rejected that alternative. And the justice system responded. Some states tightened up laws governing juveniles, decreeing that those who committed a serious crime would be charged as adults and would do serious time.

Against this backdrop, youthful offenders who commit less onerous offenses, like underage drinking, drug possession, or curfew violations, find themselves caught in a backlash. Viewing them as "criminals in the making," the law is coming down hard on these middlers. Justice is blind to their age and their naiveté. And many times bystanders, young people who may have been with the perpetrators but innocent of committing the crime, are hauled in and charged, too. So now, more than ever before, your children's friends matter.

Parental responsibility is a growing issue. There have been instances where parents have been held accountable for the actions of their children. An injured party may sue the parents and recover damages. And, in some cases, parents can be held criminally liable and actually charged for the crimes of their child.

YOUTHFUL CRIMES AND MISDEMEANORS

"How do I get my twelve-year-old son to stop taking things that aren't his— STEALING?"
   —Concerned mother

You've probably heard many crime-related terms tossed about in the movies or on TV shows. But to clear up any confusion, let's review the various types of crimes, particularly with regard to how they relate to juveniles:

- Felonies, the most serious crimes, include murder, assault, rape, burglary, kidnapping, and other violent acts. If convicted, a person is looking to serve jail time. A juvenile convicted of a felony would rarely serve as much time as an adult. The death penalty for juveniles is prohibited in some states, although there have been cases where someone who was convicted and sentenced while a juvenile was later executed after turning twenty-one.
- Misdemeanors are less serious and include acts such as

shoplifting, trespassing, drug use, and disorderly
conduct. While a light jail sentence may result, in most
cases, a person convicted of a misdemeanor will wind up on
probation or may have to perform some community
service.

- Infractions, or petty offenses, another step down the seriousness
ladder, include things like underage smoking, seat belt violations,
or littering. Punishment usually means being fined.

- Status offenses include actions that would not be a violation if
committed by an adult. This category includes juvenile-
oriented crimes like running away, curfew violation, possession
of alcohol or tobacco, and truancy.

Another way to think about juvenile crime is to group these actions
into three groups: crimes against persons (the most serious, usually
felonies), crimes against property (less serious, most often misdemeanors),
and crimes middlers commit against themselves (serious for your child because these offenses may cause him physical injury). For the purposes of
our discussion here, we will start with the least critical crimes and work
our way up. We would like to educate you about the nature of these
crimes, and analyze why middlers commit these acts. Later on, we will
give some advice for coping with the aftermath, including getting help for
your child and protecting his legal rights.

Young adolescents make mistakes. Breaking the law and being arrested
is—no doubt about it—a big mistake. The news should serve as a wake-up
call that your child has somehow gotten off track. But it doesn't necessarily
mean that he is destined for a life of crime. Yes, you have a right to be upset
and to dole out appropriate punishments (in addition to the ones that will
be handed out by the system). But keep yourself focused on the long view.
This, too, will pass. And you may all come out of it wiser and stronger.

Crimes Against Themselves

Most crimes middlers commit against themselves are acts of rebellion. Frequently, but not always, the child may be attempting to escape
an unhappy home life where she is being mistreated, abused, or neglected. Unfortunately, a middler soon discovers that she has only made
her situation worse. These offenses include:

STOP YOUR MIDDLER FROM CHEATING

"I found out that my fifteen-year-old son downloaded a term paper from the Internet. Worse yet, when I confronted him, he didn't think he had done anything wrong. 'Everyone cheats,' was his explanation. Is he right? How can I get through to him?"
—Concerned mother

"Everyone cheats" may be an overstatement but, unfortunately, not by much. Cheating, on the rise by students from the middle grades on through graduate school, is oftentimes the first evidence of breaking the rules.

- *Who's Who Among America's High School Students* surveyed 3,210 A and B-plus high school students and not only found that the majority of them had cheated, but also that cheating "didn't seem like a big deal."
- Another report from Rutgers University found that 75 percent of business school students cheat.

Why do students, of all ages, cheat? Not to be bad, but to be good. When parents pressure their children to bring home good grades, children somehow believe they must succeed at all costs. Even if success involves cheating.

Around age thirteen, children develop conscience. So now is an excellent time to talk to your middler about cheating:

Get specific. Why is cheating bad? Stealing from others short-circuits the learning process. If your child cheats to get a good grade in math, how will he sustain that effort if he hasn't truly learned the material?

Downplay perfection. Place the stress on performance rather than grades. Rather than ask, "What was your grade?" ask "Did you feel well prepared for the test?"

Consider your child's feelings. She is bound to be frustrated when other children who are cheating are bringing home better grades. Role play with her to help her deal with those feelings. Help her to devise strategies for refusing to allow others to borrow homework or copy off her test paper.

Running away. More than one million children run away from home each year. An estimated 300,000 more are homeless. (Some children actually become "throw-aways," kicked out of their homes by a parent or other relative.) In our survey of middlers across the country, 28 percent said they had considered running away. A runaway can be taken into police custody. But many young adolescents who leave home are never apprehended, and instead fall into a life on the street that can include prostitution, drug use and dealing, shoplifting, and other crimes.

Adults should take seriously a child's threat to run away. "My friend's 13-year-old stepdaughter is threatening to run away. Should she do something?" one woman asked on a message board in cyberspace. Immediate intervention may head off the problem. Getting the child into counseling or having the family enter therapy together may show the young adolescent that there are alternatives.

If your child does run away, the first forty-eight hours after her disappearance are critical. As soon as you are certain she is gone, get on the phone and contact anyone who may know where she has gone. Contact the police and provide them with as much information as possible—photographs, fingerprints, dental records, what she was wearing when she left, names of friends and relatives she may seek out for help, and places she is known to frequent.

While TV police dramas have led us to believe that a person must be missing for twenty-four hours before he can be reported missing, no such time frame exists for minors. Ask that the police enter your child's name and description into the National Crime Information Center (NCIC) computer, which will make the data available nationwide.

You can also call the National Runaway Switchboard, a toll-free number (see resources, page 283) where runaways and their parents can leave messages for each other. Check also if there are local runaway hotlines in your area.

Truancy. Ten- to fifteen-year-olds are required to attend school, with the number of school days varying by state. Many states allow children to drop out of school by age sixteen, although the trend is to increase the age for compulsory education to eighteen, a reflection that in today's world, young people need at least a high school diploma in order to find employment.

Truancy, the failure to attend school without being excused, can land a middler and his parents in trouble. Many state legislatures, in fact, have passed laws holding parents accountable when their children don't show up for class. Parents have been fined, and, in some cases, even jailed.

Aside from continuing your child's education, staying in school is important because it helps to keep your child focused and on track. When a child skips school, he is often on the streets, getting into trouble. "My fourteen-year-old son was recently caught skipping school for two days with several girls and one other boy," lamented one mother. "He went outside and shot a neighbor's son in the foot with a B-B gun. The police have been at my house twice in one week. I'm considering military school!" Any indication that your child is ducking out on school should be dealt with seriously and swiftly. Truancy is a reflection of problems and a harbinger of even more thorny issues to come.

If your child is found to be truant, he will be taken into police custody and brought into juvenile court. What happens next will depend on why your child has been missing school. If drug use is suspected, your child could be required to enter a treatment program. In the event that learning disabilities have left your child feeling frustrated, the court may suggest testing and extra help.

Curfew violations. In an effort to curb juvenile crime and gang violence, many states, cities, and local municipalities have enacted curfews, a set time when children under a certain age need to be off the streets. The ages of the children and the curfews differ from place to place. Many of these restrictions have been challenged in court as a violation of the First Amendment guarantee to free association. Most of the rules have been upheld. Before setting a curfew for your own child, check what your local law permits.

A child who violates curfew may be given a ticket or a warning by a police officer. In some jurisdictions, parents are being held liable, fined, and even jailed, when their child repeatedly ignores these time constraints.

Possession or use of alcohol or tobacco. The number of middlers drinking alcohol and smoking cigarettes is skyrocketing, as you learned in Chapter Five. In an effort to curb this usage, local governments are getting tougher with young people caught possessing or using these substances. Because drinking and smoking are legal for adults, when juveniles are caught using, these acts are considered status offenses.

The legal drinking age in all states is now twenty-one. Someone who is underage and caught drinking will be taken into custody and is headed for the juvenile court. In most cases, the middler will be put on probation or be required to perform community service. He may also be required to seek treatment.

In most states, a person must be eighteen to smoke. How your child will be dealt with if caught smoking depends very much on local laws. Some areas will let the child off with a fine, while others will deal with the youth in juvenile court. So you should educate yourself on your local laws.

Using a fake ID. In order to be served in a bar or club or purchase alcoholic beverages, a young adolescent must show proof that he is twenty-one years old. Entrepreneurs peddling fake identification cards are everywhere. Young people soon learn through the grapevine where they can purchase fake IDs.

A middler caught using a fake ID will be charged with either a misdemeanor or an offense. Claiming that the ID is real when caught by the police could earn an additional charge of false reporting.

Possession or use of drugs. Because drugs are illegal whether used by a minor or an adult, these transgressions are dealt with more critically. How critically may depend on how large a quantity of drugs was found in your child's possession at the time he was apprehended, as well as the type of drug he was carrying. Possessing a small amount of marijuana, for example, would probably be treated as a misdemeanor. On the other hand, possessing a large quantity of a harder drug like cocaine or heroin would cause the juvenile court to deal more severely with your child.

Dealing drugs. Many middlers do not understand the gravity of giving drugs to their friends. Some jurisdictions have passed laws making it a felony to provide drugs to a minor under fourteen years of age. Young adolescents may regard giving drugs in the same way as trading baseball cards or used video games. But if your child is caught, he will be in a very difficult position. He may have to serve time in a juvenile detention facility.

Gambling. It is unlawful for anyone under eighteen to gamble. Yet with casinos in twenty-six states and lotteries in thirty-eight, many young adolescents are growing up being exposed to gambling. Dr. Howard Shaffer, a professor of psychology at Harvard University, in a nationwide study of gambling addiction found that the rate of problem gambling among adolescents was 9.4 percent, more than twice the 3.8 percent rate for adults. "Young people are growing up having lived their entire lives in a social environment where gambling is promoted and socially accepted," he said. According to the Council on Compulsive Gambling of New Jersey, most who become pathological gamblers with more severe problems began gambling before they were fourteen.

Laura Letson, executive director of the New York Council on Problem Gambling, said: "According to national surveys on gambling practices, one-third of high school and college students indicated they had gambled before the age of eleven. Eighty percent had placed bets by age fifteen."

In most areas, juveniles caught gambling are fined. In other areas, they may have to undergo treatment. The signs that a juvenile is on the way to becoming a compulsive gambler include:

- preoccupation with gambling
- gambling larger amounts
- restlessness when not gambling
- missing school

A susceptible middler can find himself obsessed with game-playing; embroiled in scheming, lying, and even stealing to get more cash to bet; and ultimately contemplating suicide to end a gambling cycle gone out of control.

If you discover that your child is gambling, don't wait for him to be arrested. Talk with him first to ascertain the frequency of his gambling. If you fear he may be compulsive, seek help.

Crimes Against Property
A middler who steals or damages property, accidentally or intentionally, will probably be forced to make restitution. Depending upon whose property was involved and the extent of the damages, punishment could range from a stern warning to time in a juvenile detention facility.

Stealing. In 1997, more than 250,000 juveniles under age fifteen were arrested for burglary and larceny. Young adolescents often steal from those nearby in the neighborhood or their own house. "My fourteen-year-old son has started taking money from my boyfriend's wallet," one mother complained on a message board online. Another remarked: "I had $100 hidden under my bed and I know my thirteen-year-old son took it." One parent found a new TV set in her son's room and notified her neighbor who had reported one stolen. What she didn't anticipate was that her neighbor would call the police and that her son would end up being charged with burglary. While stealing is considered a serious offense, a young adolescent who has never been in trouble before would probably be treated with leniency the first time around and be placed on probation. Parents should be put on guard, however, and seek help immediately for their child whose stealing may be a symptom of drug use, gang involvement, or other antisocial activities.

Shoplifting. About 25 percent of those caught shoplifting are juveniles, according to Shoplifters Alternative, a nonprofit education organization. Young adolescents, like adults, often shoplift when they are stressed or angry. Getting away with the crime produces an adrenaline high that can be addictive, much like drinking or using drugs. That may be why those who shoplift once will often do it again. In fact, 33 percent of juveniles say that it is hard for them to stop shoplifting, even after getting caught.

If your child is caught shoplifting, she will probably be prosecuted and be required to undergo counseling. While this punishment would be imposed by the juvenile court, you would be wise to make sure the counseling is effective. After a second offense, your daughter most likely would be placed on probation. A third offense might bring her time in a detention facility.

Shoplifters Anonymous has developed Youth Educational Shoplifting (Y.E.S.), a home study and classroom program for young people caught shoplifting. The program's goal is to show the youthful shoplifter why she committed the act, explain how shoplifting hurts others, and help her to handle the feelings that lead to the crime. (See resources for more information.)

Vandalism. Damaging property intentionally is called vandalism and can bring severe penalties to young people who are caught. Graffiti would be considered vandalism. States where graffiti is a particular problem—California, New York, Texas, Florida—have dealt with youthful offenders harshly, often imposing heavy fines and jail time for repeat violations.

Some vandalism falls into the category of hate crimes, and in these instances the perpetrators, because of community pressure, rarely escape with a slap on the wrist. In 1998, a sixteen-year-old and a fourteen-year-old from Long Island who poured gasoline in the shape of a swastika on a ball field and set it on fire were taken into police custody. The older boy risked a year in jail while the younger one spent time in a detention facility.

Why do middlers commit such acts? Sometimes vandalism occurs when youthful exuberance goes awry. Many young people who deface property with graffiti go about the task methodically, selecting their signatures with care and boasting about where they have signed their names.

In some cases, young adolescents are bored, angry, or depressed. As with so many other disorders that crop up in adolescence, vandalism is not the disease, but the symptom. "My twelve-year-old son was brought home by the police for breaking into a junkyard and breaking a lot of car windows," one mother said. "The owners are not going to press charges. But this is the second time for something like this. I don't know what to do with him." If your child has committed an act of vandalism, don't depend on the juvenile system to send him for counseling. Arrange for it yourself.

Computer crimes. As you learned in Chapter Eight, computers and the Internet loom as an exciting new frontier for young adolescents. But there are also many ways for middlers to get into trouble. In March 1998, a Massachusetts teenager became the first juvenile to be prosecuted under federal antihacking laws when he pleaded guilty to charges of disabling airport radios and other computerized equipment. Since then, there has been a spate of other computer-related crimes committed by young adolescents.

These middlers might have committed crimes anyway if the Internet didn't exist. Others, however, get caught up in the excitement of being able to beat the system. They don't think they will get caught. Because the Internet is so visible, and because so many adults (law enforcement officials included) are fearful of this new technology, parents need to caution their children about the dangers. One middle schooler in Texas invented what he thought was a humorous web page about Chihuahuas. Unfortunately, dog breeders were not amused. The student was suspended and ordered to remove the site.

Arson. In 1997, an estimated 10,000 juveniles were arrested for arson, the act of intentionally setting a fire that causes property damage. Most children are fascinated with fire, and many cause fires accidentally. But young adolescents who develop a pattern of fire starting may have darker intentions. A middler who is taken into custody after setting a fire would probably receive a psychological evaluation. Depending on his record and the circumstances surrounding the most recent fire, he may serve time in a juvenile detention facility. In any case, he and his parents could be held liable and may be forced to pay all or part of the damages.

Crimes Against Individuals

Violent crimes, where people are seriously injured or killed, are the crimes that make the headlines. In the past few years, it seems that a disproportionate number of news stories have featured young adolescents. In fact, between 1993 and 1997, juvenile arrests for murder declined 39 percent, while arrests for forcible rape dropped 16 percent.

Assault. When a young adolescent attempts or threatens to harm someone, even if he doesn't touch the other person, he may be charged with assault. Because parents and school officials are so focused on school safety, a middler who makes threats, even in jest, may land himself in legal hot water. A playground skirmish that in the past may have been laid to rest with a handshake, now may find its way into court, the instigator finding himself charged with a serious crime. Now, more than ever, it is important for us to teach our children nonviolent ways to settle their peer disputes (look back to Chapter Ten).

Aggravated assault, a notch up the ladder, means that the perpetrator intended or threatened serious bodily harm to the victim. For example, three Illinois twelve-year-olds who put laxatives into their teachers' coffee and soda were arrested and charged with aggravated assault. They had to serve fifteen days in a juvenile jail, ninety days of home detention, and two years of probation. Aggravated assault with a deadly and dangerous weapon might mean the youth pointed a gun at someone. Whenever a weapon is involved, the crime is considered more serious and may bring time in a juvenile facility.

Rape. According to the Justice Department, more than 2,000 juveniles under fifteen were arrested in 1997 for forcible rape. Date rape occurs when two people know each other but one is forced into sexual relations (for more on date rape, look back to Chapter Ten). Even if two people consent to have sex, it may be considered rape when one person is underage as defined by state law. That act would be considered statutory rape, a felony. Aggravated rape, which involves the use of a weapon, is considered even more serious and would call for stricter penalties. Parents need to talk with both their sons and daughters about the dangers involved. A boy needs to understand that a girl has the right to say no, but that even when she says yes, if she is underage, he could get into trouble.

Homicide. The recent rash of school shootings has focused attention on young adolescents who kill. Experts blame these and other violent deaths involving juveniles on the proliferation of guns. According to the Children's Defense Fund, from 1983 to 1995, gun homicides by juveniles tripled, whereas nongun homicides declined.

Children who kill present juvenile justice with its most controversial issue. The prevailing wisdom is that children under fifteen are too young to be considered beyond rescue. That goal—to rehabilitate rather than punish—is at the heart of how young adolescents are treated when they break the law. Yet when middlers kill their parents, other adults, their classmates, or newborns, the victims are gone, beyond any hope of being saved. Why then, critics wonder, should we work to save the killers?

Right now an attitude of punishment, if not all-out retribution, is governing how young killers are being treated by the public, media, law enforcement officials, and the courts. For the young who kill, they will be facing tougher treatment that many hope will help to deter future killers.

In Jonesboro, the two shooters, one age thirteen and the other eleven, will be housed in a juvenile detention facility until they are eighteen, although the governor has declared that he will build a special facility to house the boys until they turn twenty-one. But after the sentencing was read, relatives of the victims received little solace. Their loved ones are still gone, their lives will forever be changed, and they still don't understand what could have driven two young boys to kill.

PROTECTING YOUR CHILD'S RIGHTS

For most parents, dealing with the juvenile justice system may be a first encounter with the law. It is bound to be a shocker. "I picked up the phone and a police officer said he was with narcotics and had my son in custody," recalled one mother. "I was shaking so hard I had to pass the phone to my husband. My son? In jail? I was devastated."

You want to make sure that your child's rights are protected every step along the way. State and local laws concerning juvenile crime vary, so you should always check to see what rules apply in your area. Here are answers to some commonly asked questions:

Should I hire a lawyer?

For status offenses and even some misdemeanors, you may be told your child doesn't need a lawyer. One mother, whose son was arrested for possession of marijuana, hired a lawyer to represent her child for his meeting with a probation officer. "We were told by the probation officer that we didn't need a lawyer," the mother said. "We decided to have him with us anyway. I was glad we did. Our lawyer was able to explain to us what was happening at every step along the way. I felt he was there for us while the probation officer was just doing her job. She didn't have my son's best interests at heart."

Certainly, if your child is being charged with a felony or a more serious misdemeanor, you should hire a lawyer immediately, particularly one who is knowledgeable in juvenile crime.

Does a juvenile have the same rights as an adult?

Many of the rights granted to adults also hold for juveniles. For example, juveniles are protected against unreasonable searches and seizures, self-incrimination (juveniles before being questioned should receive the Miranda warning, advising them that anything they say can be used against them), and the right to counsel. The courts have been known to examine situations where a juvenile has waived his constitutional rights, the theory being that a young person often doesn't fully grasp the seriousness of his situation and the importance of consulting a lawyer before talking.

How will I find out what my child has been charged with?

Shortly after your child's arrest, you must be provided with a written notice detailing the charges against him. Make sure that the charges are described fully and in correct terms.

How long will my child be detained before I can take him home?

The police have great latitude concerning how long a juvenile may be held in custody. A young person can be released almost immediately into the custody of his parents. If the police believe the child should be held, then a juvenile probation officer would probably be called upon to make that decision.

Will my child have to spend time in jail?

In most cases, juveniles are sent to juvenile detention centers. Most states comply with the Juvenile Justice and Delinquency Prevention Act, which requires children to be removed from adult jails. Juveniles housed in adult prisons are eight times more likely to commit suicide, five times more likely to be physically assaulted by other inmates, two times more likely to be assaulted by staff, and 50 percent more likely to be attacked with a weapon, according to the Children's Defense Fund.

There is concern, however, that juveniles are being detained improperly and for long periods of time before they go to trial. In July 1998, New York officials were criticized for housing minors, ages ten to sixteen, on a barge designed for adult inmates. The young offenders were placed in detention, officials said, because judges feared they would either disappear or commit new crimes if released.

Will my son have a trial?
That depends on his crime. If he is being charged with a status offense or even a misdemeanor, the matter may be dispensed with after a hearing before a probation officer. In these cases, your child would probably have to perform some sort of community service or enter a treatment program if drugs are the problem. He may be placed on probation for a set amount of time and have to report to his probation officer. Because the focus is on helping the juvenile get back on track, the probation officer would want assurances that the child has not gotten into any further trouble and has been attending school. She might request school attendance records.

Juveniles, like adults, have a constitutional right to a speedy trial. Depending upon the state and the circumstances, that time limit could be anywhere from fifteen to sixty days.

Will my son be tried in a juvenile court or an adult one?
Most likely in a juvenile one. But in some cases, the juvenile court could waive jurisdiction and transfer the case to an adult court. "In the last decade, states have increasingly resorted to this option in the face of rising public outrage at violent youthful offenders who seem beyond rehabilitation and very much in the need of punishment," said Deborah L. Forman, author of *Every Parent's Guide to the Law*.

Because juveniles usually receive lesser penalties in adult court—fines and probation rather than imprisonment—there is an advantage to being tried in an adult court. However, the risk is that if the juvenile is convicted, he may have to spend time in an adult jail. Forman notes that for this reason, few juveniles seek to have their cases transferred to the adult court. Most states have laws that automatically transfer the more serious crimes to adult court. The two shooters in Jonesboro were tried in an adult court but sentenced to time in a state juvenile detention center.

Will my son's offense be a permanent blot on his record?
It doesn't have to be. One of the goals of juvenile justice is that the young person not end up with an adult criminal record. The law differs from state to state, but in most cases, if the child does not get into any further trouble with the law for one year following his being taken into custody, then the record of his arrest first would be sealed and then expunged, that is, removed from the record books. In the future, anyone doing a search of his background would not turn up the history of an arrest. However, if the child were to be taken into custody again, then it would be more difficult to keep the arrest from going down on his permanent record. Expungement in some states is not automatic. You may have to bring a motion seeking to have the records sealed or expunged. Certain violent crimes are excluded from this provision in some states, and the rehabilitation period may be longer than one year, in some cases as much as ten years.

Can I get into trouble if my child commits a crime?
Increasingly, law enforcement officials and the courts are coming down on the parents when their child commits an offense. A middle school math teacher on Long Island was arrested after his teenage son hosted a weekend beer party. Even though the teacher wasn't home at the time, he was charged with violating New York State's Alcohol Beverage Control Act, which prohibits people from permitting alcohol to be provided to or consumed by minors.

What if my child is out of control? Can I ask the authorities for help?
You can ask the court to declare your child a person in need of supervision, known by the acronym PINS. Once that determination is made, your child would be placed under the jurisdiction of the court.

STRATEGIES: VALUES START AT HOME

After the Jonesboro shootings, a *New York Times* editorial asked: "How is it that teenagers, living among adults and supposedly part of a school community, can become so alienated from life that they will shoot into a crowd?" The world our children are growing up in is not the world we remember. In Chapter One, we talked about how the sanctuary of the family has been disrupted by divorce, remarriage, and the complications of families struggling with mixed race, ethnicity, and sexual orientation. The African saying, "It takes a village to raise a child," has been touted as the best method for ensuring that children absorb community values. Yet in most areas today, that "village" doesn't exist. Extended families are far-flung. Working mothers and fathers can no longer depend upon grandmothers, grandfathers, or a favorite aunt to watch their children after school. Instead, latchkey children come home alone and learn values through their peers or by watching TV.

What about schools? Ideally, teachers should serve as "last chance adults," prepared to spot problem students, alert school administrators and parents, and follow through to make sure these students receive the help and support they need. But budget cuts have led to classroom overcrowding and increased responsibilities, leaving many teachers overworked and overwhelmed. In the Springfield, Oregon school where Kip Kinkle shot and killed four students and injured twenty-two others, after shooting and killing his parents in their home, there was one social worker responsible for more than 700 students. Is it any wonder that Kinkle fell through the cracks?

While young people who break the law, particularly those who commit violent crimes, are a minuscule and aberrant minority, their actions have exacerbated the public's negative perception of today's youth. Sixty-seven percent of Americans use words like "rude," "irresponsible," and "wild" to describe today's teenagers, according to a report from the nonprofit group Public Agenda. Youngsters' failure to learn basic values like honesty, respect, and responsibility, was targeted as the key to this moral vacuum.

The Carnegie Commission has noted: "Early adolescence presents a vital opportunity for shaping enduring patterns that can set a young person on a successful course for life." How do we "shape" an adolescent's behavior? Here are some ideas:

Deliver frequent and consistent messages about morals and values. We have to speak loudly because the opposing messages coming from cultural sources oftentimes threaten to drown us out. Tell your children what you believe in—honesty, kindness, nonviolence. Don't assume they know.

Give—and communicate—your unconditional love. These are tough times to be a kid. "We didn't have AIDS, crack, all these things kids are exposed to," said a New York woman in the Public Agenda survey. Let your middler know that you love him and will always be there for him.

Keep your home free of violence. Growing up in a home where there is abuse and violence is one of the major reasons adolescents turn into juvenile offenders. If you or your spouse resorts to violence to solve problems, seek out help.

Don't tolerate inactivity. The old adage about idle minds still holds true. The time between school and dinnertime is critical. Make sure your child is involved in worthwhile activities.

Set limits. The teachers who responded to our survey sounded warning bells. The majority (55 percent) said that parents were well-intentioned but too lenient with their children. That perception may be the reason 20 percent of the teachers said they were reluctant to approach parents about serious problems. "Teachers are just not listened to in these situations," said a teacher from Georgia.

Join an organized religion. In a survey of 1,000 students ages thirteen through seventeen, by the Horatio Alger Foundation, over one third said that religion was very important to them. Younger teens rated religion as more important than older teens did. Take that as a sign. Your middler would probably be receptive to attending some kind of religious service. Perhaps you once belonged to a church or synagogue and have dropped out. If you need some help finding your way back into your faith, find someone who can offer you some spiritual guidance.

Bring spirituality into your home. If you can't accept joining an organized religion, find a way to bring spirituality into your home. Even spending some time meditating or reading poetry may help your child to tap into his inner self.

Avoid becoming jaded. Sometimes it seems we are inundated with stories of people who break the rules and survive. If we are not careful, we can develop an attitude that expects and accepts these transgressions. Don't fall into that trap. Express your disapproval, even outrage, when you see wrongdoing. Your child is listening.

Monitor your child's friendships. They do matter. Use some of the tips we offer in Chapter Two to guide you.

Find heroes for your child. Clip out magazine articles about noteworthy people. Talk to your young adolescents about what qualities make a person worthy of admiration. Should celebrities be anointed just because they are famous?

Single out heroes closer to home. Do you have a sister who fought a local environmental battle and won? Or a relative who suffered a bout with cancer and did so with dignity and courage? How about someone closer to your young adolescent's age who did something to help others? Get into a discussion about what it took to wage these battles and what your child can learn from being with these individuals.

Be an involved "villager." You can be part of that village that helps to influence and guide other children. Sign up to be a Big Brother or Sister, tutor, or mentor. Deterring one child from a life of crime will benefit all of us, your children especially.

Epilogue

*

There is nothing worse for a parent than watching a young adolescent deliberately flirt with disaster or become embroiled in a crisis. Whether dabbling in drugs, wrestling with depression, throwing away an education, or becoming bewitched by a good-for-nothing girlfriend, parents in these cases, and others, find themselves standing on common ground. Each is standing on the edge of a riverbank watching helplessly as his or her middler navigates a dangerous white-water current. Will he ultimately sink or make it back to the shoreline?

In these pages, we provided you with strategies to empower you to safeguard, rescue, and endure the crisis situations that many young adolescents bumble into. Follow our guidelines. Don't give up on your child or yourself.

Our final goal is to deliver reassurance that things will not always be this hair-raising or disheartening. Remember the dad who innocently turned on his video camera and stumbled upon his daughter's own version of *sex, lies, and videotape*? Here's how he says things turned out:

"It wasn't easy dealing with my little girl on and off that videotape. Life was filled with emotions and tears, both hers and mine. But you know what? We are now better communicators and much closer because of all this. We love each other now and we have both *proved* it."

This father is only one example of many parents who have returned to let us know how their young adolescent melodramas ended.

A mother who learned her son was drug-running ketamine across the Canadian border recently wrote, "Things finally worked out with Johnnie, but I went through a lot over the last three years. He finally turned the corner in January. Johnnie has been diagnosed with ADD. We learned that was a factor in all of his problems, starting with school and ending with his being unconscious in a van in our driveway. He is doing so well now. Hurray!"

During the years between ten and fifteen, your child's once bright, shining, smiling face may turn into a sneering, sullen mask obscuring a darker side. The open and talkative child you once loved may morph into a fresh-mouthed, selfish rebel whom you don't find particularly lovable. As children grow they do become more complicated, bringing home reasons to make us proud and reasons to make us shudder.

In the finer moments, savor the experiences and appreciate your young adolescent. In the darkest moments, know deep down in your heart that things will turn around. Sometimes they will turn around because of your efforts and your unconditional love. Other times they will turn around because time has a way of taming even the wildest and most worrisome young adolescent.

Rest assured that these battle scenes and tragic cliffhangers in most cases will become your own private and personal cache of "Rescue 911" episodes, relegated to the family album stored in your memories. Have faith and hope, and keep love center stage. Life will not always be you and your young adolescent starring in a script aptly called Parenting 911.

Recommended Reading and Resources

INTRODUCTION: PARENTING THROUGH TOUGH TIMES

Suggested Reading

The Adversity Quotient: Turning Obstacles into Opportunities, Paul Stoltz, Ph.D., John Wiley and Sons, 1997

Celebrating Girls: Empowering and Nurturing Our Daughters, Virginia Beane Conari, Conari Press, 1996

Daughters Newsletter
1808 Ashwood Ave.
Nashville, TN 37212
(800) 829–1088
Covers a variety of issues (and resources) pertaining to girls' development from ages eight to eighteen.

A 1998–1999 Directory of American Youth Organizations: A Guide to 500 Clubs, Troops, Teams, Societies, Lodges, and More for Young People, Judith B. Erickson, Ph.D., Free Spirit Publishing, 1998
www.freespirit.com

Family Digest Magazine (for African American Family Life)
696 San Ramon Valley Blvd., Suite 349
Danville, CA 94526
E-mail: FamDigest@aol.com

The Nurture Assumption: Why Children Turn Out the Way They Do, Judith Rich Harris, Free Press, 1998

P.E.T. Parent Effectiveness Training, Dr. Thomas Gordon, Plume Penguin, 1970
The classic on which many parenting classes are based. It contains many clear, helpful strategies.

The Roller-Coaster Years: Raising Your Child Through the Magical Yet Maddening Middle School Years, Charlene C. Giannetti and Margaret Sagarese, Broadway Books, 1997

A Tribe Apart: A Journey into the Heart of American Adolescence, Patricia Hersch, Fawcett, 1998
A wake-up call showing how adolescents lead isolated lives with scant parental supervision and influence.

The Way We Never Were: American Families and the Nostalgia Trip, Stephanie Coontz, Basic Books, 1993

The Wonder of Boys: What Parents, Mentors and Educators Can Do to Shape Young Boys into Exceptional Men, Michael Gurian, Tarcher/Putnam, 1996

Suggested Reading for Middlers
Chicken Soup for the Teenage Soul, Chicken Soup for the Teenage Soul II, Jack Canfield, Mark Victor Hansen, and Kimberly Kirberger, Health Communications, Inc. 1998

My American Adventure, Amy Burritt, Zondervan Publishing House, HarperCollins, 1998
A twelve-year-old girl's coming of age story which is a journey covering fifty states in fifty weeks as she sets out to meet all of our governors.

Girltalk: All the Stuff Your Sister Never Told You, Carol Weston, HarperCollins, 1997

Living with a Work in Progress, Carol Godlberg Freeman, NMSA 1996
(800) 528–NMSA
This book is for parents but very amusing and readable for middlers.

What Teens Need to Succeed: Proven Practical Ways to Shape Your Own Future, Peter L. Benson, Ph.D., Judy Galbraith, M.A., and Pamela Espeland, Free Spirit Publishing, 1998
(800) 735–7323

Organizations, Hotlines, and Websites
Boys and Girls Clubs of America
1230 West Peachtree St., NW
Atlanta, GA 30309
(404) 815–5700

National Black Child Development Institute
463 Rhode Island Ave., NW
Washington, D.C. 20005
(202) 387–1281
(800) 556–2234

National Middle School Association (NMSA)
2600 Corporate Exchange Drive, Suite 370
Columbus, OH 43231-1672
(800) 528–NMSA

Pamphlets: *HELP: How to Enjoy Living with a Preadolescent* and *MORE Help: Getting Used to Differences*

Parents Anonymous (for child abuse prevention and family strengthening)
675 W. Foothill Blvd., Suite 200
Claremont, CA 91711-3475
(909) 621–6184

ivillage.com The Women's Network
www.raisingtodaysteens.org
www.positiveparenting.com

CHAPTER ONE: FAMILY LIFE WITH MIDDLERS

Suggested Reading
The Adoption Life Cycle: The Children and Their Families Through the Years, Elinor B. Rosenberg, The Free Press, 1992

Divorce Casualties: Protecting Your Children from Parental Alienation, Douglas Darnell, Taylor, 1998

Ethnicity and Family Therapy, Edited by Monica McGoldrich, Joe Giordano, and John Pearce, The Guilford Press, 1996
This is written more for professional counselors than parents, but filled with insight for those motivated enough to explore it.

Family Outing, Chastity Bono, Little Brown, 1998

Fathering Daughters: Reflections by Men, Edited by DeWitt Henry and James Alan McPherson, Beacon, 1998

Grandparenthood, Dr. Ruth Westheimer and Dr. Steven Kaplan, Routledge, 1998

Minority Families in the United States: A Multi-Cultural Perspective, edited by Ronald L. Taylor, Prentice Hall, 1998

The Nanas and the Papas: A Boomers' Guide to Grandparenting, Kathryn and Allan Zullo, Andrews McMeel, 1998

Of Many Colors: Portraits of Multiracial Families, Gigi Kaeser and Glenda Valentine, University of Massachusetts, 1997

Raising Adopted Children, Lois Ruskai Melina, HarperPerennial, 1998

The Seven Habits of Highly Effective Families, Stephen R. Covey, Golden Books, 1998
Features easy-to-understand ideas to improve your family's communication.

Stepfamilies: Love, Marriage, and Parenting in the First Decade, Dr. James Bray, Broadway Books, 1998
Indispensable "bible" for parents pondering remarriage or in the process of building a blended family.

Stylin: African American Expressive Culture from Its Beginnings to the Zoot Suit, Shane White and Graham White, Cornell University Press, 1998

Solo Dad Survival Guide: Raising Your Kids on Your Own, Reginald F. Davis and Nick Borns, Contemporary Books, 1998

The Way We Really Are: Coming to Terms with America's Changing Families, Stephanie Coontz, Basic Books, 1997
Helps parents to move away from outdated longings and get in touch with challenges for today's real families.

"What About the Children?" Sons and Daughters of Lesbian and Gay Parents Talk About Their Lives, Lisa Saffron, Cassell, 1996

Why Did You Have to Get a Divorce? And When Can I Get a Hamster?, Anthony E. Wolf, Noonday/FSG, 1998

Suggested Reading for Middlers
Bringing Up Parents: The Teenagers Handbook, Alex J. Packer, Ph.D., Free Spirit Publishing, 1992
(800) 735-7323

Coping as a Biracial/Biethnic Teen, Renea Nash, Rosen Group, 1995

Half & Half: Writers on Growing Up Biracial and Bicultural, Claudine C. O'Hearn, Random House, 1998

How It Feels to Be Adopted, Jill Krementz, Knopf, 1988
For ages ten and older. Order from AFA (Adoptive Families of America)
(800) 372-3300

Straight Talk About Death for Teenagers, Earl Grollman, Boston Beacon Press, 1993

When a Friend Dies: A Book for Teens About Grieving and Healing, Marilyn E. Gootman, Ed.D., Free Spirit Publishing, 1994
(800) 735-7323

Who Am I? . . . And other Questions of Adopted Kids, Charlene C. Giannetti, Price Stern Sloan, 1999

Young People and Chronic Illness: True Stories, Help, and Hope, Kelly Huegel, Free Spirit Publishing, 1998
(800) 735-7323
This book will strengthen and inspire younger middlers, ages nine to twelve, to deal with their illness.

Organizations, Hotlines, and Websites
Adoptive Families of America Inc.
2309 Como Ave.
St. Paul, MN 55108
(800) 372-3300 and (612) 645-9955
Publishes a bimonthly magazine called *Adoptive Families,* and offers a catalogue of books on all aspects of adoption for parents and children of all ages.

PFLAG (Parents, Families, and Friends of Lesbians and Gays)
1102 14th St., N.W., Suite 1030
Washington, D.C. 20005
(202) 638-4200 fax (202) 638-0243
E-mail: info@pflag.org
www.pflag.org

Parent Soup
http://parentsoup.com
or on AOL (keyword parentsoup)
Bulletin boards and chats for many types

of families, for example multicultural, gay and lesbian, stepfamilies, single parents, etc.

www.geocities.com/heartland/ranch/8207/sibling.html
Contains information on loss for children

CHAPTER TWO: FRIENDS, FRIENDSHIP, AND FALLING IN LOVE

Suggested Reading
Always Friends, Alda Ellis, Harvest House, 1997
This is an interesting read because it discusses historical figures' friendships such as Louisa May Alcott and Helen Keller.

Because We're Friends: 100 Things I Love About You, Patricia Coleman, Soho Press, 1997

Enjoy Your Middle Schooler: A Guide to the Physical, Social, Emotional, and Spiritual Changes of Your 11- to 14-Year-Old, Wayne Rice, Zondervan Publishing, 1994

Good Friends Are Hard to Find: Help Your Child Find, Make and Keep Friends, Fred Frankel, Ph.D., Free Spirit Publishing, 1998 (this book is based on the UCLA Children's Social Skills Program)

The Heart of Parenting: How to Raise an Emotionally Intelligent Child, John Gottman, Ph.D., Simon & Schuster, 1997

Love Is a Story: A New Theory of Relationships, Robert J. Sternberg, Oxford University Press, 1998

Talk with Teens—About feelings, family, relationships, and the future, Jean Sunde Peterson, Ph.D., Free Spirit Publishing, 1995

Suggested Reading for Middlers
Best Friends: Tons of Crazy, Cool Things to Do with Your Girlfriends, Lisa Albregts and Elizabeth Cape, Chicago Review Press, 1998

Cliques, Phonies & Other Baloney, Trevor Romain, Free Spirit Publishing, 1998 (800) 735-7323

Written for younger children, ages eight to eleven, this book prepares them well for the difficult social realities of middle school.

Girls Know Best 2, Marianne Monson-Burton, Beyond Words, 1998

P.S. Longer Letter Later, Paula Danziger and Ann Martin, Scholastic, 1998

Understanding Guys: A Guide for Teenage Girls, Michael Gurian, Price Stern Sloan, 1999
A thorough look into the world of the young adolescent boy that a young adolescent girl will find fascinating and useful.

Websites
Cybersisters
www.worldkids.net/clubs/CSIS/csis.html
G.I.R.L. www.worldkids.net/girl

CHAPTER THREE: SEXUAL ENCOUNTERS AND FATAL ATTRACTIONS

Suggested Reading
AIDS-Proofing Your Kids: A Step-by-Step Guide, Loren Acker, Bram Goldwater, and William Dyson, Beyond Words Publishing, Inc.
(503) 647–5109

The Big Talk: Talking to Your Child About Sex and Dating, Laurie Langford, John Wiley, 1998 (a former teen runaway shares what she wishes her parents had done)

Dating Violence: Young Women in Danger, Barrie Levy, Seal Press, 1998

Going All the Way: Teenage Girls' Tales of Sex, Romance and Pregnancy, Sharon Thompson, Hill and Wang, 1995
A fascinating read for parents that sheds light on adolescent girls' sexual behavior and the process of making sexual decisions.

Not Like Other Boys—Growing Up Gay: A Mother and Son Look Back, Marlene Fanta Shyer and Christopher Shyer, Houghton Mifflin, 1997

Cracking the Love Code: Six Proven Principles to Find and Keep Real Love with the Right Person, Janet O'Neal, Broadway Books, 1999

Now That You Know What Every Parent Should Know About Homosexuality, Betty Fairchild and Nancy Hayward, PFLAG paperback, 1989
(202) 638–4200

Parents Matter: Parents' Relationship with Lesbian Daughters and Gay Sons, Ann Muller, PFLAG paperback
(202) 638–4200

The Family Heart: A Memoir of When Our Son Came Out, Robb Forman Dew, PFLAG hardcover and audio, Fawcett Books, 1995
(202) 638–4200

Venus in Blue Jeans: Why Mothers and Daughters Need to Talk About Sex, Nathalie Bartle with Susan Lieberman, Houghton Mifflin, 1998

Suggested Reading for Middlers
The Amazing "True" Story of a Teenage Single Mom, Katherine Arnoldi, Hyperion, 1998 (autobiographical story in comics format)

Cool and Celibate? Sex or No Sex, David Bull, Elements paperback, 1998

Queer 13: Lesbian and Gay Writers Recall Seventh Grade, Edited by Clifford Chase, Weisbach/Morrow, 1998

Sex, Boys, & You: Be Your Own Best Girlfriend, Joni Arredia, Perc, 1998
This book is designed to help girls make healthy, sound decisions on the tough issues they face in today's social climate.

What's Going On Down There?: Answers to Questions Boys Find Hard to Ask, Karen Gravelle with Nick and Chava Castro, Walker, 1998

Organizations, Hotlines, and Websites
CDC National AIDS Clearinghouse
PO Box 6003
Rockville, MD 20849-6003
(800) 458–5231

AIDS Hotline
(800) 541–AIDS

SIDA Hotline
(AIDS Information in Spanish)
(800) 233–SIDA

The Alan Guttmacher Institute
120 Wall St.
New York, NY 10005
(212) 248–1111 fax (212) 248–1951
E-Mail: info@agi-usa.org
www.agi-usa.org
A not-for-profit corporation for reproductive health research and public education.

The American Red Cross HIV/AIDS
Teen Hotline
(800) 440–8336
www.redcross.org
Offers peer-to-peer HIV/AIDS education programs. Local offices can tell a teen how to become a peer counselor.

Gay, Lesbian, and Straight Education Network (GLSEN)
121 West 27th St., Suite 804
New York, NY 10001
www.glsen.org
National organization of parents, teachers, students, and concerned citizens who work to end homophobia in schools.

HIV Counseling Hotline
(800) 872–2777
Monday to Friday 4 P.M. to 8 P.M., Saturday and Sunday 10 A.M. to 6 P.M.

National Youth Advocacy Coalition
1711 Connecticut Ave., NW, Suite 206
Washington, D.C. 20009
(800) 96–YOUTH 5:30 P.M.–9:30 P.M. central time, daily peer counseling

The National Campaign to Prevent Pregnancy
2100 M St., NW, Suite 300
Washington, D.C. 20037
Not Just for Girls: The Role of Boys and Men in Teen Pregnancy Prevention is an excellent booklet.

Pen Pal Program—Youth Services
LA Gay and Lesbian Community Services Center
1625 North Schrader Blvd.
Los Angeles, CA 90028
Twenty-three and under, free newsletter.

PFLAG (Parents, Families, and Friends of Lesbians and Gays)
1102 14th St., NW, Suite 1030
Washington, D.C. 20005
(202) 638–4200 fax (202) 638–0243
E-mail: info@pflag.org
www.pflag.org
Many excellent pamphlets for parents and middlers, for instance, "Our Daughters and Sons: Questions and Answers for the Parents of Gay, Lesbian, and Bisexual People"; includes list of publications and organizations, $1.80. "Be Yourself: Questions and Answers for Gay, Lesbian, and Bisexual Youth" pamphlet, $1.70

Planned Parenthood Federation of America
www.igc.apc.org/ppfa/index.html
(800) 829–7732
Offers many booklets and programs to help teens postpone sex and deal with options.

Sexuality Information and Education Council of the United States
130 West 42nd St., Suite 350
New York, NY 10036-7802
(212) 819–9770   fax (212) 819–9776
www.seicus.org/parent/pare0000.html

CHAPTER FOUR: RISKING LIFE FOR THE PERFECT BODY

Suggested Reading
Appearance Obsession: Learning to Love the Way You Look, Joni Johnston, Health Communications, 1994

Bodily Harm: The Breakthrough Healing Program for Self-Injurers, Karen Conterio and Wendy Lader, Hyperion, 1998
Written by the directors of SAFE (Self-Abuse Finally Ends) Alternatives Program in Chicago.

The Body Project: An Intimate History of American Girls, Joan Jacobs Brumberg, Vintage, 1997

Drawing on diary excerpts and media images from 1830 to present times, historian Brumberg examines girls' attitudes toward their bodies.

Cutting: Understanding & Overcoming Self-Mutilation, Steven Levenkron, W.W. Norton, 1998
An exploration of "cutters," who they are and why they do it. Also includes a rundown of the available treatment programs.

The Right Moves: A Girl's Guide to Getting Fit and Feeling Good, Tina Schwager, Michele Schuerger, Elizabeth Verdick, and Mike Gordon, Free Spirit Publishing, 1998
An upbeat guide to help girls develop a positive self-image.

The Vegetarian Way: Total Health for You and Your Family, Virginia and Mark Messina, Crown Publishing, 1996
The Messinas answer common questions about the safety and benefits of a vegetarian diet.

"What to Teach Kids About Steroids—For Parents, Teachers, and Other Caregivers," The Parenting for Prevention Information Series
Johnson Institute
7205 Ohms Lane
Minneapolis, MN 55439-2159
E-mail: info@johnsoninstitute.com
www.johnsoninstitute.com

Your Dieting Daughter: Is She Dying for Attention?, Carolyn Costin, Brunner/Mazel, 1996
Costin believes that all parents of daughters need to look at preventing eating disorders just as they work to prevent unplanned pregnancies.

Suggested Reading for Middlers
A Teen's Guide to Going Vegetarian, Judy Krizmanic, Puffin Books, 1994
Empowers teens to make lifestyle choices, explaining why vegetarianism is good for people and the planet.

It's Perfectly Normal: A Book About Changing Bodies, Growing Up, Sex, and Sexual Health, Robie H. Harris, Candlewick Press, 1994

Organizations, Hotlines, and Websites
American Anorexia/Bulimia Association
165 West 46th St., Suite 1108
New York, NY 10036
(212) 575–6200
Provides information on eating disorders,
counseling, and support groups

Anorexia Nervosa and Related Eating Disorders Inc.
PO Box 5102
Eugene, OR 97405
(541) 344–1144
www.anred.com
E-mail: jarinor@rio.com

National Association of Anorexia Nervosa
and Associated Disorders
PO Box 7
Highland Park, IL 60035
(847) 831–3438
E-mail: anad20@aol.com

The Renfrew Center
(800) RENFREW
Offers residential treatment programs at
various sites on the East Coast.

SAFE (Self-Abuse Finally Ends) Alternatives Program
Chicago, IL
(800) DONTCUT

Something-Fishy Eating Disorders
www.somethingfishy.com/ed.html
Information, support group, and resource
links

CHAPTER FIVE: DRUGS,
ALCOHOL, AND CIGARETTES

Suggested Reading
*Buzzed: The Straight Facts about the Most
Used and Abused Drugs,* Cynthia Kuhn,
Scott Swartzwelder, and Wilkie Wilson of
the Duke University Medical Center, W.W.
Norton & Company, 1998

Drinking: A Love Story, Carolyn Knapp,
Delta, 1997
This book is written for adults. It eloquently
explains an alcoholic's compulsion to drink.
If you can't fathom why anyone would drink
to excess, read it.

*Drug Abuse: A Family's Guide to Detection,
Treatment and Education,* James Gainnini,
M.D., Health Information Press, 1998

*The Edison Trait: Saving the Spirit of Your
Nonconforming Child,* Lucy Palladino,
Times Books, 1997

*How to Cope with a Teenage Drinker:
Changing Adolescent Abuse,* Gary Forrest,
Jason Aronson, 1997

*Keeping Kids Drug Free: D.A.R.E. Official
Parent's Guide,* Glenn Levant, Laurel Glen,
CA, 1998
This book includes a breakdown of all categories of drugs and many useful strategies
that parents can use to prevent young adolescents from experimenting.

*My Mama's Waltz: A Book for Daughters
of Alcoholic Mothers,* Eleanor Agnew and
Sharon Robideaux, Pocket Books, 1998

*Resiliency in Schools: Making It Happen
for Students and Educators,* Nan Henderson and Mike Milstein, NAESP
(800) 386–2377

What Works: Schools Without Drugs.
To order: Safe and Drug-Free Schools Program
400 Maryland Ave, SW
Washington D.C. 20202-6123
(800) 624–0100

*When the Drug War Hits Home: Healing
the Family Torn Apart by Teenage Drug
Abuse,* Laura Stamper, Fairview Press, 1997

Suggested Reading for Middlers
Danger: Drugs and Your Friends (the Drug
Awareness Library), E. Rafaela Picard,
Powerkids Press, 1998

*The Negative Scream: A Story of Young
People Who Took an Overdose,* Sally
O'Brien, Routledge, Kegan and Paul, 1986

Organizations, Hotlines, and Websites
Al-Anon Family Group Headquarters, Inc.
1600 Corporate Landing Parkway
Virginia Beach, VA 23454-5617
(757) 563–1600 (USA)
(613) 722–1830 (CANADA)

Alcoholics Anonymous World Services
475 Riverside Drive
New York, NY 10015
(212) 870–3400

Families Anonymous
PO Box 4375
Culver City, CA 90231-3475
(800) 736–9805

National Center for Tobacco-Free Kids
1707 L St. NW, Suite 800
Washington, D.C. 20036
(202) 296–5469
(800) 284–KIDS

National Council on Alcoholism and Drug
Dependence, Inc.
12 West 21st St., 7th Fl.
New York, NY 10017
(212) 206–6770
(800) NCA–CALL

National Families in Action
2296 Henderson Mills Rd., Suite 300
Atlanta, GA 30345
(770) 934–6364

National Inhalant Prevention Coalition
1201 W. Sixth St., Suite C-200
Austin, TX 78703
(800) 269–4237

National Urban League: Substance Abuse
Program
500 East 62nd St.
New York, NY 10021
(212) 310–9000

Parents Alert hotline
(800) 727–7044

Parents Resource Institute for Drug Education (PRIDE)
50 Hurt Plaza, Suite 210
Atlanta, GA 30303
(404) 577–4500
(800) 853–7867

Treatment Facility Referrals and Helpline
(800) HELP–111

Treatment Program Referrals (800)
DRUGHELP

www.drugfreeamerica/org.map.html
www.drughelp.org

CHAPTER SIX: YOUNG ADOLESCENT BLUES AND DEPRESSION

Suggested Reading
Does My Child Need a Therapist?
Colleen Alexander-Roberts and Mark
Snyder, Taylor Publishing, 1997
Helps parents recognize the common
warning signs of problems and explains
the different types of therapy.

"Help Me, I'm Sad," David G. Fassler
and Lynne S. Dumas, Viking, 1997
Explores all aspects of childhood and
adolescent depression, including
symptoms, diagnosis, treatment, and effect
on family.

Helping Your Depressed Teenager, Gerald
D. Oster and Sarah S. Montgomery, John
Wiley & Sons, Inc., 1995
Helps parents distinguish between normal
adolescence and serious trouble.

Suggested Reading for Middlers
Stay True: Short Stories for Strong Girls,
Compiled by Marilyn Singer, Scholastic, 1999
Brings together works from eleven distinguished authors to help girls get through
life's tough spots through self-reliance and
self-discovery.

*Girls Seen and Heard: 52 Life Lessons for
Our Daughters,* The Ms. Foundation for
Women and Sondra Forsyth, preface by Carol
Gilligan and Marie Wilson, Putnam, 1998
In fifty-two short chapters that mothers
and daughters can read together, this book
identifies and discusses major issues in the
lives of adolescent girls, when loss of self-esteem is a risk.

*Real Girls/Real World: Tools for
Finding Your True Self,* Heather Gray
and Samantha Phillips, Seal Press,
1998 In the girls' own words, ways
to foster a sense of independent
decision-making.

Organizations, Hotlines, and Websites

American Academy of Child and Adolescent Psychiatry
PARENTS, P.O. Box 9971
Washington, D.C. 20016
(800) 333–7636
www.aacap.org

American Foundation for Suicide Prevention
(212) 363–3500

American Psychiatric Association
1400 K St., NW
Washington, D.C. 20005
(202) 682–6142
www.psych.org
E-mail: m.bennet@apa.org

American Psychological Association
Disaster Response Network
(202) 336–5898

Center for Mental Health Services' Knowledge Exchange Network
PO Box 42490
Washington, D.C. 20015
(800) 789–2647

Covenant House NINELINE
(800) 999–9999
Crisis intervention, referral, and information services for troubled teens and their parents.

Mental Health Net
www.cmhc.com
An online reference guide to various mental health websites.

National Association of Social Workers
750 First St. NE, Suite 700
Washington, DC 20002-4242
(800) 638–8799
E-mail: nasw@capcon.net

National Mental Health Association
(800) 442–6642
www.worldcorp.com/dc-online/nhma/index.html

National Youth Crisis Hotline
(800) 442–4673

Society of Adolescent Medicine
1916 NW Copper Oaks Circle
Blue Springs, MO 64015
(816) 224–8010
www.SOCADMED@GVI.net

Teen Help Adolescent Resources
(800) 400–0900
Refers teens to long-term residential programs.

Youth Crisis Hotline
(800) 448–4663
Counseling and referral to young people in crisis.

Brave Girls and Strong Women
www.members.aol.com/brvgirls

Femina
(with links to magazines, books, and other websites)
www.femina.com/femina/Girls

CHAPTER SEVEN: TAKING GOOD RISKS WITH EXTREME SPORTS

Suggested Reading

"99 Tips for Family Fitness Fun"
Send self-addressed stamped envelope to:
National Association for Sport and Physical Education
1900 Association Drive, Dept. P
Reston, VA 20191-1599

"Play It Safe: A Guide to Safety for Young Athletes"
Single copy free with self-addressed, stamped business-size envelope
American Academy of Orthopaedic Surgeons
PO Box 1998
Des Plaines, IL 60017

The Romance of Risk: Why Teenagers Do the Things They Do, Lynn E. Ponton, Basic Books, 1998
An examination of why some teens take bad risks and ways to encourage good risk-taking.

The Training Camp Guide to Sports Parenting: Encouraging Your Kids on and off the Field, Rick Wolff, Pocket Books, 1998
Gives parents tips for encouraging and managing a young athlete.

Suggested Reading for Middlers

Women Who Win: Stories of Triumph in Sports and Life, Christine Lessa, forewords by Peggy Fleming and Picabo Street, afterword by Teresa Edwards, Rizzoli/Universe, 1998

Jump Magazine: For Girls Who Dare to Be Real
Weider Publications
21100 Erwin St.
Woodland Hills, CA 91367

Girls' Life Magazine
4517 Harford Rd.
Baltimore, MD 21214
(888) 999–3222
www.girlslife.com

Snowboard Magazine
Surfer Publications, Inc.
333046 Calle Aviador
San Juan Capistrano, CA 92675
All the latest information on snowboarding gear and places.

Organizations, Hotlines, and Websites

American Academy of Otolaryngology/
Head and Neck Surgery
One Prince St.
Alexandria, VA 22314
Leaflet: "Facial Sports Injuries," single copy free with self-addressed, stamped business-size envelope.

American College of Sports Medicine
PI Department
PO Box 1440
Indianapolis, IN 46206-1440
Brochure: "Nutrition, Training, and Injury Prevention" (specific to soccer players), single copy free with self-addressed stamped envelope.

American Running and Fitness Association
4405 East West Hwy., Suite 405
Bethesda, MD 20814
Brochure: "Running Injuries"; fact sheet: "Shin Splints," single copy of each free along with copy of ARFA newsletter.
Send self-addressed stamped (55-cent) business-size envelope.

GAINS (Girls Achieving in Nontraditional Sports)
Nancy Fingerhood, Father English Center
435 Main St.
Paterson, NJ 07501

Girl Power!
www.health.org/gpower/girlarea

Girl Zone
www.girlzone.com

National Association for Girls and Women in Sport
(703) 476–3450
E-mail: nagws@aahperd.org

Women's Sports Foundation
Eisenhower Park
East Meadow, NY 11554
(516) 542–4700
www.lifetimetv.com/WoSport

CHAPTER EIGHT: VIRTUAL REALITY VS. THE REAL WORLD

Suggested Reading

Easy Computing Magazine
One Park Ave.
New York, NY 10016-5802
easycomputing@zd.com
Published by Ziff-Davis
Computing magazine geared for the novice. Many "how to" articles that can help adults overcome their fear of computers and the Internet.

Failure to Connect: How Computers Affect Our Children's Minds—for Better and Worse, Jane M. Healy, Simon & Shuster, 1998
Healy, a professional educator, was once an enthusiastic promoter of computers and is now a skeptic. She evaluates the pros and cons of computers in children's lives.

From Barbie to Mortal Kombat: Gender and Computer Games, edited by Justine Cassell and Henry Jenkins, MIT Press, 1999
Barbie vs. Riot Grrls—what software should be marketed to young adolescent girls?

Growing Up Digital: The Rise of the Net Generation, Don Tapscott, McGraw-Hill, 1998

Describes how the younger generation is leading the charge into the technological revolution involving computers and the Internet.

Release 2.1: A Design for Living in the Digital Age, Esther Dyson, Broadway Books, 1998
An exploration of the new digital age by someone who has been there from the beginning.

Suggested Reading for Middlers
Zillions Magazine
101 Truman Ave.
Yonkers, NY 10703
Consumer Reports for middlers. Helps young people distinguish between what is advertised and what is actually delivered. Subscription includes a newsletter for parents.

Organizations, Hotlines, and Websites
Two online resources for teachers:
California Technology Assistance Project:
www.ctap.k12.ca.us
Wed Quest: edweb.sdsu.edu/webquest/webquest.html

Channel 1: Nationwide News Network
www.channelone.com

The Mirror: A cool culture club for teens published by the *Seattle Times*
www.mirrormirror.com

Techno Teen: Glossy site with stories written by teens with chat rooms and games
www.TechnoTeen.com

Teen Court TV: Educational site with court cases that might interest teens
www.courttv.com/teens

360° Magazine: Opinion magazine for teens
www.360.org

ZUP! Interactive webzine for girls
webcom.com/zup/welcome.html

Filtering Software
Trial versions can be downloaded from the website

Access Management Engine
Bascom Global Internet Services, Inc.
Farmingdale, NY
(516) 753–5656
www.bascom.com
Geared to schools. Company has compiled a list of useful teacher-friendly websites.

SurfWatch 3.0
Spyglass
Los Altos, CA
(800) 458–6600
www.surfwatch.com
Blocks sites that identify themselves as adult-oriented or those that are requested to be blocked.

CyBerPatrol 4.0
Microsystems Software
Framingham, MA
(508) 879–9000
www.cyberpatrol.com
Parents can block or allow sites in twelve categories.

Net Nanny 3.1
Net Nanny
Vancouver, Canada
(604) 662–8522
www.netnanny.com
Although *Consumer Reports,* in a test, was able to view twenty-two adult sites, Net Nanny has had good reviews from others. The software comes with a list of several hundred "banned" sites. Also enables the parent to receive an "audit trail," detailing where the child has gone.

Cybersitter 97
Solid Oak Software
Santa Barbara, CA
(805) 967–9853
www.solidoak.com
Uses three methods to block sites.

Chapter Nine: Failing and Succeeding in School

Suggested Reading

The ADD Answer Book: The Best Medications and Strategies for Your Child, Alan Wachtel, M.D., Plume, 1998

The ADD/ADHD Checklist—An Easy Reference for Parents and Teachers, Sandra Rief, M.A., Prentice Hall, 1998

As I See It, John Lounsbury, NMSA, 1991
Contains the essay "Homework—Is a New Direction Needed?"
(800) 528–NMSA

Beating the Odds: Raising Academically Successful African American Males, Freeman A. Hrabowski III, Kenneth Maton, and Geoffrey Greif, Oxford University Press, 1998
Written about African American families, but all families can learn how to nurture academic excellence.

Beyond the Classroom: Why School Reform Has Failed, What Parents Need to Do, Laurence Steinberg, Ph.D., Simon & Schuster, 1996

Life on the Edge: Parenting a Child with ADD/ADHD, David Spohn, Hazelden, 1998

The Middle School Companion
Totally for Teachers
Box 698
Pittsford, NY 14534
(800) 711–2665
E-mail: mscompan@aol.com
A newsletter for parents and teachers about middle school education.

Real Boys: Rescuing Our Sons from the Myths of Manhood, William Pollack, Ph.D., Random House, 1988

Safe Passage: Making It Through Adolescence in a Risky Society, Joy Dryfoos, Oxford University Press, 1998

School Is Not a Four-Letter Word: How to Help Your Child Make the Grade, Louanne Johnson, Hyperion, 1998 This author (who also wrote the book which inspired the movie *Dangerous Minds*) explains how students are motivated and how parents can become actively involved in that dynamic.

Why Bright Kids Get Poor Grades, Dr. Sylvia Rimm, Crown Publishers, 1996

Up from Underachievement: How Teachers, Students, and Parents Can Work Together to Promote Student Success, Diane Heacox, Ph.D., Free Spirit Publishing, 1991

What to Look for in a Classroom . . . and Other Essays, Alfie Kohn, Josey-Bass, 1998

Suggested Reading for Middlers

Becoming an Achiever: A Student's Guide, Carolyn Coil, NAESP
(800) 368–2377

Guide to the Best Science Fair Projects, Janice Van Cleave, Free Spirit Publishing, 1998 (ages nine and up)

The Worst Speller in Junior High, Caroline Janover, Free Spirit Publishing, 1985
This is a novel about a middler with dyslexia.

What Makes the Great Great: Strategies for Extraordinary Achievement, Dennis Kimbro, Doubleday, 1986
This book is definitely for older middlers and their parents.

Organizations, Hotlines, and Websites

Children and Adults with Attention Deficit Disorder (CHADD)
499 N.W. 70th Ave., Suite 101
Plantation, FL 33317
(954) 587–3700
fax (954) 587–4599
www.chadd.org

Coordinated Campaign for Learning Disabilities, Communications Consortium Media Center
1200 New York Ave., NW, Suite 300
Washington, D.C. 20005
(202) 326–8700
fax (202) 682–2154
www.ldonline.org

Huntington Learning Center
Call (800) 692–8400 for a center near you.

Learning Disabilities Association of America
4156 Library Rd.
Pittsburgh, PA 15234
(412) 341–1515 or (412) 341–8077
fax (412) 344–0224
www.ldanatl.org

National Association of School Psychologists
4340 East West Hwy., Suite 402
Bethesda, MD 20814
(301) 657–0270
fax (301) 657–0275
www.uncg.edu/~ericcas2/nasp

National Information Center for Children
and Youth with Disabilities
PO Box 1492
Washington, D.C. 20012-1492

National Middle School Association
(NMSA)
2600 Corporate Exchange Dr., Ste. 370
Columbus, OH 43231-1672
(800) 528–NMSA
The Family Connection, a newsletter for
teachers
Middle Ground, a magazine for teachers

National Association of Elementary School
Principals (NAESP)
1615 Duke St.
Alexandria, VA 22314-3483
Call for a catalog of resources for grades K
through eight
(800) 386–2377
www.naesp.org

National Association of Secondary School
Principals (NASSP)
1904 Association Dr.
Reston, VA 20191
(703) 860–0200
www.nassp.org
This organization has a division called The
National Alliance of Middle Level Schools
Advisory Council.

Office of Special Education and Rehabilita-
tive Services
U.S. Department of Education
Washington, D.C. 20202-2500

Parents' Educational Resource Center
1660 South Amphlett Blvd., Suite 200
San Mateo, CA 94402-2508
(800) 471–9545
fax (415) 655–2411
www.perc-schwabfdn.org
E-mail: perc@perc-schwabfdn.org

The Parent Institute
PO Box 7474
Fairfax Station, VA 22039-7474
(800) 756–5525
Offers a catalog filled with brochures
and videos for parents and educators
on a wide range of subjects from
achievement in school to substance
abuse.

SCORE Learning Center
Call toll-free (877) 726–7356 for a center
near you.

Sylvan Learning Center
Call (800) 627–4276 for a center near you.

CHAPTER TEN: DEALING WITH A VIOLENT WORLD

Suggested Reading

*Boys Will Be Boys: Breaking the Link Be-
tween Masculinity and Violence,* Myriam
Miedzian, Anchor Books, 1991
Explains the culture's tendency to push
young males toward violence and what parents can do to work against that force.

*Bullies & Victims: Helping Your Child
Through the Schoolyard Battlefield,*
Suellen Fried and Paula Fried, M. Evans &
Co., Inc., 1996
Offers parents and educators ways to deal
with and prevent bullying behavior.

Dating Violence: Young Women in Danger,
Edited by Barrie Levy, Seal, 1991
A comprehensive look at the issues surrounding dating violence, including suggestions for programs to educate adolescents
to the dangers.

*Finding Our Way: The Teen Girls' Survival
Guide,* Allison Abner and Linda Villarosa,
HarperCollins, 1995

FistStickKnifeGun, Geoffrey Canada, Beacon Press, 1995

Gangsta: Merchandising Rhymes of Violence, Ronin Ro, St. Martin's Press, 1996
A raw look at the violent world of gangsta rap written by a music journalist on the inside.

Helping Teens Stop Violence: A Practical Guide for Counselors, Educators, and Parents, Allan Crieghton with Paul Kivel, Hunter House, Inc., 1992

Keys to Dealing with Bullies, Barry E. McNamara and Francine J. McNamara, Barron's, 1997
A guide to help parents and teachers intervene with bullies and their victims.

Stay Tuned! Raising Media Savvy Kids in the Age of the Channel-Surfing Couch Potato: The Kidvidz Family Video Guide, Jane Murphy and Karen Tucker, Doubleday, 1996
Tips for managing your child's TV watching.

Viewing Violence: How Media Violence Affects Your Child's and Adolescent's Development, Madeline Levine, Doubleday, 1996
The world affects children differently at different ages. Levine shows how and offers strategies parents can use, not only in their homes, but to lobby for change outside.

Waging Peace in Our Schools, Linda Lantieri and Janet Patti, Beacon Press, 1996
A practical guide for teaching young people how to work toward peace based on the successful Resolving Conflict Creatively Program.

Suggested Reading for Middlers
The Peer Partners Handbook: Helping Your Friends Live Free from Violence, Drug Use, Teen Pregnancy, and Suicide, Jerry Kreitzer and David Levine, Station Hill, 1995
Ways adolescents can set up peer counseling programs.

Soldier's Heart: Being the Story of the Enlistment and Due Service of the Boy Charlie Goddard in the First Minnesota Volunteers, Gary Paulsen, Delacorte, 1998
A *Saving Private Ryan* for adolescents, this book tells the horrors of combat in the Civil War from the viewpoint of Charlie Goddard, who lies his way into the Union Army at age fifteen.

Organizations, Hotlines, and Websites
Cherry Creek Bullyproof Program
To order the guide, (800) 547–6747

Gay and Lesbian Parents Coalition International (GLPCI)
PO Box 50360
Washington, D.C. 20091
(202) 583–8029

Hetrick-Martin Institute
2 Astor Place
New York, NY 10003-6998
(212) 674–2400

Lambda Legal Defense and Education Fund
120 Wall St.
New York, NY 10005
(212) 809–8585

Parents, Families, and Friends of Lesbians and Gays
1101 14th St. NW, Suite 1030
Washington, D.C. 20005
(202) 638–4200

Search Institute
700 S. Third St., Suite 210
Minneapolis, MN 55415
www.Search-institute.org
Search Institute, a Minneapolis-based nonprofit group, is attempting to change the perception that young people are more violent than ever before by bringing adults and children into contact. The group promotes holding adult-children activities on a regular basis. In Dodgeville, Wis., adults and children held a Safe Night which included role-playing exercises on stereotyping and conflict resolution.

The Web of Culture: Crosscultural resources
www.worldculture.com/resource.htm
Child Help USA (800) 422–4453
RAINN (800) 656–HOPE

CHAPTER ELEVEN: WHEN YOUR CHILD BREAKS THE LAW

Suggested Reading
Before It's Too Late: Why Some Kids Get into Trouble and What Parents Can Do About It, Stanton E. Samenow, Times Books, 1999

Every Parent's Guide to the Law, Deborah L. Forman, Harcourt Brace, 1998
A comprehensive discussion of legal issues affecting parents and children from pre-birth through adolescence.

Good Kids: How You and Your Kids Can Successfully Navigate the Teen Years, Nick Stinnett and Michael O'Donnell, Bantam, Doubleday, Dell, 1996
Interviews with many happy well-adjusted teens and tips for parents for raising the same.

Suggested Reading for Middlers
Hard Time: A Real Life Look at Juvenile Crime and Violence, Janet Bode and Stan Mack, Bantam, Doubleday, Dell, 1996
A sobering look from the inside of crime by juveniles who have strayed.

Shouting at the Sky: Troubled Teens and the Promise of the Wild, Gary Ferguson, St. Martin's, 1999

What Are My Rights?: 95 Questions and Answers About Teens and the Law, Thomas A. Jacobs, Free Spirit Publishing, 1997
Written in adolescent-friendly style, Jacobs helps teens understand the laws that affect them.

Organizations, Hotlines, and Websites
Because I Love You (BILY)
The Parent Support Group
PO Box 473
Santa Monica, CA 90406
(818) 882–4881 or (310) 659–5289
E-mail: BILY1982@aol.com
www.becauseiloveyou.org
Parenting information for out-of-control preteens and teens, and a listing of regional parenting groups. If no group is nearby, you can order the program, a parent's guide for getting back in control, for $11.

National Center for Missing and Exploited Children
(800) 843–5678

National Council on Problem Gambling
(800) 522–4700

National Runaway Switchboard
A hotline operated 24-hours for runaway and homeless youths and their families.
(800) 621–4000

Shoplifters Alternative
380 N. Broadway, Suite 206
Jericho, NY 11753-2109
(800) 848–9595
This group has developed a program called Youth Educational Shoplifting (Y.E.S.) available for home or school use.

NATIONAL MIDDLE SCHOOL ASSOCIATION

Established in 1973, the National Middle School Association (NMSA) is the nation's only education association devoted exclusively to improving the educational experiences of young adolescents, ages ten to fifteen. The NMSA supports those who live and work with young adolescents, recognizing these children's future as members of an increasingly diverse population. The NMSA's membership includes principals, teachers, administrators, and parents who share the organization's goals.

The association sponsors an annual convention and numerous publications providing the most current information on learning for young adolescents. Its flagship publications, *Middle School Journal* and *Middle Ground,* serve as forums for ideas and opinions and have been solid sources of trends, current research, and innovative ideas for over twenty-five years. The NMSA also publishes many books, monographs, and position papers.

In addition to its annual convention, which attracts more than 10,000 educators and parents, the NMSA conducts an urban education conference, distance learning programs, overseas study tours, and a series of weekend workshops.

Membership information is available through the NMSA, 2600 Corporate Exchange Drive, Suite 370, Columbus, OH 43231-1672, or by calling the information line, (800) 528–NMSA.

Index

*

Language skills, 207
Lawyers for juvenile crime, 261
Learning disabilities, 133, 142, 202, 204–205, 219, 220
Lefkowitz, Bernard, 236
Lesbians, *see* Gays and lesbians
LeShan, Eda, 39–40
Levant, Glenn, 116
Levine, Madeline, 226, 227
Levine, Dr. Melvin, 202–203, 207
Levy, Barrie, 66
Lewis, Mary Ann, 62
Lifelong learning, 199
Lightsey, David, 95
Listening, active, 147
Littleton, Colorado, 222
Lopiano-Misdom, Janine, 175
Loukaitis, Barry, 222
Lounsbury, John, 196, 197, 212
Love Is a Story (Sternberg), 49

McCary, Michael, 228
McGoldrick, Dr. Monica, 28
McGwire, Mark, 92–93, 94
Maier, Thomas, 12
Maine, Margo, 89
Major depressive episode (MDE), 128, 134, 137
Manheim, Camryn, 87
Manic depression (bipolar mood disorder), 129–30
Marijuana, 101, 109–11, 135, 184
Mark Clements Research, 54
Masturbation, 64
Maton, Kenneth, 209
Matter of Time: Risk and Opportunity in the New-School Hours, A (report), 7
MDMA (methylenedioxymethamphetamine), 113–14
Media:
  body image and, 77, 78, 97
  drugs and, 117
  smoking and, 121
  sports coverage, 151, 154
  violence and, 223, 225–27, 229–31, 239
Medicaid, 71
Memory skills, 207
Menstruation, cessation of, 90
Mentors, adults, 148–49
Meth (methamphetamine), 115
Methylenedioxymethamphetamine (MDMA), 113–14
Miedzian, Myriam, 161, 227, 233

Migraine headaches, 134
Minorities, 41, 132, 146, 220
  teaching tolerance, 238
  see also Immigrants
Misdemeanors, 250–51, 261
Modem, 178
Monitoring the Future 1997 survey, 99
Mononucleosis, 134
Montgomery, Sarah S., 137
Mood swings, 101–102, 109
Moses Lake, Washington, 222
Mothers Against Drunk Driving (MADD), 107
Motion Picture Association of America, 225
Motivation to learn, 196–97, 206
Mountain biking, 152, 157, 168, 170
Mountaineering, 168
Mountain skating, 157
Movies, *see* Media
Mura, David, 29
Music, 227–28

National Campaign to Prevent Teen Pregnancy, 6, 52–53, 54, 55
National Center for Missing and Exploited Children (NCMEC), 183
National Center for Tobacco-Free Kids, 124
National Center on Addiction and Substance Abuse, 99
National Collegiate Athletic Association, 92, 94
National Commission on Adolescent Sexual Health, 73
National Council Against Health Fraud, 95
National Crime Information Center (NCIC), 253
National Football League, 92, 94
National Gay and Lesbian Task Force, 27
National Institute of Drug Abuse, 118
National Institutes of Health, 18, 108, 110, 204
National Longitudinal Study of Adolescent Health, 5
National Mental Health Association, 126
National Middle School Association (NMSA), 4, 209, 213
National Runaway Switchboard, 253
National School Safety Center, 240–41
National Sporting Goods Association, 158
National Survey on Recreation and Environment, 152

National Victim Center, 235–36
National Youth Sports Safety Foundation, 163, 166
Neonaticies, 71, 72
Neurotransmitter imbalance, 135
Newsday (newspaper), 186
Newsweek, 201
New York State United Teachers, 220
New York Times, 70, 72, 264
Nicotine, *see* Smoking
Nike, 160
1995 National Survey of Family Growth, 53
Nurture Assumption, The (Harris), 5
Nutritional Business Journal, 94

Odyssey, 178
Online, going, *see* Computers and the Internet
Oral linguistic development, 202
Oral sex, 56–57
O'Reilly, Margie, 144–45, 146
Oster, Gerald, 137
Our Guys (Lefkowitz), 236
Our Nation After All (Wolfe), 73
Overachievers, 140–41

Paducah, Kentucky, 238, 249
Palladino, Dr. Lucy Jo, 208
Parade (magazine), 92
Parents, Families, and Friends of Lesbians and Gays (P-FLAG), 73, 237
Parent Soup, 2, 190
Partnership for a Drug-Free America Tracking Study, 109
Party plans, supervising, 50
Paul, Judi, 209
Pawlowski, Wayne, 27, 73
Paxil, 143
PC Meter, 182
Pediatricians, 149
Peers:
    friendships, *see* Friendships
    harassment by, 34–35, 137, 231–32
    learning in peer groups, 200
    romantic relationships, *see* Romantic relationships
    sexual activity and, 54–55, 62–63
    sports injuries and, 166
    substance abuse and, 102, 123
Pen-pals, 51
Permissiveness, 3, 265
Personal voice, cultivating middler's, 48–49

Physical appearance, 101
    eating disorders and, *see* Eating disorders
Physician's Desk Reference, 144
Planned Parenthood Federation of America, 71
Plastic surgery, 78–80
Pollack, Dr. William, 13, 103
Ponton, Dr. Lynn E., 37, 150, 162
Pornography, 173, 182–83
"Postponing Sexual Involvement" (PSI), 62–63
Post traumatic stress disorder (PTSD), 244
Pregnancy, 54, 68–72
Prescription drugs, 124, 135, 144
    see also specific drugs
Previewing skills, 203–204
PRIDE (National Parents' Resource Institute for Drug Education), 99
Privacy issues, the Internet and, 184–86, 190
Professional help, seeking:
    for eating disorders, 80
    smoking cessation programs, 124
    for substance abuse, 108–109, 111
    warning signals and, 15
Prozac, 143
Psychiatrist, choosing a, 141
Psychologist, choosing a, 141
Puberty, 83, 162–63
Public Agenda, 264
Punishment, 60, 96, 136
    for juvenile crime, 249, 251, 260

Race, *see* Immigrants; Minorities
Rape, 106, 116, 223, 235–36, 248, 259
Raves, 112–13, 116
Real Boys (Pollack), 13, 103
Rebelliousness, 3
Rekers, George, 55
Religion, 55, 265
Reno, Janet, 247
Resnick, Dr. Phillip J., 72
Resources, 269–83
Restraining orders, 67
Ridicule, *see* Peers, harassment by
Right Moves: A Girl's Guide to Getting Fit and Feeling Good, The (Schwager et al.), 77
Rimm, Sylvia, 194
Ritalin, 143
Ro, Ronin, 227–28
Rock climbing, 157, 168

Rodriguez, Monica, 60
Rohypnol, 116
Role models, 74, 89, 92, 202, 233, 266
Roller-Coaster Years, The (Giannetti), 1, 13, 211
Romance of Risk: Why Teenagers Do the Things They Do, The (Ponton), 150, 162
Romantic relationships, 43–51
  choices, dealing with middler's, 46–50
  dating at an earlier age, 45–46
  fantasy, 44–45
  group dating, encouraging, 51
  intervening in, 50, 65–67
  with older male partners, 65–66
  the "real" romance, 45
  strategies to encourage good social decision-making, 50–51
  validating middler's emotions, 49–50
  violence and abuse in, 66–67
  see also Sexual activity
Roofies, 116
Roper Starch polls, 56
Rosa, Emily, 220–21
Rosenberg, Elinor, 23
Running away, 252–53
Rusche, Sue, 118

Safety measures, 241–44
Scapegoating, 36–39
School, 82, 102, 194–221, 264
  attitude and success in, 200–202
  computers in, 179–80, 214
  homework, 210–11
  individuality of students, 212–13
  learning process, pinpointing problems in, 202–208
  mentors at, 148–49
  motivation to learn, 196–97, 206
  safety, 241–43
  social life and, 197–200
  strategies for parents, 215–21
  substance abuse and, 101, 109, 112–13
  truancy, 253–54
  underachievement in, 4, 137–38, 194–221
  undermining importance of, 208–10
  violence and shootings in, 222–23, 225, 238–39, 249, 260, 264
School Is Not a Four-Letter Word (Johnson), 212
School Safety Center, 223
Schrodt, Christine, 164

Schuerger, Michele, 77
Schuster, Mark, 56
Schwager, Tina, 77
Science (journal), 15
SCORE, 201
Search engines, 178
Search Institute, 14, 17, 18
Seasonal Affective Disorder (SAD), 135
Self-esteem, 49, 67, 162
Self-image, 103
Self-monitoring, 204–205
Self-mutilation, 6, 79
Serotonin, 135
Serotonin selective reuptake inhibitors (SSRIs), 143, 144
Serzone, 143
Sex and the Internet, 173, 182–83
Sex education, 54, 62–63, 64
Sexual activity, 6, 14, 52–75
  abstinence after having sex, 60–61
  adopted children and, 23
  being prepared for your middler's, 74
  clarifying your beliefs, 61–62
  communication about, 53–54, 57–64
  contraception, 54, 57, 63–64, 106
  degrees of, 58–59
  helping middlers understand, 59–60
  influences to have sex, 54–57, 106
  older male partners and, 65–66
  oral sex, 56–57
  peer programs to discuss, 62–63
  pregnancy, *see* Pregnancy
  pressure to have sex, 54–55
  punishment for, 60
  refusal skills, 61, 236
  statistics, 53
  stepfamilies and, 19–20
  steps when you know your child is engaging in, 57–64
Sexual harassment, 223, 234–35
Sexually transmitted diseases (STDs), 55, 56, 63, 64, 65
  oral sex and, 57
  see also specific diseases
Sexual orientation, 72–75
  gay, lesbian, and bisexual parents, 9, 25–27
  homophobia, 27, 73, 132–33
  same-sex experimentation, 72
  see also Gays and lesbians
Shalala, Dr. Donna, 109
Shellenbarger, Sue, 212
Shepard, Matthew, 236

U.S. Department of Education, 113, 179, 214
U.S. Justice Department, 238, 247–48, 259
University of Massachusetts, 77
University of Michigan, 194
  Survey Research Center, 109
University of Minnesota, 200
University of Missouri, 210
URL (Universal Resource Locator), 178
USA Gymnastics, 90
USA Today, 155, 174
USA Weekend, 126–27

Values, 17, 264–66
  about friendships, 33–35
  sexual activity and, 55
Vandalism, 248, 257–58
Verdick, Elizabeth, 77
Video games, *see* Media
Viewing Violence (Levine), 226
Villarosa, Linda, 234
Violence, 222–46
  assessment tool for predicting, 240–41
  date rape, 235–36
  dating, 66–67
  dealing with trauma, 244–45
  examining your attitudes, 224
  gangsta rap and, 227–28, 230
  against gays and lesbians, 236–37
  guns and, 238–41
  the media and, 223, 225–27, 229–31
  against minorities, 236
  peer harassment, 231–32
  safety measures, 241–44
  sexual harassment, 223, 234–35
  see also Crime, juvenile
Visitation by noncustodial parent, 16–17, 27

Wakeboarding, 159
Wallerstein, Dr. Judith, 15
Wall Street Journal, 143
Warning signs:
  of alcohol dependence, 108
  exposure to violent programming, 230–31
  of inhalant use, 119
  for seeking professional help, 15
  of substance abuse, 101–102
  suicide, 146–47
Way We Never Were and *The Way We Really Are, The* (Coontz), 12
Web browsers, 178
Weight, *see* Body image; Eating disorders
Wellbutrin, 124
What Makes the Great Great (Kimbro), 220
What Works: Schools Without Drugs (booklet), 113
Whitewater rafting, 152, 159
Why Bright Kids Get Poor Grades (Rimm), 194
Wielgus, Dr. Mark, 101
Wilson, Wilkie, 109
Wolfe, Alan, 72–73
Wolff, Rick, 164–65
Working after school, 200
World Wide Web, defined, 177

YM, 66
Young People and Chronic Illness (Huegel), 30
Youth Educational Shoplifting (Y.E.S.), 257
Youth in Single-Parent Families: Risk and Resilience (report), 14

Zoloft, 143

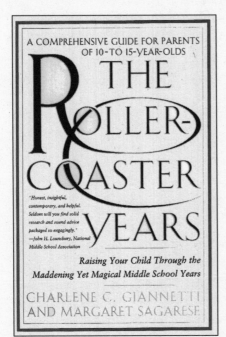

A COMPREHENSIVE GUIDE FOR PARENTS
OF 10-TO 15-YEAR-OLDS

THE
ROLLER-
COASTER
YEARS

*'Honest, insightful,
contemporary, and helpful.
Seldom will you find solid
research and sound advice
packaged so engagingly.'*
*—John H. Lounsbury, National
Middle School Association*

*Raising Your Child Through the
Maddening Yet Magical Middle School Years*

CHARLENE C. GIANNETTI
AND MARGARET SAGARESE

*The parents'
guide to
mastering
the ups and
downs
of early
adolescence*

Supported and advised by the National Middle School
Association, and with surprising insights from the authors'
own surveys, *The Roller-Coaster Years* covers every aspect of the
development of 10- to 15-year-olds. With this lively, authoritative guide in hand, seeing your child through these tumultuous years doesn't have to be a hair-raising experience.